RARE BIRDS

RARE BIRDS

FORGOTTEN AIRCRAFT
OF THE SECOND WORLD WAR

CHARLES R. G. BAIN

FONTHILL

To my parents,
Randall and Janice Bain, and my grandparents,
George and Anne Shaw—
for loving me and supporting me in everything I have done.

Fonthill Media Language Policy

Fonthill Media publishes in the international English language market. One language edition is published worldwide. As there are minor differences in spelling and presentation, especially with regard to American English and British English, a policy is necessary to define which form of English to use. The Fonthill Policy is to use the form of English native to the author. Charles R. G. Bain was born and educated in Ontario; therefore Canadian English has been adopted in this publication.

Fonthill Media Limited
Fonthill Media LLC
www.fonthillmedia.com
office@fonthillmedia.com

First published in the United Kingdom and the United States of America 2016

British Library Cataloguing in Publication Data:
A catalogue record for this book is available from the British Library

Copyright © Charles R. G. Bain 2016

ISBN 978-1-78155-524-8

Typeset in 10.5pt on 13pt Minion
Printed and bound in Great Britain by TJ International Ltd. Padstow

Preface

When I was little, I used to go to my grandparents' house whenever there was an air show. I was luckier than many in that my grandparents lived a mere ten minutes away. Moreover, their house was a few short blocks from the airport. My grandparents had a large yard, a wonderful playground and space for family barbecues, and on air show days we would all gather to sit outside and see what would fly over and to have dinner. The planes might be a little further away, but the food was homemade and the company of my parents and grandparents meant the world to me, and still does.

On this particular day, the show appeared to be over. I had seen my first F-117 Nighthawk, though at the time I had no idea what that was. I was more interested by the red replica Fokker Triplane I saw winging away, then I was called to come in for supper—the last to go inside. Just as I moved towards the house, a low rumbling started. It shook everything, the vibration passing right through me. Then, at low altitude, an Avro Lancaster came rumbling over. It flew directly over the house, and seemed to blot out the entire world. I remember so clearly that black underbelly that looked so enormous to a small child. It was so low that it looked like it almost took the aerial off the house. I'd seen very few planes up close, and I thought it was the biggest thing I had ever seen, and I was instantly hooked. I'll never forget that moment, and I suspect most of my readers won't either. That first moment of awe in the face of such machines.

It has been a long journey from there, but that incident, paired with parents who fed a voracious appetite to read and an intense historical curiosity, has led me here. My love of aviation has been enduring, and of the pre-jet era in particular. I'm not entirely sure what draws me to it; perhaps the personal aspect of it all—machines that were, at the time, frequently the pinnacle of human achievement. There is something almost hand-crafted about the aircraft of the period, an ineffable notion of effort that surrounds them.

Yet the larger historical point is, if anything, more important. These craft took part in one of the most pivotal moments in human history, and their contribution is important to understand regardless of how large or small it may have been. There is something innately fascinating about studying the war, and the people who served during the conflict. Moreover, if I have drawn any lesson from my own studies, it is that there is always something else to learn. My interests have, in general, always run to the untold and forgotten stories. This book is certainly a reflection of that—when the time came to think what my topic would be, there was only one answer.

So this book comes both from the historian I am today and also from that little kid in his grandparents' backyard. We are, after all, products of our own history.

This book is about the rare ones—the ones that may not have played a central role in the air war that raged between 1939 and 1945, yet were parts of the greater whole nevertheless. Each has an interesting and frequently underappreciated story to tell. Some were facing combat against far younger and more advanced aircraft, but bravely sallied forth regardless. Some were forgotten and failed projects, or came too late to affect the outcome via superior engineering. At least one is something of a deliberate attempt to avoid making another airplane, a Frankenstein's monster of an aircraft. All of them have stories to tell.

I feel especially privileged being the one to write their stories. Much as I was introduced to various aircraft by the work of others, I hope these words introduce at least one curious mind to a world of new information and knowledge.

Acknowledgements

I would like to gratefully thank the following people and organisations for their advice, contributions, and assistance in the creation of this work:

Hugh Alcock, Mervin Austin, Milena Balcová of the Military Historical Archive in Bratislava, Slovakia, Piotr Biskupski, Hugo Booker, Nico Braas, Tristan Broos and the *Nationaal Militair Museum*, Igor Brunclik, Jerilyn Buresh, the Coulson family and Coulson Flying Tankers, Jack Coyle, Ray Crupi, Matt Denning, Thierry Deutsch, Ron Dupas, Mark Evannier, Agnieszka Gąsiewska and PZL Mielec, Pierre Clément Got, Natasha Grunewald, Ing. Miroslav Hajek and the *Slovenské Technické Múzeum* of Košice, Thomas Harnish, David Horn, Kelly Johnson, Vincent Jones, Richard L. Kitterman, Bernhard Klein, Miroslav Khol and the Military History Institute of Prague, and Aviation Museum of Kbely. Robert Kremer, Jim Larsen and the Flying Heritage Collection, Paul Marchwica, Emily McMurphy, Marcia Mordfeld and the Canada Aviation and Space Museum, the National Museum of the United States Air Force, the National Naval Aviation Museum, Davide Olivati, Alain Picollet, Bill Pippin, Thijs Postma, Ville Ruusunen, Arjun Sarap, R. A. Scholefield, Robert W. Schoneman, Martin Stephen, Jacques Trampe, Alex Trandafir, Colin Urry, Robert Varin and the Polish Veterans Branch No. 412, Monica Walsh and the Royal Australian Air Force Museum, Cook Point, Keith Webb, and Alan Wilson.

Special thanks to Lori Brake for her photo-editing help.

Special thanks to Kate Fathers for her help in proofreading and editing.

Special thanks to Lindsy Fish for her legal advice during the process.

Special thanks to Keith Webb for the beautiful Boomerang photos for the book cover.

I would also like to thank Jay Slater and Alan Sutton, as well as the staff of Fonthill Media.

A last thank you goes out to Doug Attrell and the people of Simviation.com, who started me on this path many, many years ago.

Contents

Introduction

Aviation and the Second World War is a topic that is vastly complicated. A cursory glance might reveal a handful of stories—the Hurricane, Spitfire, and the Battle of Britain, the Bombing Campaign over Germany and Japan, and perhaps a few others, all jumbled together—but a closer inspection, however, reveals that the picture was far more complicated, with roots tracing back to the early and mid-1930s, if not before (as the case of the Polikarpov Po-2 will demonstrate, later on).

This book is meant as an introduction to that world, to the strange and weird and wonderful, the forgotten, the successes and failures, and the great might-have-beens. This book is specifically meant for all aviation enthusiasts, a community that this author has experienced and enjoyed for years. It is partially a tribute to the many good people who have been met, and partially something for us all, and it is most definitely an 'us'. It is a community of enthusiasm and knowledge, passion and learning. There will be features of this book that appeal to all, if hopefully done properly. On the one hand it will provide a general introduction and history, but also specifics of service, to fulfil the needs of the casual beginner and the experienced, detail-oriented reader.

The choices made for inclusion in this book was, primarily, to give examples of type. The choices were hard, but the final list attempts to do justice to all the participants in the Second World War who designed their own aircraft, or at least to come close. There are many that are not included, plenty of which are mentioned at the end of each entry. Each of these asides details facts and craft that may be deemed worth a reader's study, and which may be of great interest. To those who have reached this point only to be disappointed by the non-inclusion of a particular favourite, the author sends both apologies and encouragement; the field of aviation history is fuelled by passion and your interest—perhaps, one day, you will be writing your own book on your chosen aircraft, or become a dedicated modeller, remote-control flier, or part of an aviation organisation or museum.

To begin with, however, an overview of the historical events leading up to the war, as pertains to aviation, may be worthwhile.

The First World War had radically altered the picture of just what it was that aviation was capable of. The sheer rapidity with which aviation evolved in this period must be kept in mind. The Wright Brothers first made powered flight a reality in 1903, with their Wright Flyer—a machine that could, at best, manage 30 mph (48 kph), climbing to the dizzying height of 30 feet (9 metres). By 1918, a mere fifteen years later, the state-of-the-art had grown in tremendous leaps. To choose just one example, the Germans were fielding the superlative Fokker D.VII by the end of the First World War, which could reach 117 mph (189 kph), and reach up to 19,685 feet (6,000 metres). This is what can only be described as a quantum leap, and it happened despite the fact that hide-bound command structures of nearly every combatant army, in 1914, considered the aircraft a mere toy—suitable only for, perhaps (even this might be granted grudgingly), photo-reconnaissance.

By the end of the war, however, the aircraft had swept far past all of this. It was being used for photo-reconnaissance, true, and had done superbly at the task, but it had branched out into artillery spotting, air superiority, and the first attempts at strategic bombing. They were even beginning to prove their worth as anti-ship weapons. In the first few years after the war, too, the world's first purpose-built aircraft carriers would come into the ranks of the Imperial Japanese Navy and the British Royal Navy (the carriers *Hosho* and *Hermes* respectively), which was the death-knell for the battleship, though nobody yet knew it.

In essence, the prototype of what would later be seen in the Second World War was already present in 1919—nimble air-superiority fighters, armed either to counter other aircraft or engage in ground support, longer-range bombers, including some four-engined designs, and aircraft dedicated to naval duties, and the photo reconnaissance role that continues to this day as well. This quantum leap in capacity, driven by the war, came with bloodily earned experience in tactics that would point the way to future designers in all the combatants.

In the interwar years, the prophets of aviation looked forward into a world in which the aircraft could, by itself, be decisive on the battlefield. Carrier-borne aircraft, laden with bombs and then torpedoes, were proven to be absolutely lethal to the battleships and other capital warships that had been the definition of what military power was on the world stage for centuries. Quietly, with very few people noticing, the aircraft carrier was becoming one of the most critical weapons of war.

On land the situation also continued to evolve. As designs grew ever more advanced and complicated, the fastest human beings had ever gone kept being redefined in wave after wave of competition, innovation, and daring. The impetus for this was both military and civilian, and ranged far and wide. There are innumerable facets to this development, some of which deserve particular attention. First and foremost, civilians started to see and even use aircraft in the post-war world, and this developed from mere rides in surplus First World War machines to mail services and passenger transports, requiring ever greater range and ever increasing capacity. Daredevil men and women pioneered air routes to remote areas of the globe, flew across the world, competed in air races, and in general ensured that aviation was a permanent part of the public consciousness.

Each development spurred others, spurred competition, and meant that the technology continued to evolve. On 4 September 1933, a mere thirty years after the Wrights changed the world forever, a pilot named Jimmy Wedell set a speed record for a landplane over 300 mph (482 kph) for the first time, though he came nowhere close to the record for a seaplane, which stood at 407 mph (644 kph), set by George Stainforth two years earlier.

The military implications of this ever-increasing capability across the board was unmistakeable. Air power was to be a decisive power, and everybody knew it. The precise form it was to come in was unknown, but as war clouds began to gather in the 1930s, people and governments prepared for what they felt would be the worst. In the end, the worst was to prove far more horrible than anybody had imagined.

In terms of design, the biplane gradually fell in favour to the monoplane, though many still served—and did so spectacularly—during the Second World War. The struts and wires of the First World War gave way to sleek aircraft with retractable landing gear and all-metal skins, and bombers did much the same. The size and capability of bombers began to increase rapidly too, as did ambitions for their use. Many believed that invincible bomber fleets would, on the outbreak of war, range enemy countries at will, able to shoot down what precious few fighter aircraft could keep up with them.

Airmen of different nations prepared for different tactical and strategic views of the war. When war erupted in 1939, however, the early central player would be the German Luftwaffe, which the other combatant forces had been built, as best they could, to counter.

When Germany invaded Poland in 1939, the Luftwaffe possessed a technical and experience edge that simply could not be matched. Its types, as well as many of its pilots, had received extensive testing and usage during the Spanish Civil War of 1936–1939. These veterans in the most modern aircraft ran headlong into a much smaller Polish air force with older types and none of the experience advantages. Nevertheless, the Poles fought bravely, but German air superiority was assured. German strategy had evolved the famed Blitzkrieg—the close co-operation of air force and army to rapidly overcome the enemy and effect breakthroughs and encirclements with a minimum of losses and time.

In the other Allied powers, the race was on to get aircraft into service that could counter this force. In France, production difficulties meant that the large French Air Force was nevertheless inadequate to the task of defeating the Luftwaffe, despite the excellence of some of its designs and the bravery of its pilots. The British Royal Air Force was luckier in that it had larger numbers of two excellent basic fighters, the Hawker Hurricane and the Supermarine Spitfire. Once France fell, the Royal Air Force would face Germany's might alone.

The Battle of Britain was far more than the fight of 'the few' against the many. The Royal Air Force had the benefit of home-field advantage, the first extensive use of radar as an aid to air defence, and full-out production to keep replacement aircraft arriving at an adequate rate. Lastly, they had pilots who were now equal to experience to their German compatriots. These pilots were not just British, but from all over the globe—and many were valiant and highly motivated pilots from occupied nations, who would help bring the hammer down on the Germans.

It was a hard, vicious fight, but the result was always likely to be a British victory, and it redefined again what air power could do. The Luftwaffe had proven a superb tactical force, but had failed at strategic bombing. The lessons, so bloodily learned, would be turned against Germany with a vengeance in the years to come.

The air war continued to spread. Italy's entry into the war in an attempt to gain part of the glory of France's fall opened up the entire Mediterranean to conflict, and while the Regia Aeronautica was possessed of some excellent pilots and designs, it went to war in the midst of rearmament, with the bulk of its forces still older, obsolete types, and with insufficient production to meet Italy's aviation needs. There would be legends here too, of the valiant defence of Malta, of dangerous convoy runs in the teeth of elite Luftwaffe formations brought in to aid the Italians, and whirling fights over the deserts of North Africa.

In the meantime, two other developments occurred that rapidly altered the picture of the air war—the entry of the Soviet Union and the United States into the war. In the both cases, it was as the result of aggressive nations attacking them, but both would prove to be aviation superpowers the likes of which their opponents could only have dreamed of—or, more accurately, had nightmares of.

In the case of the Soviet Union, the Red Air Force that went to war in 1941 had much against it. It was huge, but most of its bulk was thoroughly obsolete. Even this proved a blessing in disguise, however, as every aircraft the Germans lost in their invasion would be brand new, while the Russians could, with their vast industry, replace their obsolete losses with newer, better types. These new types, operated at lower altitudes, became perhaps the ultimate close-support air force, almost ignoring strategic bombing. The Red Air Force and Red Army, through appalling loss and horribly gained experience, became the hammer and anvil between which Nazi power was forever shattered.

In the Pacific, Japan had realised early on the importance of a capable air force, and had put a premium on range and agility, to the sacrifice of armour and heavy firepower. They had also developed a large and modern carrier force, and this military machine was unleashed first on China and then on the entire Pacific. The strike on Pearl Harbour in December of 1941 demonstrated once and for all (as had the raid on the Italians at Taranto the year earlier) just how vulnerable navies were to aircraft. For six months thereafter, the Japanese hammered all their opponents across a quarter of the globe, their superbly nimble aircraft more than capable against the older pre-war types they encountered. Then, at Midway in 1942, the great clash of carriers versus carriers came, and the result was a catastrophic Japanese defeat. Faster, heavily armed American fighters would claim superiority, and, despite bringing new types into service as the war progressed, Japan's defeat became more and more assured after Midway.

As the naval battles and island campaigns moved closer to Japan (the largest engagements history had ever seen in some cases), the Japanese turned to a horrifying tactic—the Kamikaze. Thousands of pilots and thousands of planes were expended in suicide attacks that achieved horrific slaughter at horrific cost, and which did not alter the strategic situation at all. With their industry increasingly damaged by American attacks, and with their supplies interdicted by American submarines, Japan's newest types of aircraft could never be produced in numbers sufficient to stem the losing tide.

American production, however, was just beginning to ramp up. This vast industry, which Hermann Goering (head of the Luftwaffe) had once proclaimed could only build automobiles and refrigerators, was churning out tens of thousands of modern aircraft that their opponents simply could not match.

In Europe, the situation for the once-mighty Luftwaffe began to deteriorate. Bled white by constant use in the East and Mediterranean, they faced new aircraft that were hammering German industry, soon by day and night. By day, American bombers attempted precision bombing of German industry, and at night British heavy bombers targeted German cities. The Luftwaffe had pioneered terror bombing of civilians in Spain, and used it against the Poles and British in 1939–40, but it was perfected by the British and with increasing numbers, Germany was hammered by night and day.

It is a controversial and continuing debate as to how effective this campaign was, though the fact that it had some major effect on German industry is undeniable. It also caused unprecedented civilian casualties and damage to cities. The debate over strategic bombing will continue, and is beyond the purview of this work. However, the author would like to ask all who are reading it to consider the facts and the implications and the cost.

The result for the Luftwaffe, however, was indisputable. Despite experienced pilots and the best technology they could field, German air power was steadily ground down in attacks that cost each side badly, but cost the Germans more. While the Americans and British could replace their losses, and the sheer vastness of American industry ensured that more and more aircraft could operate over Germany, the Germans could not match this production. After the Invasion of Normandy in June of 1944, Allied aircraft would begin to target German infrastructure, rail lines, and transportation networks. While German industry continued to churn over, it could get less and less of it to where it was needed—and the advancing Soviets were taking resource after resource away from them. With Romania defecting as the Red Army approached, the Germans lost their access to the oil fields at Ploieşti, and from there the end of the Luftwaffe was merely a matter of time.

An innovation came into service, however, that would fail to win the war for Germany, but would forever change aviation and air power. The first jets had flown in 1939, and by the late war the Germans were putting jet fighters into combat, most famously the superb Messerschmitt Me 262. The Americans and British followed, and by 1945 it was becoming clear that the jet was the wave of the future. This being a mere forty-three years after the Kittyhawk.

Strategic bombing had also reached an apex—and a terrifying one. Over Japan, the American air force was setting fire to Japan's often wooden cities, and the new Boeing B-29 Superfortress could drop an unheard of tonnage of bombs from an unimagined altitude. For comparison, the first four-engined bomber was the Sikorsky Ilya Muromets, in service to the Imperial Russian Air Force. The Muromets first flew in 1913, and could fly at 68 mph (110 kph) at an altitude of 9,840 feet (3,000 metres), with 1,100 lb (500 kg) of bombs. The Superfortress first flew twenty-seven years later, and could thunder at 357 mph (574 kph) at 31,850 feet (9,710 metres), with 20,000 lb (9,000 kg) of bombs. It was the Superfortress that would bring the final act of the war to a close, dropping the atomic bombs on Hiroshima and Nagasaki in a terrifying and horrific display of just how far aviation had come in a very short time.

This, then, is what had happened in a relatively short time. It was under these conditions that all the aircraft that will hereafter be described flew and fought. These are the stories, the details, of that air war. The preceding description was broad and vague— and barely scratching the surface, and the stories of technological innovation, bravery, triumph, and tragedy on all sides throughout the war.

From here, the story becomes about individual aircraft, but the human sacrifice can never be forgotten. There are countless stories of the war, both horrible and hopeful. What follows are specific stories of specific aircraft, the lesser-known ones. There are so many more stories that cannot be told here, but that must be remembered.

1

Aichi B7A Ryusei

The story of Japanese military aviation is one of staggering achievement matched by equally staggering limitations. The result was, ultimately, army and naval air forces that conquered over a quarter of the globe's surface—although they were quickly outpaced by new Allied designs.

In the 1930s, the Japanese aviation industry and its products were little known and vastly underestimated. Much of this was based on crude, racist reasoning that held that not only were the Japanese inferior to those of 'western' countries, but that they were physically incapable of matching potential white foes. It was held by many that owing to the shape of their eyes, Japanese pilots would neither be able to fly nor shoot in a manner that could match white pilots. These opinions were—as all assumptions of innate superiority are in any era—catastrophically unintelligent. Yet, in 1941, as Japan bunched a mighty fist in order to gamble everything on a defeat of American military might, such attitudes meant that there was no clear idea of Japanese capability or their martial prowess.

It was this sort of ridiculous underestimating of a potential opponent that helped hone the legend of Japanese aircraft such as the Mitsubishi A6M 'Zero'. The Zero, and indeed the other front-line aircraft of the Japanese Navy, had all been designed with extreme range in mind. This range was matched by unparalleled manoeuvrability, but both these advantages came at the expense of armour. These aircraft were more than sufficient to fairly easily outmatch Curtiss P-40s and Brewster Buffalos, but with the advent of new aircraft in the American arsenal, control of the air shifted rapidly away from the Japanese.

Japanese aircraft ran rampant over their opponents in the early months of the Pacific War, but their deficiencies would eventually tell. The Americans began to deploy much better aircraft like the Grumman F4F Wildcat, and later the even better F6F Hellcat. There would be others too, but these two planes would swing the balance of power away from Japan's carrier aircraft. The Zero, for instance, would remain a superb fighter in manoeuvre, but faster, heavily armoured Grummans did not need to oblige it in close, turning fights.

Much like their German allies, the Japanese found themselves possessing designs that, while superb for when they were created, had been outpaced for events—and the search for replacements became critical as their enemies bore down on them. It was under these circumstances that the Aichi B7A was born.

A production model Aichi B7A2. Note the enclosed bomb bay, as well as four-bladed propeller. (*Courtesy of Thijs Postma*)

Specifications

First Flight: 1942
Powerplant: Nakajima NK9C Homare 12 radial-piston engine, 1,825 hp.
Armament: (B7A2) Two Type 99 Model 2 20-mm cannon, one Type 2 13-mm machine gun, and either one 1,764-lb torpedo or similar bombload.
Top Speed: 351 mph (565 kph)
Range/Service Ceiling: 1,889 miles (3,040 km), 36,910 feet (11,250 metres)
Dimensions: Length 37 feet 3 inches (11.4 metres), height 13 feet 4.5 inches (4.07 metres), wingspan 47 feet 3 inches (14.4 metres)
Number Built: 114 (9 B7A1, 105 B7A2)

There is a certain irony to the Aichi B7A Ryusei ('Shooting Star', Allied code name 'Grace'), in that, by the time it was ready to enter combat, the main role for which it had been intended was no longer achievable. It serves as an excellent example of the fate of many superb Japanese aircraft designs that can be simply summed up as 'too few, too late'.

The Imperial Japanese Navy operated a separate air arm from that of the army, and as such issued different requirements for its aircraft. In 1941, a new requirement was issued for a carrier-based attack bomber that was meant to replace both the Nakajima B6N Tenzan ('Heavenly Mountain' or 'Jill' to the Allies) and the Yokosuka D4Y Suisei ('Comet' and 'Judy' to her foes) aircraft, combining in one airplane the B6N's torpedo bomber role and the D4Y's dive bomber role. The new plane would be specifically geared towards the new *Taiho*-class aircraft carriers then being built for the Imperial Fleet, which would have deck elevators of larger square areas and thus would be able to operate larger aircraft than had previously been possible.

The new design was supposed to meet a bombload of up to 1,102 lb (500 kg) or be able to carry a standard 1,764-lb (800-kg) torpedo (it should be mentioned that this torpedo was one of the superb 'long lance' type torpedoes). This in turn was coupled to stringent long-range requirements. All of this necessitated a big, powerful engine, and in fact specified the Homare 11 experimental engine, preparatory to mounting the Homare 12, which was expected to become a standard engine type.

Aichi's resulting design was a large aircraft with a wingspan of over 47 feet (over 14 metres). The wings themselves were mounted mid-body and were of an inverted gull type. The mid-wing design allowed for an internal bomb bay and also provided clearance for the big, new four-bladed propeller. The inverted gull wings were necessary as a result of all this to keep the landing gear shorter. A portion of the wings folded for carrier storage, and the overall result was remarkable. For an aircraft not much larger than the B6N (though significantly bigger and heavier than the D4Y), the navy would receive a plane that was faster than the aircraft it was meant to replace, and one with an equal or superior range. As a result, the parts and labour required for two aircraft could be safely concentrated onto one. The aircraft featured impressive performance too—it could carry a hefty punch a long distance, and at a speed that was as fast as contemporary fighters. In addition, and perhaps most astonishingly, the B7A had manoeuvrability that was equal to the Mitsubishi Zero fighter. This last was accomplished by fitting drooping ailerons along with dive brakes on the craft's wings.

It was an impressive result, but the trouble came from the Homare engine. This was a new engine, and its many teething problems meant that both the testing of the Ryusei and its production and delivery to the navy was drastically slowed down. The B7A1 prototype flew in May 1942, but these problems along with changes to the airframe meant that the B7A2 production model did not begin to roll off factory lines until May 1944.

The entire history of the Ryusei seemed plagued by setbacks, and its combat history was no exception. When the first B7A2s began to arrive, the only carrier ready that could accommodate them was the IJN *Taihō*, but she was sunk on 19 June 1944 by a torpedo from the submarine USS *Albacore*. At the time, there were not even enough B7A2 examples ready to embark them.

The next carrier meant to take the aircraft was the leviathan IJN *Shinano*. The *Shinano* was a supercarrier built on the hull of a *Yamato*-class battleship. *Shinano* would have carried a total of twenty Ryusei aircraft, but this carrier was sunk a mere ten days after her completion by the submarine USS *Archerfish*.

After this, the Ryusei was limited to being based on land as no carriers existed or were likely to exist that could successfully operate them. Even then, the Shooting Star was cursed with misfortune. Eighty of the production B7A2 versions had been completed by May 1945, when a massive earthquake levelled the Funakata factory where the aircraft was being produced, wrecking nearly all further production, and this for an aircraft that

A rearward view of another B7A2 in navy colours. (*Courtesy of Thijs Postma*)

was only to be built in three total factories. Of these three, another never reached the production phase. This, coupled with the massive difficulties faced by Japan in terms of acquiring and assembling the materials needed to make aircraft while under relentless assault from the full might of the American Navy, ensured that only a further twenty-four aircraft were completed before the end of the war. In total, a mere two squadrons were equipped with it, far too few to make any meaningful impact.

The story of the Ryusei is that of an excellent design that failed almost entirely owing to circumstance. Misfortune after misfortune kept the aircraft from making any significant impact on the course of the war. There were other aircraft, discussed later, that shared a similar fate. Japan's late-war production of aircraft included numerous superb designs that could never operate in sufficient numbers to reach their maximum impact.

2

Avia B-534

Czechoslovakian aviation is not something that usually gets mentioned in connection with the Second World War, and this is unfortunate. Despite falling without a shot to the Germans, Czechoslovakia produced some interesting designs that found their way into service in the European theatre. Among these, the Avia B-534 stands out for where it ended up. The B-534 found itself as part of the Slovak National Uprising, a brave stand against Nazi tyranny in 1944. So it was that, in an unlikely manner, an older Czechoslovakian design made its mark on the history of the Second World War.

Specifications

First Flight: 1934
Powerplant: Hispano-Suiza HS 12Ydrs inline piston engine, 850 hp.
Armament: Four Model 30 7.7-inch (0.303) machine guns, up to six 44-lb bombs on underwing racks.
Top Speed: 245 mph (394 kph)
Range/Service Ceiling: 360 miles (580 km), 34,775 feet (10,600 metres)
Dimensions: Length 26 feet 11 inches (8.2 metres), height 10 feet 2 inches (3.1 metres), wingspan 30 feet 10 inches (9.4 metres)
Number Built: 665

The B-534 represents the final iteration of the biplane design as a combat aircraft, ranking with the Polikarpov I-153 and some Grumman naval fighters as being the most advanced versions of such a craft. It would be the most important—and certainly most produced—Czechoslovakian aircraft made between the creation of the country after the First World War, and the end of the Second World War. In all, 566 examples would be made, serving the Czechs and Slovaks, but also serving the Bulgarians and even seeing limited service in the German Luftwaffe.

The B-534's designer, František Novotný, crafted a design that based itself around a classical biplane configuration. By this point, the wires that had braced biplane wings of previous generations of craft were gone, with the B-534's wings supported entirely by N-struts. The rest of the design did indeed have fabric coverings, as in previous craft, but it was over a steel backbone and skeleton, giving the design more strength than many previous types. The fuselage was extensively streamlined, elongating the form, and the forward fuselage was all metal, protecting the engine. The prototype Avia B-34/2 was sluggish, so it was re-engined around a more powerful Hispano-Suiza engine, re-emerging from this conversion as the B-534/1, which first flew in August 1933 and was an immediate success. The B-534/2 prototype added another, more unique feature—a fully enclosed cockpit. There were other minor revisions, which included the landing gear and an enlarged rudder.

This second prototype was the main evolution of the form, and it almost immediately set a Czech air-speed record in April 1934, hitting a speed of 227.27 mph (365.74 kph)—a spectacular speed for a biplane. This speed, along with excellent handling features, meant that its selection for production for the Czech air arm was almost a foregone conclusion. The B-534-I, the main production version, removed the landing spats, removed the cockpit canopy, and replaced the metal propeller with a wooden one. There would be three other marks of production model, each with relatively minor changes, which were mainly expressed in terms of placement of the craft's weaponry, along with the inclusion of bomb racks. The enclosed cockpit would also be re-added to the design. The final version, the B-534-IV, added the metal propeller back to the design, increasing the maximum speed and matching the B-534 to the best biplanes in the world, if not exceeding them.

The B-534's main grace, however, was exceptional agility. This was amply demonstrated in 1937, at the Zurich International Flying Meet. The craft demonstrated exceptional manoeuvrability, establishing itself as one of the more exceptional biplane aircraft of the event. By this time, the B-534 was forming the backbone of the Czechoslovakian air force, equipping twenty-one squadrons by the time the country was partitioned in 1938.

It is worth noting that Avia attempted to create a version that mounted a 20-mm cannon that would fire through the nose, but this version had significant teething troubles and was not ready as the threat of war loomed. The project was meant to give the B-34 an armament that could be effectively used against the most modern aircraft of the Luftwaffe, but none were delivered in time—and in any event, the political outcome meant that in time Czechoslovakia was consumed by Hitler's expanding Third Reich without a shot fired in anger. As a result, it would take until the late war for this exceptional biplane to get its chance to bloody the nose of fascism.

After the occupation of Czechoslovakia, the B-534 still carried out service. Some were briefly integrated into the German Luftwaffe, though it was quickly replaced by the Messerschmitt Bf 109E as soon as more rolled off the production line and became available. Beyond that, the Germans made use of the B-534 as an advanced trainer and as a tow plane for gliders. Interestingly, the Germans also used the craft as a test aircraft for deck-landing trials in connection with Germany's aircraft carrier programme.

The Slovak puppet government, set up by the Nazis, briefly used some of the B-534s in a border war with Hungary. After that, they would see some limited service as a subsidiary part of Operation Barbarossa, Hitler's invasion of the Soviet Union. By mid-1942, however, the type had been relegated to training purposes by the Slovak government.

The Bulgarians, however, still attempted to use the B-534s in their possession in combat. They had purchased seventy-eight of them in 1940, and they were still in frontline usage in 1943. This led to an unusual incident, where a handful of biplane fighters took on the might of the United States Air Force. That August, American Consolidated B-24 Liberators had launched a failed raid on the Ploieşti oilfields in Romania, attempting to knock out Germany's largest fuel source. Having already dealt with both Romanian and German fighter opposition, the bombers were on their return flight when they were challenged by Bulgarian B-534s. Despite their technical obsolescence, and a slower speed than the American bombers, the B-534s made two passes at the bombers, scoring hits, but not managing to down any of the powerful Liberators given the relatively light armament used by the biplane. No B-534s were lost, and so this rare Czechoslovak design managed the singular feat of being perhaps the only biplane used in combat against American heavy bombers in the European theatre.

The Bulgarian B-534s have a further distinction of having taken part in combat on both sides of the war effort. After the coup that saw Bulgaria switch sides on 9 September 1944, B-534s started to be used in ground attacks against the Germans. On the 10th, six of the Avias entered into a low-altitude dogfight with an equal number of Messerschmitt Bf 109s. One of the B-534s was lost, but the 109s broke off combat, wary of both the low altitude and the superior manoeuvrability of the biplane.

All of this points to a unique and frankly remarkable historical position of this forgotten biplane, but its story was not yet complete. For a while it had already accomplished many unexpected things, and it had still not fired its guns in anger at the Germans in the hands of its own pilots. However, as Germany's allies deserted her, and the Soviet Red Army began to close in, the opportunity arose to employ the remarkable little bird in her intended role—to strike a blow for Czechoslovakia against German power. It would do so in a remarkable, and also frequently forgotten, campaign of the war, the Slovak National Uprising.

The Slovak National Uprising erupted in 1944, but had its roots as early as 1943. The head of the Czechoslovakian government in exile, Edvard Beneš, had been in contact with various dissident groups within the Slovak Army in order to plan a revolt against the collaborationist government under Jozef Tiso. In what was called the 'Christmas Treaty', the various groups that would be involved all agreed to a joint declaration that both recognised Beneš' leadership, and to the recreation of Czechoslovakia after the war. These groups ranged from the government in exile, and democrat groups, the Communists, and the Slovak Army. They stockpiled cash, and various military supplies. By early 1944, they had formed into the First Czechoslovak Army and the Czechoslovak Forces of the Interior.

Events fell into motion quickly as Soviet troops approached the border of Eastern Slovakia. Partisan attacks increased in frequency and ferocity all through the summer, and by the time Romania defected from the Axis on 23 August, the Germans were ready to occupy Slovakia. This was the start of the uprising proper, and by 10 September the rebels had occupied large parts of central and eastern Slovakia—including two crucial airfields, which the Soviets used to fly in supplies.

From there, however, momentum slipped from the rebels. The Germans rushed in tens of thousands of SS soldiers, and the Soviets both failed to deliver enough aid and blocked the other allies from providing aid. At the same time, inner squabbles doomed a concerted effort, and as the rebellion collapsed the SS and other pro-Nazi forces put down the rebellion, the former with their typical brutality and wide-spread war crimes. Partisans and the remnants of the rebel forces continued to fight from the mountains, and while the uprising failed to achieve its objectives, it tied down significant amounts of German troops who could have been used to reinforce the collapsing Eastern Front.

As involves the Avia B-534, the Slovak rebels managed to get hold of a small motley air force that had been organised into the Slovak Insurgent Air Force. The force initially included four Avia B-534s, three Letov light bombers, and two obsolete Me 109E4s. This was later reinforced by two Me 109Gs and a Focke-Wulf Fw 189.

The rebels had great trouble supplying their air force, but nevertheless managed to fly 923 sorties that resulted in the destruction of forty Axis aircraft. As the uprising was being overrun in October 1944, the leader of the Slovak Insurgent Air Force, Rudolf Viest, withdrew the remaining Slovak air forces to airfields already secured by the Red Army in Poland. Most of the insurgent pilots then joined up with the 1st Czechoslovak Combined Air Division, which took part in the liberation of Czechoslovakia in 1945.

The Avia B-534 was an unlikely candidate to still be in service in 1944, let alone fighting against the Axis, given the circumstances of Czechoslovakia at that time. Yet the aircraft not only had lasted in service, but was able at the end to strike a blow against those who had occupied Czechoslovakia in 1938. The Avia B-534 even scored the last recorded aerial victory of a biplane fighter—downing a Junkers Ju 52. It was also the first aerial victory of the insurgent air force. As such, the Avia B-534 has most certainly earned its place in history for doing sterling service against the Axis, despite having been obsolete almost throughout its existence.

All too frequently the biplane is written-off as an obsolescent footnote to the Second World War, and in strictly technical terms this is true. After all, as jets began to appear in service, what world was there for a type of plane that had reached its maximum combat potential in the early to mid-1930s? Yet in truth, the story was vastly more complicated. As will be seen later, biplanes played unexpected and successful roles elsewhere in the war, and often under adverse circumstances. It is fitting to start with the Avia, which faced perhaps the most adverse conditions and still found success. Clearly, for the Avia B-534, 'obsolete' was not a term that carried much weight.

No original Avia B-534s survive today, but there are two replicas that were constructed using some original parts. The first is at the Prague Aviation Museum in the Czech Republic, and the other is held by the Slovak Technical Museum in Košice.

3

Bachem Ba-349 Natter

As the war progressed, German aircraft design moulded itself to the desperate situation facing the deteriorating Reich. Increasingly, as Allied bombers pounded German territory in ever-growing numbers around the clock, potential solutions were given the go-ahead for development that, perhaps, should have stayed on the drawing board.

Looking at the German designs from 1943–1945 is an intriguing glimpse into the future of aviation design. Some of the projects are eerily advanced, and as such have become the frequent pieces of science-fiction and other forms of entertainment—the products of 'Nazi Science'. Whether or not any of the projects were truly feasible given the technology of the day can be debated extensively, and in any event the course of the war rapidly outpaced them all. Some designs, however, should have been left to the minds of fantasists.

One of these radical designs was the Bachem Ba-349 Natter or Viper. The idea was for a simple and cheap solution to the problem of vastly superior Allied air forces. The reality was a nightmare.

Specifications

First Flight: 1944
Powerplant: Walter 109-509A-2 rocket motor, plus four Schmidding 109-553 booster rockets, 2,640-lb thrust not counting boosters.
Armament: Twenty-four Föhn unguided missiles.
Top Speed: 497 mph (800 kph)
Range/Service Ceiling: 24.8 miles (40 km), 45,920 feet (12,000 metres)
Dimensions: Length 19 feet 8 inches (6 metres), height 7 feet 5 inches (2.25 metres), wingspan 13 feet 1 inch (4 metres)
Number Built: 35

By 1943, the Luftwaffe was beginning to suffer greatly. There was little hope for the future either, with resources beginning to dwindle and increasing attacks both on German industry and on the infrastructure of the Luftwaffe itself. The need for new solutions other than piston-based fighters was starting to become urgent. One solution was the Luftwaffe's advancing jet and rocket fighter programme, which would result in such aircraft as the Messerschmitt Me 163 rocket fighter and the superb Messerschmitt Me 262

Captured Bachem Ba349 on display, likely late 1945. (*Courtesy of Thijs Postma*)

jet fighter. Another solution was the surface-to-air missile, a field that the Germans were developing, but only slowly. A stopgap measure would be a piloted rocket interceptor that was essentially used as a piloted version of the same thing. The RLM issued a call for submissions for what was termed the Emergency Fighter Programme. A number of radical concepts were developed for the programme (including the Heinkel He 162 Volksjäger ('People's Fighter') and the Bachem Werke submitted one of the most radical designs amongst a field of radical designs.

Erich Bachem's design, the BP-20, was meant to be as cheap to produce as possible, requiring no proper airfield at all—a far-sighted suggestion given the increasingly precarious situation Luftwaffe airfields would find themselves in as time progressed. The construction used mainly wooden parts, held together with glue and nails. Some of the relatively few metal parts would be the engine, an armour-plated bulkhead between the pilot and the BP-20's weaponry, and a bulletproof glass windshield.

The rocket motor used was the same one being used in the Me 163, but in addition a bevy of four Schmidding booster rockets would be provided. These boosters would run for ten seconds on take-off, adding 10,600 lb (4,800 kg) of thrust. The aircraft was designed to be launched straight up a vertical tower, and the launch thrust was supposed to ensure that the craft was going fast enough when it left the tower that its own control surfaces would be able to keep it under control.

From here, the idea was that an autopilot would guide the craft to the enemy bombers. Then, the pilot would take control and aim and fire the mass of rockets that constituted the plane's armament. An early proposal that it use a concrete nose and ram enemy bombers was rejected as Bachem insisted the plane was not to be a suicide weapon. Initially it was to carry nineteen R4M rockets, but was soon redesigned to carry twenty-four—though in the end the Föhn rockets were used.

Following this attack, and almost certainly out of fuel, the pilot would dive in what was now essentially a glider, then level out, and then eject the nose of the aircraft. A small parachute would be deployed from the rear of the craft, and the sudden deceleration would eject the pilot, and both the pilot and rocket motor would safely drop back to the ground to be re-used. All of this was proposed by August 1944, and development proceeded immediately.

The first M1 prototype was ready by October 1944, with glider tests started on 3 November. The first glider was taken aloft by a Heinkel He 111. While the tow cables interfered with the results and made them difficult to interpret, the first free flight in the M8 proved that the aircraft could indeed fly normally. This test occurred on 14 February 1945, by which time the need for Emergency Fighters was already beyond critical.

By the beginning of March 1945, sixteen prototypes had been built and tested—including some unmanned tests on the launching tower. The decision was made that it was time for a manned test flight, which was scheduled for the end of February, even before the unmanned tests finished.

Berlin was, by this point, pressuring Bachem to hurry. On 25 February, a test flight was made with a dummy pilot and all went to plan—except for the fact that the engine exploded when it made contact with the ground. Bachem was concerned that the test programme was too short, but a volunteer pilot from the Luftwaffe, Lothar Siebel, was ready to attempt the flight. The date chosen was 1 March.

What happened when the Natter tried to launch is difficult to fully determine, and it fully depends on which source one consults. Some believe that the cockpit latch was faulty, others that the cockpit latch was not fully closed when the boosters ignited. Whatever the case, the canopy flew off almost immediately, and, as the pilot's headrest was attached to the canopy, Siebel's head was snapped back against the rear bulkhead, either rendering him unconscious or killing him instantly. The Natter itself continued to ascend until the motor stalled about fifteen seconds into the flight, at which point the craft plunged back to earth, destroying the vehicle entirely.

What would have happened from here is uncertain. The SS, who had taken control of the project early, were already preparing launch pads for its use, and it is uncertain how many Natters were actually built. Whether or not its problems could have been solved—and Bachem believed that with automated take-off near the bombers that they could—events swiftly overtook the programme. By 25 April, the Bachem works had fallen to French soldiers, and the dispersed parts of the programme were either destroyed by the SS or captured by advancing American or Soviet troops. In addition, there were pilots already training for the use of the Natter in combat, and sites prepared for its launch, but the sites were overrun before the theoretical start date of 25 April 1945.

Readying a serpent's strike—a Ba349 prepared for a test launch. Note the late-war paint scheme (*Courtesy of Thijs Postma*)

It is difficult to assess the Bachem programme, and it might be easy to write off the Ba-349 as a suicide machine created by a desperate Germany. Different sources will either view it as one of many advanced aircraft using revolutionary power sources in order to stem a desperate tide, while others will view it as a fundamentally flawed concept that would have just proved lethal to its own side.

What can be said is that it was a design born of desperation that attempted to fulfil nearly impossible conditions under which Germany sought to fight as her war situation deteriorated. That Bachem found a solution to the problem, despite it being beset by misfortune and overwhelmed by events, is remarkable in and of itself. It is also remarkable as it provides an example of how varied German late-war projects were, and how strange and unreal these may look to modern eyes.

The Natter was part of numerous strange and unusual designs created by the Germans in the late-war years. Some were highly advanced pieces of technology that would influence aviation design for years afterwards, while others were desperation projects seeking to stem the tide of Allied bombers. Indeed, German science has become a major source of interest in popular culture ever since. It can be difficult sometimes for even an experienced student of history to differentiate between fact and fiction. A good starting point if one is interested in the strange German aviation projects from war's end can be found by looking up the Luft '46 website at www.luft46.com.

The one surviving full Natter has been stored in the Smithsonian's Gerber facility, in apparently bad condition. Parts of another have been used to create a replica in the Deutsches Museum in Germany. In addition, there are several replicas that can be visited by the public. One is at the Planes of Fame Air Museum in Chino, California. Another is at the Fantasy of Flight in Polk County, Florida.

4

Bell P-59 Airacomet

The history of the jet fighter in the Second World War is often remembered as a story of German technological marvels. To be fair, German projects in this regard were many and varied—and the spectacular Messerschmitt Me 262 is one of the most recognisable aircraft of the war. Yet it is far more accurate to say that each of the major powers created jet fighters during the war, though often in small numbers or far too late to see any significant operational use. On the American side, their first jet fighter—the first of many contributions the United States would make to the jet age—was the P-59 Airacomet.

Though it would never garner fame or see combat, the P-59 was America's first step, providing technical expertise and learned experience—a critical start for the American jet age.

Specifications

First Flight: 1942
Powerplant: Two General Electric J31-GE-5 turbojets, 2,000-lb thrust.
Armament: One M4 37-mm cannon, three 0.5-inch machine guns, all nose mounted
Top Speed: 409 mph (658 kph)
Range/Service Ceiling: 400 miles (644 km), 46,200 feet (14,080 metres)
Dimensions: Length 38 feet 10 inches (11.84 metres), height 12 feet 4 inches (3.76 metres), wingspan 45 feet 6 inches (13.87 metres)
Number Built: 66

In technological terms, the United States benefitted greatly as a result of their alliance with the United Kingdom. As part of the normal transfers of information between the two nations, the work of Sir Frank Whittle was given to the American aircraft industry. Whittle was the genius behind England's jet programme, a programme that would ultimately result in the Gloster Meteor. In April 1941, American General 'Hap' Arnold was present at a test of Whittle's prototype Gloster E.28/39, and he took the plans for the powerplant, the Power Jets W.1, back to the United States, and by the start of September 1941 General Electric had been offered a contract to replicate the engine. General Electric was, in the main, chosen for its convenience. The company had extensive experience with turbines dating back to the turn of the century, and this expertise was considered invaluable to ensuring a quick start to the air force's nascent jet programme.

Bell Aircraft Corporation was approached to build an aircraft that would house the new engine when it was completed, also for reasons of expediency. They had a good geographical location in relation to the GE plant that would be building the engine. The head of the company, Lawrence Dale Bell, immediately agreed to the project, and work began on three prototypes. To preserve secrecy, the craft was given the designation XP-59, to tie it to an already cancelled and more conventional Bell project.

The design chosen was ultimately fairly conservative. An early vision of the XP-59 programme had seen a pusher design with slightly swept wings and a twin-boom tail design. The XP-59 that was rapidly being constructed was to be a standard mid-wing monoplane, with a pair of the new engines, one on each side of the fuselage under the wings. The reason for this was, once again, practical. Much like in almost all early jet fighters, the early gas turbine engines had only limited thrust. This problem plagued the entire first generation of legendary jet fighters, such as the Messerschmitt Me 262 and Gloster Meteor. The other problem would prove to be engine reliability, another across-the-board issue that the first generation of jet fighters was plagued by. The only other unconventional feature of the design was the landing gear, far out on the wing and onto the nose, the entire idea being to build around the needs of the engine. The tail sloped upwards too, in order to ensure the control surfaces were well clear of the turbojets.

The Americans moved relatively quickly. General Electric proved a good choice for the engines, as did Bell, for the prototype XP-59A took to the air on 1 October 1942—only

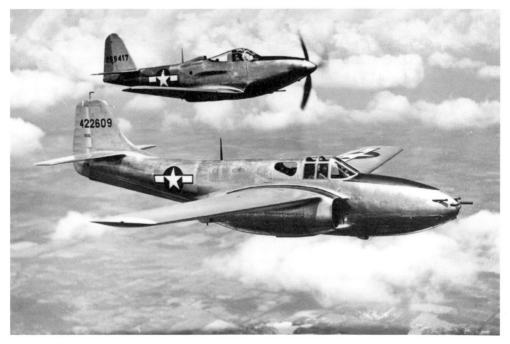

One of the production-model P-59A Airacomets, in company with a P-63 King Cobra. (*Courtesy of the National Museum of the United States Air Force*)

a few months behind the Messerschmitt Me 262, and far ahead of the Gloster Meteor, which first flew in March 1943.

From this ostensibly promising start, however, the project ran into difficulties. The engine performance was far from what had been desired and its reliability was somewhat suspect. The XP-59 also failed to live up to performance expectations, and was at best somewhat sluggish. As a weapons platform, it was also far from stellar. Nevertheless, a contract was still placed for eighty production versions, officially designated as the Bell P-59A Airacomet.

Bell would complete fifty of these, twenty being the P-59A and the remainder being the slightly improved P-59B. Even though the P-59B came with an improved engine, her speed was still inadequate, its maximum speed actually being slower than that achieved by mid- and late-model P-51 Mustang fighters. Many of the delivered fighters had open-air observer's cockpits put into the nose, much like those of much earlier biplanes. These dual-cockpit P-59Bs were used for the interesting purpose of being drone-control aircraft. Drone operation was in its infancy in the latter stages of the Second World War, far from the major component of aerial warfare they are as of the time of this writing. These operations were an early signal to the future.

The P-59s were ultimately mostly operated by the USAAF's 412th Squadron, concerned initially with putting the production aircraft through their respective paces, but then began to use the aircraft as advanced trainers for the other jet aircraft starting to come into American service. The testing of the P-59 began in late 1943, and while by itself the aircraft would not prove to be a combat-worthy aircraft, it would serve as both testbed and trainer to familiarise pilots with the dawning jet age.

It is difficult to recall, looking at the P-59 from decades on, that it was still a revolution in design and a massive leap in what aircraft were and could do. There was, at the time, a lot of excitement about it, despite its sluggish performance. One man who flew it stated:

I have flown the Army's new jet-propelled fighter, the Bell *Airacomet* [P-59A], and found it nothing short of amazing. Soon it may be flying circles—literally—around the remnants of enemy air power.... Let me give you my first impressions of my first *Airacomet* flight. I felt like a Hallowe'en witch riding astride a vacuum cleaner instead of a broom and being pushed through the air faster than anyone has ever flown before.

Charles M. Fischer, *Flying Magazine*, 1944

In the end, the P-59 was not a success and by 1950 there were no airworthy examples left in service. They had been expended in various training purposes to familiarise pilots with how to handle jet aircraft, and then often written-off. Other American jets were coming into play, most notably the Lockheed P-80 Shooting Star, which would prove a vastly superior design. The P-59 Airacomet was nevertheless the first jet fighter in the arsenal of the United States, the starting point for a long tradition of aviation excellent. It is all the more remarkable that such technical prowess and achievement came from such humble beginnings. The Airacomet was the genesis point, testbed and teacher, for all that came after it.

Despite its decidedly lacklustre career, the P-59 is remarkable in one respect—a frankly astounding rate of survival. Out of a mere eighty that were constructed, six are still on display today. Given how few of these early jets were built, and the hard test use to which they were put, it is truly astonishing. All six are can be viewed by the public. One, naturally enough, is on display in the Milestones of Flight area at the Smithsonian National Air and Space Museum, in Washington, D.C. This aircraft is one of the early XP-59s. A P-59A rests at March Field Air Museum in California, and three P-59Bs can be found at Edwards Air Force Base, Pioneer Village, in Minden, Nebraska, and at the National Museum of the United States Air Force in Dayton, Ohio. In addition, a single YP-59, a development of the design evaluated by the US Navy for potential carrier use, is under restoration to flying condition by Planes of Fame of Chino, California.

5

Bloch MB.152

French aviation often gets short shrift in histories of the Second World War. The standard narrative, applied to all levels of the French military, is of a large, but obsolete force faced by an onslaught of modern German equipment operated by superbly trained soldiers, in turn controlled by masterful tactical and strategic planning. There is some truth to the stereotype. French designs were frequently older than those of their German adversaries, and more to the point French strategic thinking was woefully unprepared for the invasion of 1940 planned by German general Von Manstein, which would knock France out of the war in a mere six weeks.

In the catastrophe that came with the German Blitzkrieg, the French Armée de L'Air was outmanoeuvred, although not technically outmatched. While some of its aircraft were behind the times, the French also had very modern craft that were in service when the Germans attacked. Had they been available in larger numbers, their influence on the campaign may have been far greater than it was.

The Bloch MB.152 was one of these modern craft, an attempt to match the high-performance German fighters. While its performance was not that of a world-beater, the Bloch MB series demonstrates that French aviation was not an outdated concept during the Second World War.

Specifications

First Flight: (MB.152 Prototype) 1938
Powerplant: One Gnome-Rhône 14N-25, or 14N-49, radial-piston engine, 1,100 hp.
Armament: Four 7.5-mm (0.295-inch) machine guns, or two similar machine guns and two 20-mm cannon.
Top Speed: 320 mph (515 kph)
Range/Service Ceiling: 373 miles (600 km), 32,810 feet (10,000 metres)
Dimensions: Length 29 feet 10 inches (9.1 metres), height 9 feet 11 inches (3.03 metres), wingspan 34 feet 7 inches (10.54 metres)
Number Built: Approximately 663, all models.

The French had many varied designs on the drawing boards or just entering service when the Second World War began. It is much fairer to assess French aviation as having

An early prototype Bloch MB.151. (*Courtesy of the Nico Braas Collection, 1000aircraftphotos.com*)

a wide stable of potential aircraft, many of which were overtaken by events. The Bloch MB.150 series is an example of this. Had it been able to reach its full potential, a world-winner could have been in French service. As it stood, the aircraft never quite measured up to expectations, but still proved itself a good combat fighter.

In the interests of precision, it should be noted that the MB.152 is the ultimate combat expression of the line. The initial prototype was the MB.150, and the early production models were labelled MB.151. The 152 was the last of the series to be built and see combat, but the series as a whole must be discussed to adequately explain its development.

The initial impetus for the MB.150 series came from a French Armée de l'Air requirement in 1934 for a new monoplane fighter. Ultimately, the Morane-Saulnier M.S.406 would win the competition and end up as France's main frontline fighter when the war began, but the Bloch entrant was promising enough that further development was authorised. The first prototype MB.150 made its first attempted flight in 1936, when the craft resolutely refused to become airborne. Despite what many designers would have considered a rather comprehensive failure, the Bloch team went back to work and made extensive modifications. The modifications included a larger, stronger wing, new landing gear, and a more powerful engine that finally got the MB.150 into the air in October 1937.

This prototype was handed over for testing, and, after further revisions, SNCASO was awarded a production order for twenty-five aircraft (in explanation: the *Société nationale des constructions aéronautiques du sud-ouest* was an amalgamation of several French aircraft firms that started operation in 1938). It was at this point that another problem arose—the MB.150 design was discovered to be utterly unsuited to mass production. A further redesign, with yet another new engine, resulted in the MB.151.01, which first flew in September 1938. Despite the increasingly urgent need for new fighters, a grand total of four aircraft had been delivered by April 1939.

Simultaneously, however, SNCASO was improving the design yet again, with another engine—this time the Gnome-Rhône 14N-21, which ended up being upgraded before it was even handed over for testing to the 14N-25. The result, however, was a success— undoubtedly a huge relief to the harried designers involved—and a production order was placed for 400 aircraft, 340 of which were to be the new MB.152, as this version was known.

Then, once again, things went wrong. Despite all the modifications to ensure smoother production, the actual building of the craft was still agonizingly slow. The first aircraft was delivered in early May 1939. By the outbreak of war, only between 123 to 129 of both the MB.151 and 152 had been completed. Precisely none of these could be deployed for combat, since none of them had gunsights and at least ninety-five of them still had no propellers (this latter problem being something that would plague the aircraft right until the defeat of France). By November 1939, only 358 were complete—despite the emergency situation—and 157 still had no propellers. When the German invasion rolled westwards, 140 MB.151s and 363 MB.152s were in service, but a mere thirty-seven and ninety-three of the respective models were in functional order.

The French Air Force, however, did everything it could to get these fighters into service, despite indifference and political intrigue within the French government. Though slightly inferior in terms of speed and manoeuvrability to the Bf 109, the MB. 152 was definitely superior to the M.S.406 that equipped the bulk of French squadrons—had more been available, the Luftwaffe would undoubtedly have had a tougher time of things. The other problematic element was the craft's rate of climb, which was slower than its German opponent. The problems of French manufacturing also became apparent, with the radio equipment being only sporadically in working order, and what propellers that had been manufactured were unreliable.

When the aircraft was used in combat, it could achieve its objective, but it was never used with the impact it should have had. It was used instead in bits, here and there, failing to impact the conflict. On 3 June, the Germans mounted one of their rare attempts at strategic warfare, known as Operation Julia. The Luftwaffe gathered 500 planes for a series of strikes against airfields and railway junctions around Paris, and the French responded as best they could, shooting down twenty-six German aircraft for the loss of seventeen of their own. The MB.152 was used extensively, with the largest French formation of the defence including twenty-two of the aircraft. It was a capable aircraft, but even here, in decently heavy numbers, it was unable to exert a heavy enough response to be decisive.

Some of the Bloch's pilots were men who had, until recently, been flying the M.S.406, and the MB.152 was a radically different experience in combat. One pilot, Pierre Courteville, found it to be a much bigger fighter, and significantly more robust. Another, Henri Gille, noted that it was in nearly every way a superior aircraft, but the complaint of both of these pilots was that it was significantly slower than the Bf 109E, putting it at a significant disadvantage in a dogfight. The problem for the pilots was not the quality of the aircraft so much as the problems facing them. Replacement aircraft were available, but in the chaos of the war they might be missing parts. In Courteville's case, the replacement MB.152s his unit were allotted were lacking propellers. Overall, the pilots were drained by constant operations and the slow attrition of both men and machines. In the chaos, more than one MB.152 was lost to an accidental cause. Perhaps most notable in this regard was the loss of six Bloch fighters on 10 June, all of which landed in a river. These pilots, of GC I/8, more than likely mistook the river for a wet runway in the chaos of the retreat. The unit would lose another pilot shot down by the local peasants, and still two more aircraft that collided in a clear sky. All of these disasters occurred within ten days, almost as deadly to the unit as fighting the Germans had been.

Ultimately, by the time of the Fall of France, the MB.151 and 152 would equip eighteen squadrons of the French Air Force, and gave good account of themselves in combat. The final kill ratio of the type tallied at 159 aircraft shot down compared to fifty-nine lost. The rapid fall of France, however, combined with small numbers of the aircraft, prevented it from exerting a major effect on the course of events.

After the fall, the Vichy Air Force maintained a few *Groupes* of these fighters, with some sold off to the Romanians. In total, Vichy equipped six *Groupes* with it, a total of 320 aircraft. Combat against the Allies and other causes would reduce this number. Design improvements were still made too, in the apparently endless development process the series endured. These ultimately resulted in the superb MB.155, which was

A production model MB.152. (*Courtesy of Thijs Postma*)

too late to see combat in 1940, and of which around twenty were ultimately produced. These briefly served with the Vichy forces until the Germans occupied the rest of France in late 1942, upon which all the remaining aircraft, totalling 173 planes, were confiscated by the Luftwaffe. The Germans utilised these aircraft as advanced trainers before passing twenty MB.151 and MB.152 fighters off to Romania as well.

The MB.152 was the expression of a good design that, despite numerous setbacks, still somehow made it into service. The dedication of the designers to producing a fighter, and the herculean efforts of the French military to hurry it into service, are worthy of remembrance in their own right. Yet, beyond that, the MB.152 serves as proof of the fact that the French were far from technically outmatched by German aviation design—that it was a matter of production and politics that kept the French from having a force that could have challenged and even matched the best the Luftwaffe had to offer.

The ultimate expression of the Bloch 150 series would be found in the exceptional MB.157, of which one prototype had been completed by the Fall of France. Bearing a remarkable resemblance to the Republic P-47 Thunderbolt, the MB.157 had a 1,580-hp engine and could hit the then-incredible speed of 441 mph (710 kph). Sadly, this remarkable fighter ended up having its engine removed by the Germans for testing, with the airframe being left on the ground to be destroyed in a later Allied air raid.

6

Boeing P-26 Peashooter

If the Peashooter is remembered at all today, it is as a strange-looking craft that was part of America's woeful unpreparedness in dealing with the Japanese onslaught after Pearl Harbour in December 1941. Indeed, by 1941 the Peashooter was obsolete and outclassed by its Japanese opponents. Yet it was not always so. The Peashooter that was unable to stop the Japanese would see its last combat mission in 1954. Additionally, it had been seeing combat since 1937, and demonstrated a surprisingly long combat career as well as an accidental achievement that marks the P-26 Peashooter out as a unique aircraft that should not be simply written-off.

Specifications

First Flight: (XP-936) 1932
Powerplant: Pratt & Whitney R-1340-27 radial engine, 500 hp.
Armament: Two 0.5-inch (12.7-mm) machine guns, or one 0.5-inch gun and one 0.3-inch (7.62-mm) gun, plus two 100-lb (45-kg) bombs, or five 31-lb (14-kg) anti-personnel bombs.
Top Speed: 200 mph (377 kph)
Range/Service Ceiling: 360 miles (597 km), 24,400 feet (8,350 metres)
Dimensions: Length 23 feet 7 inches (7.18 metres), height 10 feet (3.04 metres), wingspan 28 feet (8.5 metres)
Number Built: 139, including export models.

The Peashooter started life as a company funded venture. Boeing was working on the airframe long before the United States Army Air Corps agreed to supply engines and instruments for a trio of trial aircraft, which was tentatively named the XP-936. This was in 1931, at which point the design that would become the Peashooter was still a highly advanced design. It would, in fact, become the first American all-metal monoplane fighter, following what was then the parlance of the US Army Air Corps and being termed a 'pursuit plane' (thus the 'P' designation for American fighters that persisted until the end of the Second World War).

The design was, in some ways, a very strange one. For a start, despite being a revolution in what the Air Corps had been stocked with, it still featured an open cockpit. Moreover,

A photograph of a Boeing P.26 Peashooter. (*Courtesy of the United States National Naval Air Museum*)

despite Boeing's experience installing retractable landing gear on its designs, the Peashooter would have fixed landing gear, with full spats. In addition, despite cantilever wings being increasingly common, the Peashooter's wings would be braced in the old way, by external wires.

Interestingly, all of these strange decisions would later be rectified in another prototype, the Model 264, otherwise known as the YP-29. This prototype, which flew in 1934, was never selected for production, but is an interesting vision of what the Peashooter might have been.

The first Model 266, the Peashooter's original designation, flew in March 1932, and each of the three completed models were sent to different air bases for testing. The tests went very well, since Boeing shortly thereafter received a production contract for 111 aircraft, which was later increased to 136. These were the P-26A, the first of which was delivered at the start of 1934, with the rest delivered by the end of the year. The most remarkable feature of the entire programme was that the Peashooter went from initial conception to its maiden flight in just over nine weeks, an astonishingly short time frame even for aircraft of the day.

A number of slight modifications were made to the production models to bring down the landing speed and protect the pilot's head in case of a rollover crash. This latter feature was, unfortunately, somewhat common. The early Peashooters had a proclivity to flip over on landings if they were not handled with care. A higher headrest was installed as a necessary feature after an accident that killed the pilot. Further modifications resulted in an order for twenty-five P-26B aircraft, which came with a fuel-injecting Pratt & Whitney

Wasp engine, then a further twenty-three P-26C aircraft, which had made changes to the carburettor and fuel system. As the P-26B was demonstrably the better-powered aircraft, many of the existing Peashooters were converted over to that as a standard. The resulting aircraft was, for its day, a representative of the peak of aviation design. It was a more advanced design than any fighter in the US arsenal, which makes its transitional nature to 'true' monoplane fighters all the more interesting. It was the first monoplane fighter the US would have, but also the last to feature an open cockpit design—a feature that was, apparently, mainly a concession to the older aviators still in the War Department.

While faster than anything the USAAC had ever experienced before, and an aircraft well-liked by its pilots, the technological development of monoplanes in the 1930s made it rapidly obsolete, and by the outbreak of war the Peashooter was considered woefully out of date. Despite this, between 1932 and 1934 the Peashooter set records for both speed and altitude, and started to make its way around the globe. By 1938, the craft was very officially obsolete and remained in American service only in Hawaii, Panama, and the Philippines.

This, however, is where the irony came in. The P-26 did all of its service after it was officially out of date, and it managed to do so across the globe in many different hands. A single P-26 export version, known as the Model 281, became part of the Spanish government's fight against Franco's fascist-backed Nationalists, and fought until it was shot down in 1937.

A further eleven Model 281s were purchased by the Chinese government, by this time fighting for its life against Imperial Japan. As a result, the P-26 not only became the first Boeing fighter to gain actual combat experience, but also the first to score an aerial victory. On 20 August 1937, a flight of six Peashooters shot down four G3M2 bombers and suffered no losses. Over the rest of the year, the craft would be used up in heavy service and were replaced by the Gloster Gladiator.

Therefore it was that the Peashooter saw combat in the skies both of Europe and of Asia, and its service was far from over. In the Philippines, the Peashooter would once again meet the Japanese in combat, and it would acquit itself rather well, despite its utter obsolescence. As late as 1940, the Peashooter made up the entire strength of the Army Air Corps in the islands—a total of twenty-eight aircraft. By 1941, despite reinforcements, these Peashooters were still there as part of a woefully unprepared force to counter the Japanese onslaught that began on 8 December 1941. The Japanese struck many American planes still on the ground, but the Peashooters that got aloft downed at least one Japanese bomber, and are believed to have accounted for two, possibly even three Mitsubishi A6M Zeros—a fighter that was almost a quantum leap forward in aviation design compared to the compact little P-26.

The very last Peashooters were retired from the Guatemalan Air Force in 1957, bringing to an end a remarkable career that had lasted for twenty-three years, and spanned the globe. The Peashooter is an object lesson in pointing out that 'obsolete' does not necessarily mean the same thing as 'useless' and was a remarkable aircraft in its own right.

The Peashooters that survive (as well as reproductions) are wonderful craft. They show off the vibrant paint schemes of the pre-war USAAC, and while they may seem somewhat alien to those familiar with later fighters there is something visually appealing about them. The two survivors are at the Planes of Fame Museum in California, and the National Air and Space Museum in Washington. Replicas are viewable at the National Museum of the Air Force in Ohio, the San Diego Air and Space Museum, and two more replicas are being constructed by the Golden Age Aeroplane Works of Seymour, Indiana. In addition, there is a flying replica of the Peashooter held by the Military Aviation Museum in Virginia.

7

Boulton Paul Defiant

The Boulton Paul Defiant is usually written-off by historical texts. At best, it is treated as an intriguing experiment that didn't manage to live up to expectations. At worst, it is written-off as a poor idea that utterly failed in its assigned task. The truth of the matter is rather different. Initially designed as a daytime interceptor, the Defiant is usually summed up as the plane that was mistaken for a Hawker Hurricane, which then used its rearward facing, turreted armament to spring a nasty surprise on German Messerschmitts. The story continues that the Defiant was withdrawn from service when the Germans grew wary of the trick. Thus, ultimately, the Defiant is written-off, but this is far from the truth. In reality, the Defiant continued on as a successful night fighter, bridging the gap until radar-equipped aircraft such as the Bristol Beaufighter could be thrown into the fray. It would serve elsewhere too, and is more than worthy of remembrance and not just as a trick that soon went sour.

Specifications

First Flight: 1937
Powerplant: Rolls-Royce Merlin XX inline piston engine, 1,280 hp.
Armament: Four 7.7-mm (0.303-inch) machine guns in a fully powered dorsal turret.
Top Speed: 313 mph (504 kph)
Range/Service Ceiling: 465 miles (746 km), 30,350 feet (9,250 metres)
Dimensions: Length 35 feet 4 inches (10.77 metres), height 11 feet 4 inches (3.46 metres), wingspan 39 feet 4 inches (11.99 metres)
Number Built: 1,064

The Defiant was not the only craft of its sort constructed—contemporary aircraft of a similar configuration were the Blackburn Roc and the Hawker Hotspur. The Defiant, however, found a better niche than either of these two aircraft, which by itself should serve as a partial repudiation of the 'brief trick' analysis.

The concept of a turret fighter had first emerged as early as 1935, as aviation theory began to evolve. British doctrine of the early to mid-1930s held that the greatest threat that would be facing Britain would be massed formations of unescorted bombers, as fighter ranges were still unequal to the task of long-distance escort missions. Moreover,

Trainer version of the Boulton-Paul Defiant, *sans* the four-gun turret. (*Courtesy of the David Horn Collection, 1000aircraftphotos.com*)

there were bombers at that point in time that could outrun the biplane fighters that were then in frontline service. The main British fighters at the time were craft such as the Bristol Bulldog and Gloster Gauntlet, the latter of which was in major service in the late 1930s. Such fighters were inadequate to the task of countering the new bombers that would face Britain in a future war.

Moreover, the British were certain that their own bombers would be able to successfully defend themselves against conventional fighter attack, and it was safe to assume that the same would be true of the fledgling Luftwaffe, which was accurately perceived as the enemy of the future. So the theory that formed the Defiant ran that a turret-equipped aircraft would separate responsibilities. The pilot could manoeuvre to the most optimal point, below or to the sides. From there, a separate gunner could concentrate on aiming precision gunnery.

The resulting specification from the Air Ministry, F.9/35 for a two-seater fighter to operate at any time of day, and Boulton Paul prepared a submission, already highly experienced with turret design from their previous bomber designs. Despite seven prototypes being ordered, only two were ever built, one of them being Boulton Paul's P.82.

The resulting aircraft was a monocoque design, meaning that the elements are supported by the external skin of the plane. The various pieces were bolted together, making the craft relatively easy to assemble. The turret itself would be a powered design, featuring four Browning machine guns. Quite an advanced design for its day, the guns were fired electrically, and cut-off mechanisms ensured that the turret would not be able to fire into any part of the airplane, including the propeller disc, as the Defiant's turret was to feature a nearly unlimited ratio of fire. The gunner could even rotate the guns fully forward and then transfer fire control to the pilot. This was very rarely done in reality, however, as the pilot lacked a gunsight and the guns had a minimum elevation in that position of 19 degrees.

The first Defiant rolled off the assembly lines in 1937 and without its turret the resemblance between it and the Hawker Hurricane was easily noted. The Hurricane was, by that point, coming into service as the main front-line fighter of the Royal Air Force. The cockpit and turret were designed to reduce drag. In addition the landing gear and the large radiator under the fuselage further enhanced the resemblance. The first flight was on 11 August 1937, a year ahead of its competition, the Hawker Hotspur. Once the turret was installed, the prototype was evaluated and approved as the victor of the turret fighter specification. Production, however, was initially extremely slow as Boulton Paul were already turning out Blackburn Roc aircraft for the navy. As a result, a grand total of three aircraft had been delivered when war broke out.

In October 1939, the first Defiants started to arrive in RAF service, and was the subject of a disinformation campaign put out to the public saying that the Defiant carried the astonishing total of twenty-one guns. Initial training befitted the Defiant's dual-role design—the first crews to receive Defiants were trained against British medium bombers as night bombers.

The first combat usage of the Defiant, however, came in daylight in the Low Countries. In May 1940, the Defiants were thrown in to stem the tide of the German advance, and proved successful against Luftwaffe bombers. German fighters, however, were a tougher proposition, and they took their toll of Defiants—already learning to engage them in frontal attacks.

As France fell, the Defiants were thrown into combat again over Dunkirk, engaging in heavy fighting both with German bombers as well as the swarms of Bf 109s. Their best success, however, would come during the early stages of the Battle of Britain. In the event, two squadrons would operate the Defiant, No. 141 and No. 264, and they would be thrown into the battle immediately, taking advantage of German methods before experience could alter their tactics.

German fighter tactics called for quick attacks from behind before speeding away, and these 'boom and zoom' tactics had served them well. Against Defiants, however, which were very easy to mistake for the Hurricane, they could prove a lethal error. On 29 May 1940, the Defiant would have its best day—Squadron No. 264 cut a swath through the Germans in two sorties, downing nineteen Ju 87 dive bombers, nine Bf 110 heavy fighters, as well as eight Bf 109s, and a lone Ju 88. This was balanced against the loss of a single gunner. This was, unfortunately, in a time period where the Defiant's time as a day fighter was already limited.

The British may well have been pleased at this early performance, but outside observers were unconvinced. Writing in June 1940, the *Science News Letter* noted British reports of the Defiant's success, though they immediately added that the craft they termed 'mystery fighters' would be far too few in number to change the outcome of the battle then raging in the skies over England. This pessimism went deeper still. They went on to note that the Defiants were indeed exploiting a vulnerability in the German bombers, but accurately predicted the limitations of the type:

> Superiority of the Defiant can be attributed mostly to its armament and not to other features. A single-engined twoseater, its top speed of less than 330 miles an hour makes England's 'secret weapon' slower than most fighters, little faster than most bombers and not as fast as some of the newest. Single-engined multiseaters have been abandoned by the U. S. Army Air Corps for that reason, but it should not prove impossible to utilise the Defiant's principle of gun-power on twin-engined combat planes.

The Science News Letter, 15 June 1940, p. 374

While this may be seen as accurate with the benefit of hindsight, the Germans were quick to respond to the Defiant. The Luftwaffe adapted tactics rapidly, attacking from different positions and overwhelming the Defiants. Losses began to mount, particularly amongst gunners, who had difficulty baling out under combat conditions. Even while it was still enjoying success, the Defiant's losses were already becoming intolerable. On 13 May, six Defiants of No. 264 Squadron went into combat with Bf 109s and they lost five of their number. Boulton Paul attempted to concentrate by proposing the Mk II Defiant, which came with the Merlin XX engine, as well as a bigger fuel tank and rudder. Meanwhile, Defiant pilots came up with practical and effective counter tactics to hold off German fighters, but the decision was still made to minimise losses by transferring Defiant operations to night fighting, the other role for which it was originally designed. The order to remove them officially went out on 28 August 1940. The planners of the 1930s had not been prepared for bombers that were under near-constant escort by fighter planes. The irony, then, was that the designers had predicted daytime combat and instead the Defiant would carry out the original purpose under cover of darkness.

Four squadrons would ultimately take the Defiant into night combat over the capital during the height of the Blitz. This number would rise to a grand total of thirteen squadrons after the battle, until the type was replaced in 1942. They attacked from below and behind, in a manoeuvre that the Germans would later use successfully in their *Schräge Musik* tactics. These Defiants shot down more enemy aircraft than any other type of night fighter, and a show of their success is that the RAF tried to fit turrets to the Defiant's successors, such as the Bristol Beaufighter and de Havilland Mosquito.

The Defiant was only withdrawn from service as larger numbers of Beaufighters and Mosquitos became available, which offered high enough performance to supplant the older turret-fighter, and they also came with built-in radar. Even after this, the Defiant soldiered on, operating as a trainer, a target towing aircraft, as an air-sea rescue vehicle, and as an electronic countermeasures aircraft. It would last in the air-sea rescue role until the middle of 1943, seeing service with five RAF squadrons. Here the Defiant would be replaced in wartime, in this case by older, converted Supermarine Spitfires Mk IIs. The last major use of the Defiant was testing ejection seats, starting in December 1944. The chief drawback of the Defiant, in retrospect, was not the turreted design. This, in itself, was not the flawed idea that stereotype makes it out to be. The chief downside of the turret was its lethality to the gunner. The design meant the turret had to rotate fully in order for the gunner to bale out, which often was not possible in combat. Moreover, the combat suit that the gunners were forced to wear had its own limitations. The turret left no room for the standard parachute, so the gunners were forced to wear a single-piece garment known as the 'rhino' suit. This suit also frequently failed to operate properly. One air gunner, Frederick 'Gus' Platts stated:

> The Rhino suit we had to wear on Defiants was a bear but I couldn't come up with an alternative, even though it killed dozens of us. I forget the details of it but we could not have sat on our chute or even keep it nearby as in other turrets, so you wore—all in one—an inner layer that fitted a little like a wetsuit of today. The chute fitted around this, and then the dinghy and the outer clothing. There was inner webbing and pockets that literally fell apart (I presume) when one baled out.
>
> Nijboer, p. 150

This multi-role career, and its sterling service during the Blitz, puts paid to the myth that the Defiant was a 'one-trick pony' and ultimately an unsuccessful aircraft. In truth, the Boulton Paul Defiant took on many roles during the war and was successful at all of them.

A single Boulton Paul Defiant survives today and is on display at the RAF Museum in Hendon. Revealingly, it is painted in its night fighter colours, not as a daylight fighter.

8

Breda Ba.88

Italian aviation during the war is, perhaps, the most easily discounted of the major combatants. The combat performance of Italian arms during the war is considered legendary to this day only in its incompetence. The story tells—with a good deal of justification—of poorly led and poorly equipped men being thrown against armies that frequently annihilated their Italian foes in short order.

In the air, however, there is another, quite different story to be told. The Regia Aeronautica came from a proud aviation tradition, and produced interesting and highly useful designs both before and during the war. Moreover, while some of their mainstay craft were outdated or flawed by the time the Second World War started, there were others that most definitely were neither. As a result, Italian designs sort, as will be seen, into either of these categories. The other examples in this book are mostly of the latter type. The Breda Ba.88, however, sorts neatly into the former category. The supreme irony is that it showed so much promise, but reaped utterly no reward.

Specifications

First Flight: 1936
Powerplant: Two Piaggio P.XI RC 40 radial-piston engines, 1,000 hp.
Armament: Three Breda-SAFAT 0.5-inch (12.7-mm) machine guns mounted in the nose, one 0.303-inch (7.7-mm) machine gun on a flexible rear cockpit mount, plus 2,204 lb (1,000 kg) of bombs within the fuselage, or three 441-lb (220-kg) bombs carried semi-exposed in the belly.
Top Speed: 304 mph (490 kph)
Range/Service Ceiling: 1,019 miles (1,640 km), 26,245 feet (8,000 metres)
Dimensions: Length 35 feet 5 inches (10.79 metres), height 10 feet 2 inches (3.1 metres), wingspan 51 feet 2 inches (15.6 metres)
Number Built: 149

Italian arms, much like those of the French, are often given short shrift in histories of the Second World War. Admittedly, there is a good deal of evidence to back up a bleak overall picture. It is unfair, however, to attribute this to incompetence on the part of Italian soldiers—it is far more accurate to place the blame at the hands of the

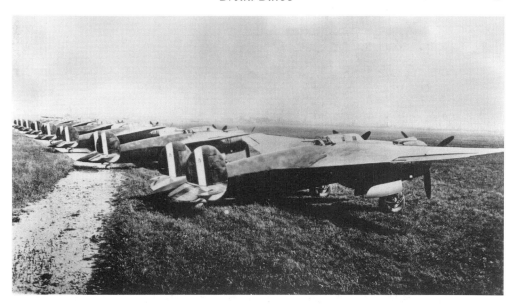

Rear view of a line of Breda Ba.88s. (*Courtesy of the Ron Dupas Collection, 1000aircraftphotos.com*)

high command, most of whom had reached (and retained) their positions by being politically reliable to Mussolini. Much like in Germany, the entire system revolved around the power at the centre, as is the case in every totalitarian state. Throughout history, such systems have also been accompanied by incompetence and corruption given the requirements of survival in the higher echelons. Germany, for instance, made its share of incompetent industrial and design decisions, but this was offset by being a highly industrialised power, meaning that better equipment was always on hand in significant—if not sufficient—numbers.

Italy did not have this advantage, never possessing the level of industrial power required to support Mussolini's egotistical dreams. This, combined with favouritism and corruption, meant that many Italian industrial decisions and design imperatives were not made under ideal circumstances. In this case, it led to an excellent idea rapidly becoming a terrible idea.

It is all the more remarkable, therefore, that the Italian Air Force produced a stable of fantastic designs during the war. Forgotten in a story dominated by Hurricanes and Spitfires, Bf 109s and Fw 190s, Thunderbolts and Mustangs, they are easy to forget. As this book will demonstrate, however, there were many Italian types that could equal or even surpass their counterparts, designed with a superb mastery of technical problems. However, there were exceptions. The problem for Italy was that it went to war far sooner than it expected to. It went to war in 1940 to take advantage of French weakness, but its frontline equipment was, for the most part, still of an older generation. This weakness was particularly felt in the air. Italian aircraft in 1940 were agile and quick, but already obsolete in almost every respect. The main fighters of the war, the Fiat CR.42 and Macchi MC.200, were both open-cockpit, which imposed significant restrictions on performance. Agile, yes, but insufficient to meet the enemy. Replacements were arriving in every type, but the lack of industrial might meant that, much like the French, there were simply never enough to alter the course of events.

Italy had a proud heritage of sleek design for its vehicles, impressive civilian craft that set speed records throughout the 1930s. It was only natural that thinking would turn to converting them for military use. In the case of one particular Breda, however, the difference between the civilian craft and its military equivalent was that of a bright day descending into an abysmal night.

The initial requirement for the Breda Ba.88 'Lince' (Lynx) came from the Regia Aeronautica's desire for a heavy fighter-bomber that could make a maximum speed of 329 mph (530 kph), which was faster than anything on the drawing boards or in service. If this craft lived up to the expectation, it would be a true world-beater, coming in with an armament that included 20-mm cannon and a range of 1,240 miles (2,000 km).

The trouble came in the construction. Breda's designers made some mistakes in how they designed the aircraft. For a start, the fuselage was streamlined and strong, but was made with a complicated and outdated structure, meaning the bomber would be slow to produce. In addition, this attempt at streamlining meant that a full bomb bay could not be fitted, which meant that the bombload would be carried semi-externally, which had a huge effect on aerodynamics. The structure also made the aircraft heavy, and the only armour carried was on the self-sealing fuel tanks.

Despite the structural liabilities, the single-tailed prototype set speed records after it first flew in 1937. It rapidly gained a reputation as the fastest aircraft in the world, and between February and December 1937 the aircraft shattered four French and German air-speed records, one after the other, with apparent ease. At this juncture, the designs' shortcomings did not undermine its capabilities. The design was fast, tough, with an excellent range and as much horsepower as medium bombers at a fraction of the weight. Had this been converted to a liaison or reconnaissance aircraft, the story of the Breda Ba.88 might have turned out much differently. Unfortunately, once all the military equipment was added, the performance loss was catastrophic. Self-sealing fuel tanks, four machine guns in total, as well as the bomb payload rapidly brought up the maximum weight, without any corresponding changes to offset the rather massive drop in maximum speed and agility this produced.

The Ba.88 was, as a result, cancelled. For political reasons, production was resumed to keep the production lines of Breda and IMAM operating. Some modifications were made to try to deal with the worst of its problems, and the Ba.88 got its second chance. Two *Gruppi* were equipped and in the absence of fighter opposition were able to use the type with limited success. In its first appearance, this was entirely due to a lack of opposition. In anticipation of a French invasion of under-defended Sardinia, the first few Ba.88s were rushed to the island. They would, on 19 June 1940, attack enemy airfields successfully without loss to themselves and without any defensive fire from the ground or the air to meet them. Nevertheless, the pilots complained bitterly. They complained that the aircraft had instability in the air and was plagued

Another view of the Breda Ba.88, showing off some of the sleek likes that held such promise. This particular one is likely the original, successful model before military equipment was added. (*Courtesy of Thijs Postma*)

by poor handling. They were even more upset, perhaps, about the small canopy's very limited vision, and lateral and ground views were cut off almost entirely by the radial engines.

This, combined with the dismal speed, should have been enough, but Italy was in no position to withdraw the Ba.88. The Italian attempt to take Britain's North African holdings was going appallingly badly, and several dozen Ba.88s were thrown into the conflict in an attempt to stop British armoured columns. To serve in North Africa, anti-sand filters had to be fitted. The result was somehow even worse. Pilots of the 7th *Gruppi*, who were equipped with the type, reported that it was so underpowered with all the extra weight that two of them were unable to take-off at all. A third aircraft, once it was airborne, was so heavy and slow that it couldn't execute a turn. Every last attempt to lighten the craft and improve its performance failed completely.

The ignominious end came quickly. Within five months of Italy's entry into the war, the Ba.88 was withdrawn from service, leaving Italy without a heavy fighter-bomber for the rest of the war, forcing the Italians to rely on outdated types such as the Fiat CR.32 and Breda Ba.65. In the short run, it meant that they had little in the way of light bombing and ground-attack that could help stem British tanks, which were causing major strategic problems. Perhaps worst of all, the remaining aircraft were scattered around airfields to be used as decoys for attacking British fighters.

A last attempt was made to renovate the design into a ground-attack aircraft shortly before the Italian Armistice in 1943, but if any worthwhile results were achieved, circumstances meant the project went no further. These aircraft were tested by the Luftwaffe and apparently discarded. Another attempt was designated the Ba.88M, designed to be dive bombers and equipped with a lengthened wing, lower horsepower engines, and a new armament—this also went nowhere. Overall, most of the Ba.88 production run was simply scrapped, having made no contribution whatsoever to Italy's war effort. In fact, building the aircraft ended up detracting from it by soaking up some of Italy's scant production resources.

The Breda Ba.88 was an outstanding design in theory—before it was equipped to fight a war. As a record-setter it was superb, and had it been used for a similar purpose it might have gone down as a useful aircraft for Italy. It is also a prime example of what happens when political concerns and a lack of alternatives overwhelm common sense. It looked good, it looked like a world-beater, but irrevocable errors in the design process, and trying to use the aircraft for a purpose it could never fulfil, ultimately ensured the Ba.88 would be one of the most spectacular failures of the war.

9

Brewster F2A Buffalo

History enjoys the concept of duality. It is a simple, easily understood concept in any period; to pit two concepts against each other to compare them—two sides, two figures, or two ideas or ideologies. It is one of the basic units of storytelling, and as such is one of the most basic concepts of human beings as a whole. Therefore, it can be applied to the history of aviation during the Second World War.

After all, who can forget the legendary duels of the Supermarine Spitfire and the Messerschmitt Bf 109 in the skies over England during the Battle of Britain? Or the legendary duo of P-47 Thunderbolt and P-51 Mustang? Or indeed that of B-17 Flying Fortress and B-24 Liberator? Yet there is one aircraft that manages to be, in a way, two very different aircraft. One was a sluggish, outpaced fighter that has been unloved by many historians of flight. The other gave sterling service against a powerful foe, etching out a permanent and proud space for itself in the history books and becoming a legend.

Both of these aircraft were, in fact, one. The Brewster Buffalo demonstrates, perhaps more than any other aircraft during the war, just how important circumstances can be to a larger historical outcome. The Buffalo was also a stepping stone in path that would lead to the triumph of American aerial might. It was the duality made into one.

Specifications

First Flight: 1937
Powerplant: Wright R-1820-40 Cyclone radial-piston engine, 1,200 hp.
Armament: Four 0.5-inch (12.7-mm) machine guns, and two 100-lb (45-kg) bombs.
Top Speed: 321 mph (517 kph)
Range/Service Ceiling: 965 miles (1,553 km), 33,200 feet (10,120 metres)
Dimensions: Length 26 feet 4 inches (8.03 metres), height 12 feet (3.66 metres), wingspan 35 feet (10.67 metres)
Number Built: 509

Because of her less-than-stellar performance under American and British control, the Brewster Buffalo is often written-off as a failure or, in some sources, as one of the worst aircraft of all time. In this author's opinion, such a designation is an appalling overstep. In reality, the Buffalo served a similar role to the Bell P-39 Airacobra and P-63 King

A Brewster Buffalo in flight. (*Courtesy of the United States National Naval Aviation Museum*)

Cobra. While they failed to impress their initial owners in their originally intended roles, they found their niche in unexpected places and in different ways.

The origins of the Brewster F2A came from a requirement put forth by the US Navy in 1936 for a new generation of carrier-borne aircraft. The requirement was extensive and called for a very modern design. It designated an enclosed cockpit and retractable landing gear, wing flaps, and arrester gear specifically to aid carrier take-off and landing, and lastly specified that the plane was to be a monoplane. The only competition of the Brewster design was Grumman's early XF4F, which would one day become the famed Wildcat; however, in 1936, it was under development as a biplane. The US Navy kept the XF4F as a backup as the Brewster F2A was selected as the first monoplane fighter in the history of the navy.

The prototype Buffalo took to the air for the first time in December 1937, a stubby looking aircraft indeed. However, it went into production the very next month, with the early production Buffalos immediately equipping the aircraft carrier USS *Saratoga*. It was in naval service that the aircraft's problems began.

Never superbly manoeuvrable, it was found in the Pacific that the engine was prone to overheating. The top speed would also prove to be significantly less than that of its eventual Japanese opponents. Brewster made constant improvements, their last model being the F2A-3, but it was never liked by the navy, and by late 1940 was considered obsolete.

Many were passed off to the British for use in that country's Pacific holdings, where the RAF pilots assigned to it had a litany of complaints, mostly along the same lines as their American counterparts. Nevertheless, when the Japanese invaded Malaya, Singapore, and Burma, the export version of the Buffalo, designed B-339E, made up the bulk of Britain's fighter defence. Against some older Japanese types, the Buffalo did quite well, but in combat with the Nakajima Ki-43 (the main fighter of the Japanese Army) it simply could not keep up. The Ki-43 was extremely nimble and when the Buffalo encountered the Mitsubishi A6M Zero, it had even less chance of success. Though it gave good account of itself against Japanese bombers, the vast majority of Buffalos were lost.

In the Dutch East Indies, a partial solution to the Buffalo's problems were found. By lightening the fuel and ammunition load in the wing, the Buffalo's turn radius could at least be matched to the Ki-43, though the Zero remained superior. Though the Dutch employed their Buffalos bravely, the outcome of the air war was never in doubt.

One of very few combat uses of the Buffalo by American pilots came soon after, at the Battle of Midway. Here, operating from Midway Island, the Buffalo was once again thrown at Japanese fighters with superior manoeuvrability. Consequently, the Buffalos suffered greatly, losing thirteen out of twenty aircraft. Soon afterwards, the increasing availability the Grumman F4F and F6F pushed their Brewster cousin out of service.

Here the story might end, sounding rather similar to the Breda Ba.88—a good idea that never lived up to expectations. That would be the case except for the other theatre in which the Buffalo served extensively—Finland. Here, in colder climates that negated the engine overheating problem, the Buffalo would forge a superb reputation against invading Soviet aircraft.

The US government was only too happy to offload some of its Buffalos onto the Finns, for a price, but the Finns immediately removed all the specifically naval gear, which lightened the aircraft. With its engine running fine, and with an already superb range, the Buffalo quickly became a favourite. It became known as a 'Gentleman's travelling plane' and, despite being vastly outnumbered by their Soviet foes, the Buffalo was the mount that created fighter ace after fighter ace for the Finns.

Even if one posits a low level of proficiency amongst Soviet pilots, the results were still astonishing. For example, between 1941 and 1945, Fighter Squadron 24 claimed 477 kills, with losses of merely nineteen Buffalos—a staggering 26:1 loss ratio. Although, it must be recalled that this was a single unit. Despite the later availability of newer types, the last Buffalos would only leave Finnish service in 1948. Finland's highest-scoring ace, Ilmari Juutilainen, would go on to claim that if the Finns had possessed Buffalos during the Winter War of 1940 (rather than their major role during the Continuation War against the USSR starting in 1941), no Soviet planes would have flown over Finland. High praise indeed for a design nearly everyone else had written-off long before.

It is difficult to categorise the Buffalo as either a 'success' or 'failure'. In its original, intended role, it did not perform well, but in unexpected roles it performed superbly. Perhaps it is best to say that circumstances dictated what the Brewster F2A Buffalo was, and sometimes it was capable of being an extremely successful surprise.

There are several replica Buffalos in existence today, as well as a single original. The original can be seen at the Aviation Museum of Central Finland in Jyväskylä. Two replicas are held by the Cradle of Aviation Museum in New York, with one painted in Dutch markings and the other in US Navy markings.

The original aircraft has followed an interesting path. In June 1942, Lieutenant Lauri Pekuri downed two Soviet Hawker Hurricanes before a third set his Buffalo on fire. He put it down in Lake Kolejärvi and then swam ashore. His Buffalo remained there until 1998, when it was rescued and briefly ended up at the National Museum of Naval Aviation in Florida. It was returned to Finland soon thereafter, and the Finns made the decision to not restore it. The Finns have been described as revering the Buffalo as a symbol of their courage and suffering against the Soviet Union. The aircraft is on display as if raised from the lake mere days before the viewer saw it, as seen in the above photograph.

10

Caudron C.714

The advent of fighters such as the Messerschmitt Bf 109 was a watershed in the history of military aviation. They rendered an entire generation of aircraft obsolete, and schools of design that traced their antecedents to the earliest days of aviation were consigned to the past. The response to their arrival was a flurry of activity in order to match them, and the Caudron C.714 was born of that scramble.

The C.714 was not the best French design by far, and in fact was an inadequate attempt to match the growth of German might. Caudron's new fighter was meant to be a parry that brought the French air force up to par with their oncoming foes. If that were the only facet of its existence to be considered, it would have to be written-off as an abject failure. Yet inadequate though it may have been, the C.714 still took its place in the brave fight against fascism—and the result is a tale more than worthy of telling.

Specifications

First Flight: (C.710 prototype) 1936
Powerplant: Renault 12Ro1 inline piston engine, 450 hp
Armament: Four 0.295-inch (7.5-mm) machine guns.
Top Speed: 301 mph (485 kph)
Range/Service Ceiling: 559 miles (900 km), 29,855 feet (9,100 metres)
Dimensions: Length 28 feet 3.875 inches (8.63 metres), height 9 feet 5 inches (2.87 metres), wingspan 29 feet 5.125 inches (8.97 metres)
Number Built: Approximately 90

The concept of a light-weight fighter was something that, while never particularly in vogue amongst designers, was a concept that was pursued before the war as a theoretical component of achieving future superiority in the battlefield skies. The results were wildly varied, with the Caudron C.714 being at least one of three aircraft to be completed in line with the concept. One result that turned out spectacularly was the Yakovlev Yak-3. The Yak's light construction, with most of the plane being of wood rather than metal, made this derivative of the Yak-1 into a spectacular fighter, dreaded by the Luftwaffe. The Yak-3 would carve a path through Germany's best fighters, with extraordinary agility at low levels over the battlefield. On the other end of the spectrum was the Curtiss-Wright

A Caudron C.714 in French service. (*Courtesy of Thijs Postma*)

CW-21. The CW-21 started life a bit differently from the Caudron in being born from an advanced trainer rather than a racer. The prototype even shot down an Italian medium bomber over China in early 1939, but the Chinese did not accept it for service. This was a wise decision, for when it was used by the Royal Netherlands Air Force in the Dutch East Indies, the Japanese fighters it faced in early 1942 made mincemeat out of it. The Caudron C.714 would be France's attempt at the concept. In the event, it would not achieve the Yak-3's brilliant performance, but nor would it do as badly as the CW-21.

The C.714 began life far from the notion of a fighter. It was a development from several superb racing planes that Caudron had manufactured in the mid to late 1930s. Chief Designer Marcel Riffard's darting little aircraft created quite a bit of performance from relatively little plane, and when the French military issued a requirement in 1936 for a 'light fighter', Caudron stood ready.

The gist of the requirement was for a mostly wooden aircraft, which could be built rapidly, without disrupting existing French production. Given what has been demonstrated about the state of French production of aircraft, this was a far more crucial requirement than it might otherwise appear. The need to build up an arsenal of modern fighters was extremely pressing, and Caudron's C.710 prototype seemed ideal. It beat out the competition, the ANF-Mureaux 190, and certainly had the pedigree of a winner. Riffard's previous racers for Caudron had been tearing up the international racing circuit, consistently beating or at least providing major opposition to heavier, more conventional racers. One prime example of this came in 1934, when a Caudron C.460 piloted by Michel Detroyet won the Thompson Trophy race with an average speed of 264 mph (424.8 kph), and a maximum speed of 304 mph (489 kph)—this seemed to hold great promise. The C.710 prototype first flew in mid-July 1936, and immediately seemed to justify a sense of optimism. This was true despite the prototype coming with fixed landing gear, which by the mid-1930s was an obsolescent feature. The tiny, light little fighter could also deliver quite a punch for its size, coming equipped with a pair of 20-mm cannon.

In December 1937, the development of the prototype, the C.713 'Cyclone', first flew. It was generally similar, but with retractable landing gear. This evolved into the C.714, which flew in the summer of 1938. The C.714 incorporated all of the improvements of the previous marks, but with a stronger structure and a better set of wings. Handed over for testing, it performed well enough to result in an order for 100 aircraft. Here one other change took effect; the pair of 20-mm cannon were swapped for four machine guns, although the wing was too thin to mount them conventionally. Thus the machine guns were mounted in streamlined pods under the wings.

The plane was still mostly wood, though the control surfaces had an alloy framework and fabric covering. The final design was remarkably quick for a plane that really had a very light engine. The major disappointment was its rate of climb, which would ultimately lead to the cancellation of its contract.

Production did not enter full swing until 1940, and many of the early Caudrons produced were meant to go to Finland (only a handful ever made it as events and chaos overtook France). In the event, the aircraft's problems would be so significant that the Finns, desperate for every plane they could get their hands on, would not use the Caudrons in combat. Unfortunately, this international order had been fulfilled first before domestic needs, so regardless of its capability domestic production proceeded slowly. Therefore, when the Germans invaded, there was a relatively tiny handful of Caudron Cyclones in service with the French air force.

In actual combat, the rate of climb and the limitations of the powerplant that the Finns had clearly sensed became apparent. The design—much like the Messerschmitt Bf 109 would later find—had reached its maximum potential, and could not be changed to fit a more powerful engine. Since sufficient numbers were unavailable to make up for its deficiencies, the French authorities ordered the Cyclone withdrawn from combat only a week after it was introduced.

However, events took a hand. The Cyclone had been used to equip the French *Groupe de Chasse Polonais I/145* (otherwise known as the Warsaw Squadron). These Polish pilots were, as would prove true everywhere else they served, extremely eager to strike at the Germans. The Poles, commanded by Major Josef Kepinski (in collaboration with the First World War French ace Major Lionel Alexandre de Marmier), were supposed to be equipped with Bloch MB.152s, but in the event production was not keeping up, and German bombing of the factories in the Lyon area where the Poles were based was hardly helping. The only aircraft available to them were the C.714s. With the order to withdraw the Cyclone, they would be left without aircraft to fly, as no replacements were forthcoming. In a practical decision, they chose to simply ignore the order and took their Cyclones into combat, despite the misgivings they themselves had voiced about the type. Polish bravery and skill could, it seemed, make up for a good deal of technological deficiency, and the Cyclone lanced into German formations despite being inferior in every respect to the Bf 109E that it would frequently face. In three vicious battles between 8 and 11 June 1940, the Poles accounted for a dozen victories, losing nine of their own aircraft, although another nine were lost on the ground.

The Poles faced all the type's shortcomings. It took far too long for them to take-off and land, making them vulnerable at the beginning and end of their missions. The variable-pitch mechanism for the propeller was also prone to failure, and the landing gear jammed frequently. The rate of climb never improved, remaining abysmal. Above all, the engine gave constant problems. It had frequent difficulty starting, was prone to overheating, leaked both fuel and oil on a regular basis, and had a weak crankshaft. For all these shortcomings, if the choice for the Poles was to fly them or remain grounded, the choice was clear.

The Poles took over the airfield at Maison la Blanche, at Dreux, and the civilian engineers from Caudron's factory arrived to oversee the cranky engines, to soothe them into a semblance of reliability. Within a day of taking over their base, the Poles struck with their new Caudrons, downing a pair of Heinkel 111 bombers. On 8 June they struck again, shooting down a pair of Bf 110 heavy fighters, with one C.714 slightly damaged in return. Two more probable, but unconfirmed victories were scored by 2Lt Czeslaw Glowczynski, who had scored three and a half victories against the Germans during their invasion of Poland in the PZL P-11c, which will be examined later in this book.

This luck could not hold out forever, not even for the valiant and skilled Poles. The next day, they ran into a formation of Dornier Do 17s, escorted by Bf 109 fighters. The Poles' radios were malfunctioning, so they could not coordinate their attack as they wished. One Caudron attacked the Germans, while the rest ended up tangling with the fighters. Lt Glowczynski struck first, demonstrating the power of experience to overcome even the worst limitations. Diving out of the sun, he shot down one of the Bf 109s, and the 109 trying to pursue him was shot down in turn. However, three Polish pilots were killed in the course of the battle, and most of the rest returned to base with damaged Cyclones. The Poles' losses were mounting, and replacements were not forthcoming.

By 10 June, a mere eight days after entering combat, the Poles had just thirteen aircraft left, with only a dozen being operational. The next day, after still more furious combat, they turned in eleven of these for repair, which the French promptly burned to keep them out of the hands of the advancing Germans. The last dozen Caudrons issued were again prohibited from flying shortly thereafter, with some of the Poles passed to another group, GC.I/1, to finally fly the Bloch MB.152. The remaining Poles naturally ignored the order for a second time, continuing to fly any plane they could, be it Bloch or Caudron. On the 20th, however, the Poles were evacuated to Britain, their French campaign over.

Precisely how many Cyclones were ultimately delivered is a matter of some confusion.

Given the chaos of France in 1940, this seems understandable. Estimates range from between fifty-three and ninety-eight production aircraft—with only two squadrons of Poles (one of them a training squadron) making use of the type before France was overrun. A total of thirty aircraft survived to be captured by the Germans, though they were all technically part of the Vichy regime. After this event, a total of nine Cyclones were used as fighter trainers by the Vichy regime, which then passed them on to the Germans for the same purpose. There is no confirmed record that the nine Vichy aircraft were ever actually utilised by the Germans. For some of the Poles who had flown the lightweight fighter, however, there was a final irony. Several of them would find themselves in Russia, as part of the Normandie Regiment—utilising the other lightweight fighter, the Yak-3, which they flew until the Germans surrendered.

In summation, the C.714 Cyclone was the best it could be, but given the limitations of its design it could not hope to match the aircraft that opposed it. Nevertheless, in brave and determined hands, this tiny, unexpected, and above all forgotten little fighter overcame its own inadequacies to strike a blow against the Nazi war machine.

There are two surviving Caudron C.714s. One is owned by the Aviation Museum of Central Finland, which is on loan to the Polish Aviation Museum in Krakow. The other is in France and still flies, held by a company named Préservation du Caudron Cyclone.

11

Commonwealth CA-13 Boomerang

Australian aviation was not exactly considered a major factor in the air battles of the Second World War. While Australian soldiers and sailors did make a formidable reputation for themselves, this was not matched in historical memory by the role of its air force. This is a grossly unfair notion, as Australian aviation during the war faced a unique hurdle—it had to create itself, hurriedly, to meet the threat of the Japanese.

From this hurried process came the excellent Commonwealth Boomerang, notable both for its unique origins and also for the fact that it became Australia's first combat aircraft made entirely by their own efforts. It was, from start to finish, designed and built in Australia, and this alone should warrant enough merit to be included in such a volume. Yet there is a greater story beyond this, one that makes the Boomerang's inclusion all the more important. Namely, the unique and pressing circumstances of its birth.

Specifications

First Flight: 1942
Powerplant: Pratt & Whitney R-1830-S3C4-G Twin Wasp radial-piston engine.
Armament: Four Browning 0.303-inch (7.7-mm) machine guns, and two Hispano-Suiza 20-mm cannon.
Top Speed: 305 mph (491 kph)
Range/Service Ceiling: 1,600 miles (2,575 km), 34,000 feet (10,365 metres)
Dimensions: Length 25 feet 6 inches (7.77 metres), height 9 feet 7 inches (2.92 metres), wingspan 36 feet (10.97 metres)
Number Built: 250

As war clouds loomed, Australia was faced with some difficult circumstances. While a vast land, they were extremely isolated from reinforcement by the British Empire. The Americans were even more distant. As events were to prove, British power in the Pacific would collapse rapidly in late 1941 and early 1942, leaving a vulnerable Australia with the full juggernaut of Japanese imperial might seemingly right on their doorstep.

Before the war began, British aircraft manufacturers made up the bulk of deliveries to the Royal Australian Air Force. By 1941, however, deliveries were thin on the ground. British resources had been devoted to simply surviving in 1940, and the Southern Pacific

A Commonwealth Boomerang on the ground. (*Courtesy of the Royal Australian Air Force Museum*)

was right at the bottom of the priority list. The Royal Air Force in the European and later North African theatre took almost all new production, while even British commands in Asia had to make do with whatever they could get. Moreover, by and large, what they did receive was inadequate both in design and in numbers to what the Japanese were fielding.

Once the Japanese began to fight their way across the Pacific, the situation became increasingly dire. The Japanese advance brought nearly a quarter of the world's surface under the aegis of the Rising Sun, and brought the war to Australia's doorstep, with the Dutch East Indies falling and the Japanese advancing across Papua New Guinea. Japanese planes were in range of the Australian mainland itself. While the entry of the United States into the war theoretically added the vast productive capacity of the American aircraft industry to the fight, the sheer distances involved meant it would be some time before any aircraft arrived, presuming the Japanese did not manage to interdict supplies. Small numbers of American aircraft ended up based in Australia after the losses of previous campaigns, but the amount was insufficient to the need.

The best solution, it seemed, was for the Australians to design and build their own fighter, and the Commonwealth Aircraft Corporation quickly took up the challenge, and what a challenge it was. Only two types of aircraft were then in production in Australia. The first was the Bristol Beaufort bomber, already well on their way towards obsolescence, and the second was the CAC Wirraway—an armed trainer and ground attack aircraft, built on the North American NA-16 trainer. The Beaufort was unsuitable as a basis for a fighter, but its engines were not. They were powerful Pratt & Whitney Twin Wasp engines, under licensed production (for comparison to a better-known aircraft, these same engines powered the F4F Wildcat).

The Beauforts supplied the engines, and the Wirraway provided the basic idea. The entire process was done at speed in an *ad hoc* fashion. For instance, there were no 20-mm cannon produced in Australia, so a British made Hispano-Suiza gun—apparently collected by an Australian airman as a souvenir in the Middle East—was hurriedly reverse engineered.

At the same time, the design itself was proceeded apace. The main designer of the aircraft would be Fred David, recruited by the head of Commonwealth, Lawrence Wackett. Wackett made a superb choice, but there was a hitch—David was technically an enemy alien. David was an Austrian Jew, who had fled to Australia as a refugee from Hitler's tyranny. His work was absolutely essential, however, since he had worked on Heinkel's most advanced designs, as well as having done some work for Aichi and Mitsubishi. There is quite a deal of irony that his expertise and work experience also made him suspicious in the eyes of the government. However, his work for the Japanese meant that David was uniquely aware of the challenges an Australian fighter would face, and had a working knowledge of some of the world's more advanced fighter designs. His work was, therefore, essential, and necessity put him onto the project, even if Australian authorities did not realise that David's loyalties were unlikely to lay with the Axis.

Getting David was a critical achievement for the programme, and design work commenced in late December 1941. It was meant from the beginning to be a stopgap aircraft, produced as quickly and easily as possible. To do this, the original intent was to use as much of the Wirraway as they possibly could, as every shared component spared a little bit of time and development work. This, however, did not work as planned— design priorities shifted, putting an emphasis on the craft's manoeuvrability against its most likely opponent, the Mitsubishi A6M 'Zero' of already legendary fame and supreme lethality. The resulting aircraft was very small, being a mere 25.5 feet long (7.7 metres), with a wingspan of 36 feet (11 metres). It was built for the stresses of manoeuvrable warfare, with a light aluminium frame, which was wood-sheathed.

It is the best proof of the necessity of the programme that the Australian government already ordered 105 of the CA-12 (the Boomerang Mk I) before the prototype even flew. In fact, the order was placed in February 1942, and the first prototype didn't fly until the end of May. The initial tests were promising, but showed some problems. In tests against other aircraft modified to simulate a Zero (one of them being a Brewster Buffalo), the Boomerang could outrun them, and it had a heavier punch, but it couldn't match the manoeuvres. The bigger problem was that performance fell off sharply above 15,000 feet (4,600 metres).

The problems were partially solved in other variants, such as the re-engined CA-14 that never entered production. The late model Boomerangs, produced as model numbers CA-12, CA-13, and CA-19, were considered to be the equal of the Spitfire Mk V, or early model P-47 Thunderbolts or P-51 Mustangs. In the end, a total of 250 aircraft of all the marks would be produced, until such time as British-built Spitfires and license-built Mustangs began to arrive in significant numbers.

The first Boomerangs were delivered to training/conversion squadrons in April 1943, and by mid-May the Boomerang was flying its first missions to counter Japanese bombers; although, on the first mission, the Japanese bombers dropped their loads wide of their target and headed back to base before they could be engaged. In defence of Australia, the Boomerang achieved little more success. Its higher-altitude performance meant that it was too slow to truly intercept Japanese bombers, which had usually fled by the time it could draw near.

At a lower altitude, where the Boomerang operated at its best, it would find a much better niche. The Boomerang turned out to be a superb ground-attack aircraft, a role vital to the ground wars that were moving across the South West Pacific theatre. The Boomerang was at its most manoeuvrable there, but it also had superb range to move across the necessary battlefields at will. It was also renowned as being easy to fly, which meant getting in to very close range to make its attacks as precise as possible was a simple matter. It could also, in the process, flit over obstacles in the terrain. All the while, even when faced with ground fire, the Boomerang proved able to absorb a good amount of damage owing to its rugged construction. By the end of the war, the Boomerang would be operated by a total of seven squadrons before being passed out of service in favour of newer aircraft.

A pair of Commonwealth Boomerangs in flight. (*Courtesy of the Royal Australian Air Force Museum.*)

The Boomerang was a superb first fighter for Australia, especially given the circumstances of its birth. Born out of chaos, worry, and confusion, the Boomerang nevertheless managed to succeed—if not as it was originally meant to. More importantly, though, it gave Australia the ability to produce a fighter for itself when it could not acquire them from anywhere else. The Boomerang succeeded in what it was meant to do, and found new roles of itself. It was Australia's only fighter of the war, and one very worthy of remembrance.

Three Boomerangs are still in existence today. They are all in Australia and located at the Army Aviation base near Oakey, the Temora Aviation Museum in New South Wales, and at Classic Jets Fighter Museum, Parafield Airport. These last two remain in flying condition. A replica is also viewable at the Amsterdam airport.

Personal Impressions of Flying a CAC Boomerang Fighter

In preparing this work, the author came in contact with Matt Denning, a man with intimate knowledge of the Boomerang. He was kind enough to prepare this short piece, which is included in its entirety here:

> She might be approaching her 72nd birthday however this grand old lady still stands tall and looks ready for action (you can't keep a good woman down). This mighty CA-13 Boomerang, with former Royal Australian Air Force serial no. A46-122, was my first foray into the warbird restoration world, having acquired her mortal remains (essentially a skeletal fuselage frame) in 1976 and exercising a dogged determination to return her to the skies in my spare time over the next 27 years. She was originally delivered to the RAAF from the Commonwealth Aircraft Corporation located on the fringe of Melbourne, Victoria on the 18th August 1943 and spent her entire service life with No. 83 Squadron.
>
> I've witnessed her reincarnation and coaxed her back to airworthy status, which was confirmed on the 14th February 2003 when she took flight again for the first time since April 1945, a hiatus of almost 58 years. Owing to the complete disassembly of every component for inspection and repair as required, along with a freshly overhauled engine, propeller, instrumentation and new fuel lines, new hydraulic pipes, hoses and seals, new electrical wiring and new control cables, this old gal was as good as new. But what is she like to fly? The answer is fantastic! Definitely worth the 27 year wait.
>
> With a displacement of 1830 cubic inches (30 litres) her Pratt & Whitney twin row 14 cylinder radial engine pumps out 1200 horsepower at full throttle which creates an impressive acceleration on take-off for a relatively small airframe (remember two of these engines are used on a DC-3 which carries 28 passengers or a good freight load). Care needs to be taken not to apply too much power too early during the take-off roll as the torque effect of the engine along with the gyroscopic forces of the 11 foot diameter three-blade Hamilton Standard propeller as the tail comes up will pull you off your

intended path down the runway centreline if you are not careful. Holding a slightly taildown attitude will see the Boomerang lift off at around 80 knots and feeling like a homesick angel. At full power the manifold pressure is sitting on 48 inches with an engine speed of 2700 rpm … and gulping down 130 gallons per hour (600 litres per hour) of avgas in the process. Having established a positive rate of climb the landing gear can be tucked away and climb power settings selected, usually 34 inches MP and 2350 rpm. A scan over the other instruments confirms that cylinder head temperatures are remaining under 230 degrees Celsius, oil temp is under 90 degrees and oil pressure is sitting on a solid 80 pound per square inch.

A good rate of climb can be achieved whilst indicating 140 knots and before long she is ready to try out a few aerobatic manoeuvres. A few clearing turns and a radio call gives some reassurance that this patch of sky belongs to the Boomerang. Rolls in this machine are effortless with the ailerons being very light and responsive. The rudder provides good authority whilst the elevators are effective, although slightly heavy. She was borne out of urgent times however the handling qualities are sound considering the development time from drawing board to first flight back in 1942 was a matter of only 16 weeks. The high roomy cockpit combined with a sliding canopy that can be opened in flight makes this a superb touring machine also. When set up in cruise at 165 knots she can be flown with feet off the rudder pedals. Those two 20mm cannon, 4 Browning .303 machine gun ports and camouflage pattern on the wings are constant reminders though that this was a war machine built for a specific purpose. For the ground-based spectator the Boomerang is music to the ears, developing a combination of a low pitched growl from the engine and a unique whistle from the open machine gun ports. This is definitely one relic from a bygone era that's more than worthy of a return to the skies.

Matt Denning
16 August 2015

12

Dewoitine D.520

As has been mentioned previously, French aviation during the war has been frequently dismissed when it should not be. While some of its designs were inadequate to meeting the threat posed by the German Luftwaffe, others were superb craft that, had they arrived in greater numbers, may have tipped the historical balance. While it is idle speculation to wonder how aircraft such as the Dewoitine D.520 could have altered the outcome of the campaigns of 1940, it is an intriguing thought nevertheless. France had perhaps her most superb design in the D.520, a worthy successor to the proud line of French aviation that had stretched all the way back to the dawn of aviation.

The D.520 was the most modern design in the French arsenal, and the best chance the French possessed for beating back the German menace.

Specifications

First Flight: 1938
Powerplant: Hispano-Suiza 12Y 45 inline piston engine, 935 hp.
Armament: One HS 404 20-mm cannon, engine mounted, with four wing-mounted MAC 34 M39 0.295-inch (7.5-mm) machine guns.
Top Speed: 332 mph (534 kph)
Range/Service Ceiling: 950 miles (1,530 km), 34,450 feet (10,500 metres)
Dimensions: Length 28 feet 3 inches (8.6 metres), height 8 feet 5 inches (2.57 metres), wingspan 33 feet 5.33 inches (10.2 metres)
Number Built: Approximately 900.

As has previously been described, France attempted to rearm at high speed in the mid-1930s to counter the gathering war clouds. The story of the Dewoitine D.520 is precisely the same as that of the Bloch MB.152 and Caudron C.714 previously mentioned in this book—none of these projects reached their full fruition, and the numbers were unfortunately never there to have a major impact. The difference between these three planes was that the Dewoitine was, perhaps, the best of them all. A truly superb fighter, the D.520 was a match for the best in the world in 1940. Yet again, however, it would never arrive in time and in amounts necessary to assert a dominant role over the battlefield.

Émile Dewoitine had something to prove. His company, Société Aéronautique Française (Avions Dewoitine), was still relatively new, having been founded only in 1931. His independent company had been folded into the amalgamation of 1936, though Dewoitine continued to make independent designs. His previous fighter concept had been the Dewoitine D.513, of which only two prototypes were ever built. Unfortunately for Dewoitine, it lost out in competition to what would become France's main frontline fighter of the early war, the Morane-Saulnier M.S.406. While a good fighter, the M.S.406 was inadequate to the tasks to which it would be put. Though manoeuvrable, the Morane-Saulnier was outperformed by the Bf 109E, and even as it was rolling off the assembly line replacement fighters were already in the works.

The French government had placed an order for a high-performance fighter in 1936, and Dewoitine rose to the challenge. The specific requirements were for a fighter that could reach 26,000 feet (8,000 metres) in a mere fifteen minutes, and attain a maximum speed of 310 mph (500 kph). In the end, the D.520 would reach, at its absolute best, 347 mph (560 kph). Dewoitine was also determined to learn from the loss with the D.513, and sought to construct the most modern fighter he could. As a result, the construction techniques were to be state-of-the-art, and the sleek craft would be paired to the most powerful engine that was available. This was the brand-new Hispano-Suiza 12Y-21, with 890 hp.

This was only a start, however. As things moved from the prototype phase towards production, progressively more powerful engines were fitted, meaning that the D.520 continually gained more power. It was also designed to carry a heavy punch, with four machine guns and a 20-mm cannon, meaning that it would be close to performing equally against the best the Luftwaffe would be able to field in the early war years. In actual combat, the D.520 could in many cases outmanoeuvre Messerschmitt's best, though the Bf 109 would always retain a slight speed advantage.

In other ways, too, it was a superb design. It carried a total fuel weight of 636 litres (131 gallons), giving it longer legs than any of its British, German, or Italian contemporaries. When France fell, this meant that a large number of D.520s were able to escape to Africa simply by making a dash for it. The airframe was almost entirely metal, excluding the ailerons and tail surfaces. The pilot could count on armour for himself, as well as on self-sealing fuel tanks. Even in a maximum dive of up to 520 mph, the Dewoitine remained a stable gun platform. The D.520 even came with a fire suppression system, activated from the cockpit.

Also rare for the era, the D.520 was fitted with numerous maintenance panels to speed its repair and systems checks in the field—a look at the future of aviation design. Rearming was also apparently a very rapid operation, meaning that the turnaround time for a D.520 was considerably quicker than might be expected for such an advanced design. All of these were useful features for a combat aircraft in the chaos that was France in 1939–1940. The only real drawback to the design was the cockpit location. The sleek shape also meant that while most of the pilot's views were excellent, seeing forward when taxiing on the runway was a bit limited. This could be considered a rather unimportant problem in view of the sterling flight characteristics, heavy weapons, long maximum range, and most important of all the absolutely urgent need for the aircraft in operational service.

In June 1939, Dewoitine's efforts were rewarded with a production contract for 600 aircraft, though this was reduced to 510 the next month. The outbreak of war, however, meant that the order requirement for this superb aircraft shot up to 1,280, with production supposed to be hitting 200 per month by May 1940. The French Navy then requested 120, and then the order was increased once again to 2,250 aircraft, with the production quota reaching 350 a month.

There was, however, an early teething problem. The engine cooling was troublesome and the top speed was limited, meaning that the craft managed to fail acceptance tests. Redesigned components were thrown in as quickly as possible, but this meant that the D.520 was not rated as combat ready until April 1940. While production was ramping up too, it would never come close to matching that of the Bf 109E, and there would never be enough Dewoitines reaching the frontline to stem the tide, despite the French government actually managing to reach its production quota for the type in June 1940. Considering that the complete collapse of France was at hand, this is perhaps the acme of 'too little, too late'. This was compounded by the very recent arrival of the D.520 by the time combat was joined over France. The first unit to equip the type was GC I/3, who started to equip with the aircraft in November 1939. However, owing to the devastating production delays, even this first unit had not gotten up to strength in the type until May 1940.

When the German invasion rolled into Western Europe on 10 May 1940, 228 D.520s had been produced, but only seventy-five had been accepted with the balance still being refitted as required. *Groupe de Chasse* I/3 was ready, however, and in its first engagement the D.520 scored three kills and suffered no losses. It also could out-turn the Bf 109, but displayed some vicious tendencies when leaving that turn, frequently spinning out of it. A total of four more *Groupes de Chasse* would become operational with the type—GC II/3, GC III/3, GC III/6, and GC II/7, though the latter did so too late to see combat. One naval squadron also saw combat with the type.

The units equipped with the D.520 could post heavily unequal kill ratios against numerically superior German forces. Against the Italians, it did even better. The Fiat and Macchi fighters that equipped the Italian units facing the French proved to be easy prey. On the 13 June, for instance, pilots of GC III/6 had been engaged with the Italians and had just landed at their base at Le Luc in the Riviera. Others were still airborne, however, when Italian aircraft arrived. One French pilot, Adjutant Le Gloan, provided an ample demonstration of the Dewoitine's deadly skills. In this one engagement, he shot down four biplane fighters and savaged a bomber.

The fighter remained a deadly opponent in the skies over France. Czech fighter ace Vaclav Cukr, who was part of the French air force, wrote later in vivid terms about the situation and the usefulness of the D.520 in combat. He had first flown the Morane-Saulnier MS.406, and was one of the lucky pilots re-equipped with the Dewoitine:

We flew to Toulouse for the D.520s. Holland and Belgium collapsed. France awoke herself from her lethargy. The Germans are at Sedan. We went to Bouillancy and the first time we took off, all was in flames around us! Lieutenant Jaroslav Gleich shot down a Do-17 and a Messerschmitt Me-110. A French pilot, Hericourt, was killed. The Germans have three times more planes than we. Without the D.520, we would be dead!

Vasiscek, p. 68

Though it did well, especially against the Italians, the D.520 was too late to alter the outcome. On 16 June, the order came down that all units flying certain aircraft were to fly to North Africa to keep them out of German hands. This list included the Curtiss P-35 Hawk, the Bloch MB.152, and, perhaps most importantly, the D.520. In the chaos, only the fighters and their pilots were to fly there—the ground crews had to find their way there by any means they could find. By the time of the armistice, a total of 351 of this exceptional craft had been delivered. After the surrender, through a complicated deal with the Germans, the Vichy Government that ruled over the 'independent' parts of France (independent only so long as the German Wehrmacht allowed this to be the case) were able to resume production. A total of 550 were ordered to replace all other fighters then in service, adding to the 165 D.520s that had been evacuated to North Africa. A total of three had flown to Britain to continue service under the Free French banner, but the next time the D.520 fired its guns in anger, it would be against its former allies.

In the Syria-Lebanon campaign, the D.520 would feel its advantages slip away, through little fault of its own. The campaign is little known today, more than likely because Allied censors and high-ranking authorities felt it unseemly to detail the often vicious fighting between former allies there. Between June and July 1941, the territory would be conquered and handed over to the Free French.

The D.520's part in the campaign is most remarkable in how it was achieved. Given its long legs, the decision was made to fly the aircraft from France all the way to Syria. These were gruelling flights for any single-seat fighter, especially a 1940 one. Most of the aircraft flew through Italian territory, with stops in Rome, then either Brindisi or Catania, with a final stopover in Rhodes. The Catania–Rhodes portion was the worst—over 1,200 kilometres flown over open water. Much of the rest was mountainous. Nevertheless, the D.520s made it, as did the vast majority of other aircraft sent with them. Unfortunately, the infrastructure to support them and keep them in the air was severely lacking. This herculean feat was not matched by sufficient ground crew, nor was there anywhere near an adequate amount of anti-aircraft weaponry protecting the Vichy airfields. After initial successes, the D.520s were bled white through attrition against experienced Allied pilots—who could much more easily replace their losses—and most importantly through attacks on under-protected airfields.

The D.520 would fight the Allies again during the Torch landings of 1942, but by this point the D.520 was becoming increasingly obsolescent against new developments in fighter design. After 1942, as Vichy forces defected, well over 100 D.520s switched sides—

though after a few patrols, they were relegated to training duties by 1943. A few were still in France when liberation came in 1944, and some scratch air units used these against isolated pockets of German resistance on the Western coast.

The Axis countries also made use of the type. The Italians in particular were eager to get their hands on the D.520 to supplement their agile, but lightly armed and obsolescent Macchi MC.200 fighters. The D.520s in Italian service were used in attempts to intercept B-24s bombing Italy itself, and were the only suitable interceptor available to the Italians in even small numbers for such a task. These served with the Italians until Italy also switched sides in 1943, after which a very small number continued in Italian service against the Germans. The Germans themselves kept a handful of D.520s for training purposes before passing on the lion's share to their ally Bulgaria. The Bulgarians used the D.520 with limited success as a bomber interceptor as well, challenging British and American bombers, although the P-38 and later P-51 escort fighters proved more than a match for an aging design.

After the war, what few D.520s were left in France became trainers for the French Air Force, soldiering on until the late 1940s when they were replaced. This was a quiet end for a type that had seen extensive service on many fronts, and one that seems far too much of a whisper for an aircraft that had possessed such a potential roar. The main weakness of the D.520 was simply that it ceased to evolve. With France prostrate under German occupation—and with Vichy a mere rump state—the D.520 received none of the upgrades and redesigns that fighters such as the Spitfire or Bf 109 received. It stayed, as if preserved in amber, in 1940—other improved developments only ever received a single prototype, at best, before France had fallen. Without any improvement, with scant resources, and no hope of replacement, the D.520 was thrown into combat again and again against adversaries who could field vastly numerically superior air arms, with constantly improving types. That the D.520 could be any sort of threat at all, in that environment, is testament to what had been a superb design.

Moreover, it was one of the best fighters in the world in 1940. 'What if?' questions are, as ever, difficult to ask for those involved with history, as well as aviation enthusiasts. There seems little doubt, however, that the main limitation on the D.520 was her late arrival and the small numbers available. Had more of this superb aircraft been available to counter the German invasion of 1940, it seems likely it would have exercised a critical role on the battlefield. As it stands, it remains a symbol of France's tragic fall, and an elegant tribute to the heights to which French aviation design could aspire.

Three D.520s are known to survive today. A fourth was destroyed in a tragic, fatal accident in 1986. The remaining trio are on display at the *Musée de l'Air et de l'Espace* in Paris, the *Conservatoire de l'air et de l'espace d'Aquitaine* in Bordeaux-Mérignac, and the third is undergoing restoration work at the French Naval Museum in Rochefort.

There are also, in some circles, persistent rumours that some D.520s saw service with Romania. There is no extant evidence, at least none seen by this author, for this—it is more than likely that any seen in or around Romania were on their way to Bulgarian service via the auspices of the Luftwaffe, or in other words were just passing through.

13

Dornier Do 19

When it launched itself into Poland in 1939, the German Luftwaffe operated a magnificent force of aircraft that was unmatched in the European skies. The craft had been perfected in fighting during the Spanish Civil War, and along with this the Luftwaffe had gained precious operational and tactical experience that its opponents in 1939–1940 could not match.

For operations in Poland, Norway, France, and the Low Countries, the Germans had a stable of excellent bombers as its mainstays—the Heinkel He 111, Dornier Do 17, and the Junkers Ju 88. The first two craft had been built as passenger craft that could be easily converted to bombers when Germany refuted the Versailles treaty, while the Ju 88 was a purpose-built bomber. This trio wrought havoc across Europe, backed up by the infamous Junkers Stuka dive-bomber for close-support.

However, when it came time to launch a campaign against England, the Luftwaffe found itself in a disadvantageous position. While it is true that the Germans enjoyed a nearly 4:1 superiority in numbers, they were faced by daunting challenges. Firstly, the British had made extensive use of radar, so they were better able to concentrate their response to German raids. Secondly, every aircraft lost over England represented a total loss to the Germans, whilst Royal Air Force pilots who survived the loss of their craft could potentially return to service. Thirdly, the Luftwaffe was operating at the extent of its range and effectiveness—attempts to move beyond the range of short-legged Luftwaffe fighters could prove disastrous, as attempts to attack England from bases in Norway proved.

The most serious deficiency was that the Luftwaffe could simply not deliver the tonnage of bombs required for effective strategic bombing, or indeed at the range needed for effective strategic purposes, and, as the war progressed, the Germans had no response to Allied air fleets that operated superb heavy bombers. Thus, while the Allied powers could damage German industry from far-off bases in England, Allied industry sat almost unaffected.

In fact, the Luftwaffe heavy bombing programme had failed to get very far at all and the Dornier Do 19 was a major example of what might have been.

Specifications

First Flight: 1936
Powerplant: Four Bramo 322H-2 radial-piston engines, 715 hp each.
Armament: (Intended, never mounted) two MG 15 0.31-inch (7.92-mm) machine guns, one in the nose and one in the tail, two 20-mm cannon meant for a pair of ventral and dorsal turrets, and up to 3,527 lb (1,600 kg) of internally stored bombs.
Top Speed: 196 mph (315 kph)
Range/Service Ceiling: 994 miles (1,600 km), 18,370 feet (5,600 metres)
Dimensions: Length 83 feet 6 inches (25.4 metres), height 19 feet (5.77 metres), wingspan 114 feet 10 inches (35 metres)
Number Built: One finished prototype, two incomplete prototypes

Germany had, from the end of the First World War in 1918, been secretly planning new military hardware to defend the Reich. The work was carried out in secret, in every facet of German armaments. For instance, the Krupp firm built submarines in the Netherlands that would prove to be test designs for the Germany navy. In another instance, tank designs were disguised under the label of 'tractor', though one design for a 'heavy tractor' was accidentally submitted complete with turret and main gun.

In the realm of heavy bombers, by the time Hitler came to power in 1933, the still nascent Luftwaffe had multiple potential candidates. The heavy bomber programme was

The Dornier Do.19 V1 on the ground. (*Courtesy of Thijs Postma*)

spearheaded by the Luftwaffe's first chief of staff, *Generalleutnant* Walter Wever. Amongst the high command, Wever was practically unique. Much like Cassandra of Greek myth, Wever looked into the future and saw clearly what others did not, and suffered much the same fate—namely, having others around him unable to see the truth of his vision. Wever understood that heavy bombing on a strategic basis would be a key aspect of any future air war, and was the strongest advocate for German heavy bombers.

The Dornier 19 was, in part, the result of Wever's vision. The first designs were finalised as early as 1933, far in advance of other competitors, such as the British. The first prototype flew at the end of October 1936 at Löwental. It was a surprisingly advanced design for the early 1930s. A cantilever mid-wing monoplane, the Do 19 had fully retractable landing gear—then still not a universal feature of aircraft design. While the aircraft was mostly metal, including the square cross-section fuselage, the twin tail unit contained fabric covered rudders. The V1 prototype was also unique in being fitted with an Askania-Sperry autopilot. The Do 19 was, in point of fact, the first aircraft fitted with the system.

While the specifications for the Do 19 may not seem stellar to the eyes of a modern observer, at least one familiar with those for bombers of the Second World War, it must be remembered that it was still a prototype aircraft. It would have undoubtedly been improved in order to see combat service, and moreover would have led to the development of other, more advanced aircraft. As it stood, the Do 19 prototype took to the skies three years before the Short Stirling did in 1939, the first of Britain's wartime heavy bombers.

Unfortunately for the Luftwaffe, both propaganda and strategic doctrine were weighing against the project. On the propaganda side, larger fleets of twin-engined medium bombers could be produced far more easily, which increased the perception of German aerial might in better ways than did smaller numbers of four-engined heavy bombers. Moreover, the Luftwaffe was being designed specifically for the Blitzkrieg tactics that would erupt across Europe in 1939. As such, strategic bombing was far less important than was close and medium-range bombing to knock out airfields and assist the advances of the Wehrmacht on the ground. Despite the advancement of at least parts of the Do 19's design, and its early lead, there was very little enthusiasm for heavy bombers as a result.

Wever was the sole exception. Unfortunately for German bomber design and doctrine, Wever was killed on 3 June 1936, when his Heinkel Blitz crashed, along with his flight engineer. The impetus for strategic bombing as a major part of German planning and design died with him. Ironically, the design specification for a heavy bomber that would eventually result in the Heinkel 177 was issued on the day of his death.

With Wever gone, there was no counterbalance in the Luftwaffe to voices such as Ernst Udet or Hans Jeschonnek, who favoured close support and battle-ground destruction of enemy air forces. A month later, in July 1936, all design work was ordered to halt on the Do 19 prototypes then under assembly. The Reich Air Ministry (the RLM) stated that there was no intention to put the bomber into production, and the project was abruptly terminated.

The cancellation orders, stemming from Hermann Goering himself, pointed to the insufficient top speed given by the current engines. This despite the improved aircraft engines then in production by German factories that could have been fitted to further prototypes or developments. Even the support of the Defence Minister could not reverse the decision. Therefore, it was that the Luftwaffe was locked into development of medium and light bombers, ensuring that when the crucial strategic moments came, German aviation would prove unequal to the tasks assigned to it.

As for the Do 19 V1 itself, it completed eighty-three test flights at Rechlin, which was the Luftwaffe's main testing ground before and during the war. After that, at the specific instruction of the RLM, the Do 19 prototype was scrapped, as were the incomplete prototypes, and all heavy bombers were deleted from the planning programme. Wever would certainly have pointed out that this constituted a catastrophic decision, and events were to prove him right. Aside from the use of the Focke-Wulf Fw 200 Condor as a maritime anti-shipping aircraft, the Luftwaffe would possess absolutely no aircraft capable of proper strategic bombing until the arrival of the flawed Heinkel 177 Greif in mid-1942, at which point that aircraft's teething troubles and then the deteriorating strategic situation rendered it a case of 'too little, too late'.

The Dornier Do 19 definitely qualifies as one of those fascinating 'might-have-beens' in military aviation history. Any student of history who is interested in posing and discussing 'what if?' questions will immediately wonder at the impact proper heavy

The Dornier Do.19 V1 on one of her test flights. (*Courtesy of Thijs Postma*)

bombers, ready in 1939–1940, might have done to alter the strategic balance of Europe. However, perhaps the impact the loss of the programme had was best stated by the Germans themselves.

Writing to *Generalfeldmarschall* Erhard Milch, the President of the Association of the German Aviation Industry pointed to an optimistic and confident vision of what might have been. Admiral Lahs, writing in 1942, noted that had the Do 19 and Junkers 89 been properly developed, the types would have proven superior to those fielded by both the Americans and the British.

Another casualty of the sudden cancellation of heavy bomber development was the Junkers Ju 89. Much like the Dornier 19, the Ju 89 did not make it past the prototype phase. It was, again like the Dornier, a four-engined bomber with a theoretical bomb load of up to 4,408 lb—significantly more than the Dornier. In other categories, it also outstripped Dornier's entry. It had a top speed of 253 mph, and would have possessed a range of 1,850 miles. Had the two planes entered competition to see which would be picked as the Luftwaffe's mainstay heavy bomber, it would have proved interesting. On paper, as they stood, the Junkers design had superior capabilities, yet the Do 19 had other advanced features, and more to the point would have been improved as it advanced from the first prototype. It is difficult to say which of the two may have ultimately been selected, if indeed the answer wouldn't have been that both went forward. The first two prototypes of the Junkers Ju 89 flew, and the third was nearing completion with its armament when the order came down to convert it to use as a heavy transport. Shortly after that, in 1937, it too was cancelled, robbing the Germans of yet another potentially capable heavy bomber. While a student of Second World War bombers might point out that the theoretical load of the Ju 89 was vastly inferior to that carried by aircraft such as those the Allies possessed during the war (indeed, its load is only slightly higher than that carried by a Heinkel 111 medium bomber), it was an early stepping stone. The sudden stopping of development ensured that the Germans had to eventually restart their heavy bomber programme without the benefit of experience provided by either aircraft's continued development.

A further note would be that the late-war German heavy bomber programme is fascinating in and of itself, and the focus of numerous works worth pursuing for any student interested in the history of the Luftwaffe or indeed of the secret projects of the Second World War. The casual reader will find accessible books available, and, for those more interested in the engineering, technical data is also available in books and online.

14

Fisher P-75 Eagle

In aviation history, there are often cautionary tales. There are the designs that are poor ideas terribly executed, or the ones made by outright charlatans. The former could be represented by the Bachem Natter seen previously in this volume. The latter could be represented by the Christmas Bullet, a design made by one Dr Christmas in an attempt to bilk the United States military that universally came apart on take-off. However, the Fisher P-75 Eagle perhaps represents a 'third way' in terms of poor design—the possible deliberate failure.

Specifications

First Flight: 1943
Powerplant: One Alison V-3420-23 24 cylinder double-banked Vee piston engine, 2,885 hp
Armament: Ten Browning 0.5-inch (12.7-mm) machine guns, six mounted on the wings, four in the fuselage, plus two 500-lb (227-kg) bombs on wing racks.
Top Speed: 400 mph (644 kph)
Range/Service Ceiling: 3,000 miles (4,828 km), 36,000 feet (10,975 metres)
Dimensions: Length 40 feet 5 inches (12.32 metres), height 15 feet 6 inches (4.72 metres), wingspan 49 feet 4 inches (15.04 metres)
Number built: 13

The P-75, at first glance, looks like what people in the past might have thought the future would be. The design itself is undoubtedly futuristic looking, sleek and built around two contra-rotating propellers. All views of the P-75 enhance this picture, with the surviving examples shining silver and so brightly that it seems like one could use the fuselage as a mirror. Yet on closer inspection by the trained eye, certain elements begin to stand out— namely that some of the parts look very familiar indeed. The wings have some curious similarities to those of a Curtiss P-40 Warhawk. The tail bears a striking resemblance to a Douglas SBD Devastator or, depending on what source one consults, the Douglas A-24. The landing gear, perhaps a bit less obviously, looks like that of a Vought F4U Corsair. There are even wing centre-section panels that would, on close inspection, look much like those from the P-51 Mustang. All of these coincidences are, to reveal the rather obvious, because they were indeed parts for those aircraft. Like Frankenstein's Monster,

Prototype XP-75 on the runway. (*Courtesy of the National Museum of the United States Air Force*)

the P-75 was assembled out of existing parts around an engine. The reasons why this was done could either be practical or, to take another theory, disingenuous.

First, however, attention must be turned to the background history. In 1942, a new priority was sinking into American industry as the B-29 Superfortress programme began to move forward. Boeing could build a relatively small number of Superfortresses, given its existing commitments to supply B-17s. Thus it was that the government would have to direct many factories from many companies in constructing this massive and complicated new craft. This would, as an aside, lead to Boeing sharing out design schematics of what was at the time one of the most advanced pieces of technology on earth. This move seems alien to modern eyes—it is difficult to imagine modern corporations cooperating so readily with potential post-war competitors.

At the same time, the US Army Air Force had a need of a new, quick-climbing fighter plane. General Motors' Fisher Body Division rose to the challenge with an unusual proposal. They would marry existing parts already in mass-production to the most powerful engine then in production, the Alison V-3420-19 engine, which was really two V-1710 engines bound together side by side. Fisher Body promised the new aircraft would be ready for testing as early as April 1943, but the first prototype wasn't ready until November of that year. At least some in the military blamed the delay on incompetence and over-optimistic estimates.

What eventually appeared, however, certainly looked impressive. The XP-75 was over 41 feet long, with a 49-foot wingspan. The engine was behind the pilot, driving the two propellers via a long shaft, much like in the P-39 Airacobra. The plane was, in a marketing flourish undoubtedly native to General Motors, given a good deal of press and described as a wonder plane with the designation harkening back to a famed French artillery cannon of the First World War.

In the air, however, the Eagle failed to live up to its press. It was sluggish at many manoeuvres, and its speed fell short of what had been envisioned, and indeed promised, by Fisher. The early testing programme was not helped, in addition, by fatal crashes—or by the fact that the 10 ton weight of the fighter did nothing to aid the craft's performance. There was also the small matter of the Allison engine installed not often being able to deliver the designed horsepower in actual use. Moreover, by the time it had flown for the first time, the Air Force's requirements had shifted to long-range escort fighters, roles in which the existing P-38 Lightning and P-51 Mustang were admirably suited.

In essence, then, the P-75 was already an airplane surplus to requirements. Nevertheless, the Air Force placed an order for the plane contingent on Fisher making improvements to meet new requirements for a long-range fighter, which resulted in the slightly improved P-75A production model. This took to the skies in November 1944, after eight Eagles had already been built and flown. The requirement it was built to fulfil, however, had been withdrawn in September. Thus the Eagle project was terminated, after a total of thirteen aircraft had been built.

Here the story might well end, that of a project that never lived up to its hype and ultimately was relegated to the dustbin. Yet some sources claim another intriguing aspect to the story that has a lot to do with corporate politics. Here, the previously mentioned need for the B-29's construction to be spread out comes very vibrantly into play.

According to this reading of history, General Motors did not want to be part of the Superfortress project, but GM facilities were already earmarked for participation in the programme. The only way out was to put those facilities into use fulfilling another requirement, one that put less strain on what GM considered to be already overstretched commitments on their part. Thus it was that Fisher Body, with no experience of aircraft design, produced the P-75 Eagle. In this context, the Eagle can be seen as an elaborate ruse to escape building the Superfortress. Since General Echols, head of the USAAF Materiel Command, could compel companies into what was deemed essential war production, any escape GM planned had to at least be theoretically legitimate. Thus, the hybrid Eagle.

In the end, General Motors submitted a bill in May 1945 for $4.7 million. The P-75 had ultimately cost them $9 million, and so the most charitable description of the P-75 project would be of an expensive disappointment. Yet taken another way, the expense may have seemed justified—General Motors never took part in the Superfortress project.

There is a surviving P-75 Eagle on display at the National Museum of the United States Air Force in Dayton, Ohio.

15

Focke-Wulf Fw 187 Falke

Military aviation is usually never the product of sheer luck. Sometimes the unexpected does occur, like taking a superb American airframe and replacing a sluggish Allison engine with a magnificent British Merlin and creating the legendary P-51 Mustang. However, for every occurrence like that, there are a far greater quantity of service aircraft made via painstaking work and competitive trials.

It is an exhausting process in which competing designs are matched against each other and tested in every way that could conceivably measure any potential usefulness. This process is sometimes influenced by outside factors, including political concerns as well as personal pressure and influence. Ostensibly, the best aircraft wins. Yet, while the winner frequently goes on to a well-remembered historical role, the question one naturally comes to wonder is: what happened to the other one? To the one not quite selected?

Such is the case with the Focke-Wulf Fw 187 Falke, an aircraft that was perhaps superior to the aircraft that was chosen over it, and offers an interesting look into a historical 'might-have-been'.

Specifications

First Flight: 1937
Powerplant: Two Junkers Jumo 210G 12-cylinder inverted Vee piston engines, 700 hp
Armament: Four MG 17 0.31-inch (7.92-mm) machine guns and two MG FF 20-mm cannon
Top Speed: 329 mph (529 kph)
Range/Service Ceiling: Maximum range unknown, 32,810 feet (10,000 metres)
Dimensions: Length 36 feet 6 inches (11.12 metres), height 12 feet 7.66 inches, wingspan 50 feet 2.33 inches (15.3 metres)
Number Built: 9

German industry was not necessarily the efficient force that stereotype would have one believe. In point of fact, Germany's industrial production during the Second World War was plagued by conflicting priorities, production being drawn in too many directions, and the large industrial concerns competing via any means necessary to secure contracts. Given the fact that Nazi authority was frequently crisscrossed with multiple departments or major figures vying for Hitler's favour, this often led to confusion. Moreover, industries

The Focke-Wulf Fw187 Falke. (*Courtesy of Thijs Postma*)

weren't always producing what was best for Germany's needs. Krupp, for instance, played on Hitler's mania for the grandiose to produce the titanic Dora gun, officially the Schwerer Gustav. It was an 80-cm railway gun, meant to annihilate the Maginot line, though it was finished too late for that. It was used rarely, only able to hit massive static targets, and was in every measure (except size) relatively useless—yet each unit cost the Reich 7 million RM.

This is a necessary background to what comes next, as well as an instructive lesson on how Nazi Germany actually functioned, if such a word can be applied to a violent tyrant-state. The point being that competition for contracts was fierce, but also that the best designs were not necessarily selected for use. In a state run by men like Hitler, who often made choices based on instinct, whim, and even romantic delusions, this meant that short-sighted choices were made that impacted the future of Germany as a whole.

In this regard, the Focke-Wulf Fw 187 is a perfect example of such a decision. It was a superb design that was rejected primarily because the highest echelons of German power could see no reason for it, picking the tactical objective over the strategic goal, and once again hampering Germany's entire air war.

The Focke-Wulf Corporation was destined to produce some of the Luftwaffe's best aircraft, and it owed much of its success to a single person—Dr Kurt Tank. Tank's designs would encompass the Fw 200 Condor, the superb Fw 190 line of fighters (culminating in the Ta 152 evolution of the design, bearing his name), and his career would continue even after the war, across the globe.

In 1935, however, Tank had the idea for a twin-engined fighter that would surpass all known performance marks for fighter speed. In the mid-1930s, it looked for a brief time as if the bomber was pulling away, literally and metaphorically, from the fighter. The newest twin-engined bombers, such as the Dornier Do 17, were capable of outpacing all known fighter interception. A need was perceived to counter such aircraft, which would result in multiple projects such as the Westland Whirlwind and Grumman XF5F, seen later in this work. In the brain of Kurt Tank, it spawned the Falke.

The concept for the Fw 187, predicted to have a top speed of 350 mph (560 kph), was unveiled at a 1936 exhibition of new weapon technologies and prototypes, in front of the high-ranking Nazi party members, including Hitler. Unlike the twin-engined Messerschmitt Bf 110, the idea for the Falke was to have a twin-engined fighter that would have the performance of a single-engined fighter, with additional speed. Though it would not possess the range of a longer-range heavy fighter, it would be able to compete against the swiftest bomber.

The RLM was persuaded to sign off on a few examples of a single-seat, twin-engined fighter, which was supposed to be powered by the new Daimler-Benz DB600 engines that were being developed. Tank passed off the detail design to his assistant, Obering R. Blaser, and the result was a superb, modern design. The Fw 187 was all-metal, a sign of the path to come for fighter design. It also had a super-thin fuselage, so thin that the cockpit did not have its full instrumentation. Instead, the instruments that couldn't be fitted in the standard positions were located on the inboard side of the engine cowlings, so they could still be seen by the pilot.

Had the Fw 187 been fitted with its originally planned Daimler-Benz engines, it would have been faster than the Messerschmitt Bf 109E, but this was not to be the case. Tank took the design to the chief of development for the RLM's research and development division, Wolfram von Richthofen. Richthofen, cousin to both of the First World War flying aces of the same name, was dubious of the idea that bombers would remain faster than fighters—a view that can be justified by later events. In the moment, however, Richthofen struck the Fw 187 programme a mortal blow by insisting that production of a few examples could only happen if the engines were substituted. As the DB600 engine was in such short supply, the Fw 187 would receive the Junkers Jumo 210, a reliable, but significantly less powerful engine.

The V1 prototype flew for the first time in late spring of 1937, and even with the less powerful engine it still achieved a speed of 350 mph (563 kph). The entire design had been crafted to achieve speed, with extensive use of streamlining and the absence of any support struts, all the supporting mechanisms being carried internally. Uniquely, the engine radiators were retractable, to further increase high-speed performance. Initial testing went very well, despite the lower-grade engines. It was found that the aircraft was 50 mph (80 kph) faster than its contemporary, the Messerschmitt Bf 109B—this despite having double the range and double the weight. The Falke's climb and dive rates were either at par with, or superior to, the Bf 109B as well. The RLM officials complained that these results were caused by faulty instruments rather than being indicative of the type's

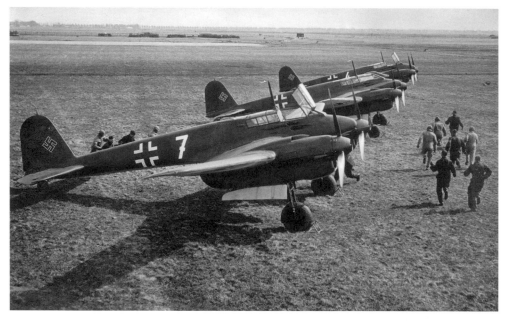

Propaganda photo of Focke-Wulf Fw187s. (*Courtesy of Thijs Postma*)

actual performance, but further testing ruled this out. The Falke was proving, even in the prototype phase, to be superior to the early mark 109s.

The RLM, however, remained unconvinced. Messerschmitt had good relations with the higher-ups, and his 109 would be produced more cheaply than the Falke. As such, the Falke was already doomed to never take on the role intended for it. Further testing also went poorly, through no fault of the aircraft itself. The V2 prototype, which removed the fancy radiators, with some minor changes and upgraded Jumo engines, crashed on landing when one of its landing gear collapsed. The V1 was also lost on 14 May 1938 when pilot Paul Bauer was at the controls. After making a high-speed pass over Focke-Wulf's Bremen factory, he pulled up too sharply, causing a stall, and the aircraft spun into the ground.

Though damaged by all this, the programme limped along, and in fact seemed to see new light ahead. Richthofen had been replaced by Ernst Udet at the RLM. Udet was a devotee of the single-engined design, believing firmly in manoeuvrability's importance, and utterly certain that a twin-engined design could never match the agility of a single-engined design. Nevertheless, he instructed Focke-Wulf to continue development of a two-seater version to potentially replace the Messerschmitt Bf 110 in the role of bomber destroyer.

The Falke had always been intended to be capable of this role, but as a single-seater. Yet the cockpit was extended to suit this requirement, which changed the centre of gravity, necessitating changing the engine nacelles. Further, there was no room in the high-line fuselage for a rearward facing gun, meaning the second crewmember would be exclusively a radio operator. Though the two-seater Falke was supposed to have a heavier punch, with two 20-mm cannon to be fitted in place of machine guns in a theoretical production model, there were issues. Namely, the redesigned two-seater, with the Jumo engines, had performance that did not warrant it being adopted as a replacement for the Bf 110.

The final prototype, however, had a surprise in store. It had a new evaporative cooling system, but, most importantly, it finally had the DB600 engines it was supposed to have in the first place. The V6 would prove to have cooling problems as a result of the new system, but in October 1939 it achieved a speed of 395 mph (634 kph) in level flight, the fastest in Germany.

In the end, a very small production run of a development of the V3 prototype was ordered (a measly three aircraft) fitted with the lacklustre Jumo 210 engines. Designated Fw 187 A-0, these generated no interested within the Luftwaffe, who bluntly stated that without defensive armament they were not interested in the aircraft as a *Zerstörer* like the Bf 110. They were returned to Focke-Wulf, who used them through 1940 as a defensive squadron for their Bremen factory. The Falkes were used mainly as propaganda, and it was claimed they had scored several kills over the Bremen works. They also showed up in Norway in 1941, promoted as a replacement for the Bf 110, though any such plan was long dead. In reality, the aircraft were utilised briefly by a *Zerstörer Staffel* of the Luftwaffe's JG 77 for trial purposes. These trials, perhaps expectedly at this point, went nowhere. Again returned to Focke-Wulf, it is likely they served as testbeds during the initial stages of Tank's Ta 154 programme, when the Luftwaffe belatedly decided it needed a twin-engined fighter after all.

By all accounts, pilots loved the Fw 187, preferring it greatly to the Bf 110, and proving that the design was one unduly rejected. It is interesting to speculate what would have become of continually improved production versions of the Falke, mounting the superior Daimler-Benz engines. The usefulness of the twin-engined fighter concept was proven instead by aircraft such as the American P-38 Lightning, which would carve out a fearsome reputation against the Luftwaffe.

The Falke was not the only aircraft programme that was jinxed by requiring the scarce DB600 series engines. Another victim was the superb Heinkel 100 fighter, which was also a rejected design used for propaganda purposes. A direct competitor to the Bf 109, the Heinkel He 100 set a world speed record in 1939, and the type could regularly achieve a speed of 416 mph (670 kph)—a spectacular speed for any fighter. Why it was rejected is a reason of some controversy, with multiple claims made. The Heinkel side of the story holds that it was politics and favouritism towards Messerschmitt, while another blames the RLM's production strategy that favoured numbers over types, which seems illogical given the sheer variety of vehicles the Germans frequently produced for a given role, and also that the Focke-Wulf 190 was on the cards at the same time the He 100 was cancelled. Still a third holds that it was the extensive problems with the DB-series engines that doomed the project. Whatever the reason, the Heinkel He 100 is another fascinating aircraft worth examining, to the student of rare and lesser-known Second World War aviation.

16

Fokker D.XXI

Anthony Fokker's company did sterling service to his native Dutch air force. His post-First World War contribution has unfortunately been frequently forgotten by historians. The D-series of fighter aircraft that had begun in the First World War continued onwards, marching all the way through the 1920s and 1930s with a series of designs, all of them at the very least competent aircraft. By the time the Second World War began, Fokker would find itself supplying the lion's share of Dutch fighters (to say nothing of his export contracts), which would be used against Fokker's former employer, Germany. It was a somewhat ironic situation, given the legendary role of Fokker aircraft in German military history, but both the man himself and his aircraft had not lost their abilities.

One of Fokker's forgotten craft was the basic, rugged Fokker D.XXI, which proved to be a mainstay for not only the Dutch, but also the Finnish air force. In this role, the D.XXI would face two leviathans: the full might of the Luftwaffe at the height of its power, and the Soviet Air Force in all its vastness and increasing technical proficiency. The D.XXI would spend its career outnumbered by vast margins, making its sterling service to both the Netherlands and Finland all the more remarkable.

Specifications

First Flight: 1936
Powerplant: Bristol Mercury VIII 9-cylinder radial-piston engine, 830 hp
Armament: Four 0.31-inch (7.9-mm) machine guns, two in the wings and two in the upper-engine cowling.
Top Speed: 286 mph (460 kph)
Range/Service Ceiling: 590 miles (950 km), 36,090 feet (11,000 metres)
Dimensions: Length 26 feet 11 inches (8.2 metres), height 9 feet 7 inches (2.92 metres), wingspan 36 feet 1 inch (11 metres)
Number Built: 148

The D.XXI may look obsolete to modern eyes, and by its arrival in combat it was—at least in part. Yet it was originally a quantum leap forward in terms of the designs that Fokker was producing, jumping almost immediately from biplane fighters and high-wing monoplanes directly to a mostly modern low-wing monoplane, albeit with fixed landing gear.

Fokker D.XXIs in formation. (*Courtesy of Thijs Postma*)

The Netherlands army air division had contracted Fokker for a prototype in 1935, for the purposes of evaluating its potential use in Dutch overseas possessions, specifically the Dutch East Indies. The aircraft was originally planned around the Rolls-Royce Kestrel IV engine, but these were never acquired. The aircraft would instead receive the Bristol Mercury VIII, which was a significant blessing for the project as it led to a large increase in available horsepower. The prototype, however, had to make do with a Mercury VI-S radial engine, which had a total of 645 hp. Those reading the specifications above will notice the vast difference in performance between the VI-S and the VIII in terms of power delivery. Its punch would be delivered by four machine guns, two in the fuselage and two in the wings.

The prototype would fly in February of 1936 at Eindhoven, and almost immediately be ordered into production. It was meant to fulfil Dutch air doctrine at the time, which could be summed up as bombers at home, fighters abroad. The Dutch government was certainly more interested at that point in using its fighter strength primarily in its far-flung colonies, where the ability to use smaller airfields with less required maintenance would undoubtedly make fighters the more economical choice.

The increasing belligerency of Nazi Germany, however, caused a hurried re-thinking of strategic priorities. In 1937, the government ordered the Fokker for home use, with the better engine. At the same time, Fokker began to make foreign sales of the aircraft, with seven being ordered for the Finnish air force, with a license arrangement concluded thereafter so that the Finnish State Aircraft Factory, located at Tampere, would be able to build them. Finland would certainly get its money's worth from the design, as events were soon to prove. It is worth noting that the main differences between the Finnish-built D.XXIs were the frequent use of skis instead of the spatted landing gear, and that the Finns mounted all four guns in the wings, rather than the standard Dutch configuration.

Though they would play little role in upcoming events, Fokker also made sales to Denmark's tiny air force, delivering some D.XXIs, while at least ten were built by the Danes themselves at the Royal Army Aircraft Factory in Copenhagen. The difference in this export model was more pronounced—the Danish examples retained the slower, older Bristol VI-S engines, but instead of the paired machine guns over the engine mounted a single 20-mm cannon. This resulted in an interesting trade-off between less power, but more punch.

Another early purchaser was Spain, with the Republican government also acquiring a license to produce D.XXIs. This effort did not, however, get very far before the production lines were seized by Francisco Franco's Nationalists. As far as is known, no D.XXIs were completed before the capture, and none were finished by the Nationalists after the fact.

Back in Holland itself, the first D.XXIs began to arrive in service in July 1938, beginning the usual evaluation and training period. By the time war was declared in September of 1939, a grand total of thirty-six had been delivered. This was a pitifully small number with which to defend against a German onslaught, and there was worse to come. When the Germans invasion of the Low Countries and France began on 10 May 1940, there were only twenty-eight operative D.XXIs in service.

Nevertheless, despite the overwhelming odds, the D.XXI gave very good account of itself. It was a particularly nimble aircraft, and was proving to be a difficult little opponent for the Luftwaffe. Unfortunately, the speed of the advance meant that Dutch resistance lasted a mere five days before collapsing. In that time, however, the D.XXI scored one notable feat against the overconfident Germans. On the first day of the invasion, the D.XXIs pounced on a formation of Junkers Ju 52 trimotor transports, which had crossed the frontier as part of the early morning start of the invasion. There were a grand total of fifty-five Junkers in the air, and the D.XXIs accounted for thirty-seven of them destroyed—an absolute slaughter.

It is also worth noting that efforts were in hand before the invasion to once again upgrade the type's engine. Before the war began, the durable airframe served as a testbed for numerous engines, including the Hispano-Suiza 12Y (used by the Avia B-534, Dewoitine D.520, and Ikarus IK-2), as well as the Rolls-Royce Kestrel V. The incomplete plans were for one to mount the Bristol Hercules, and another to mount the Daimler-Benz DB600—a likely major increase in engine power. Perhaps most interesting, however, was the version labelled Project 151, which was to gain the legendary Rolls-Royce Merlin engine. Each of these new projects was to have fully retractable landing gear and other aerodynamic improvements, each of them being a fascinating 'what if?' situation.

In Finland, however, the D.XXI had more time to prove itself, and prove itself it did. The Finns would produce the greater part of the D.XXIs that were ever built, and they served in both the Winter War of 1940 and the Continuation War until 1944. Fitted with 'snowshoe' landing gear, the type did sterling service for the Finns, with the last ones lingering in service until 1948. Many of the later Finnish-built examples came with Swedish-built Pratt & Whitney Twin Wasp engines, owing to a scarcity of the original types.

The evidence suggests that the D.XXI is yet another of the aircraft that, despite being an excellent overall design, simply did not exist in enough numbers to have a decisive impact on events. When it did serve, it did so very well, even against vastly superior enemy forces. Therefore, it was that Fokker continued to design nimble, capable craft, right up until the capitulation of his native country, to the country he had once worked for.

There are two surviving examples of the D.XXI viewable today. One is held in the Aviation Museum of Central Finland, at Tikkakoski. While it was restored with parts from others, the airframe itself is FR-110, the most successful of the D.XXIs in Finnish service, which scored ten kills. There is also a replica D.XXI at the Militaire Luchtvaart Museum in Camp Zeist, in the Netherlands.

It should also be noted that while the D.XXI was the last of Fokker's fighters to enter production, it was not the last fighter desinged in the 'D' series. The line that began with the superlative fighters of the First World War, actually ended with the Fokker D.XXIII, a strange departure from anything Fokker had previously designed. It was a twin-engined fighter, but with one propeller mounted conventionally, while the other was a pusher-engine mounted at the rear of the fuselage. A twin-boom tail design completed the strange-looking aircraft. Only one prototype was completed, and flew in May 1939. Work was still being undertaken to improve the type for potential future service when the Germans invaded and the project was abruptly brought to a close.

17

Fokker G.1

The name Fokker is one of the most legendary in the history of military aviation. While the Dutch-born Fokker is most closely associated with the aircraft he designed for the Germans during the First World War (most famously the Dr.I triplane), Fokker created for far more than just the Germans. The company Fokker created produced famed and important aircraft such as the Fokker F.VII—better known in North America as the plane that took Admiral Byrd to the North Pole. Beyond this, though, is a fact that is easily and frequently forgotten. Namely that the company produced numerous combat designs, especially those for the Dutch Air Force.

As cataclysm engulfed the Low Countries and France in 1940s, these designs would be put to the test. Vastly outnumbered and technologically surpassed, the machines and their pilots fought with courage against an overwhelming and determined foe. In so doing, they carved out a role for themselves worthy of remembrance.

Specifications

First Flight: 1937
Powerplant: Two Bristol Mercury VIII 9-cylinder radial-piston engines, 830 hp each
Armament: Eight 0.31-inch (7.9-mm) machine guns mounted in the nose, with a ninth in a rearward-facing, pivoting mounting, plus up to 882 lb (400 kg) of bombs.
Top Speed: 295 mph (475 kph)
Range/Service Ceiling: 870 miles (1,400 km), 30,500 feet (9,300 metres)
Dimensions: Length 35 feet 8 inches (10.87 metres), height 12 feet 4.8 inches (3.8 metres), wingspan 56 feet 3.48 inches (17.16 metres)
Number Built: 63

The Fokker G.1 was one of many heavy fighters that were developed in the 1930s, and one of the more interesting designs. The G.1 started life as a private venture by Fokker's chief engineer, Dr Erich Schatzki. The G.1 was designed to fulfil two roles: to be a standard air-superiority fighter, and also to be a bomber destroyer. Later thinking would add ground attack and light bombing to its designed responsibilities.

The G.1 was also a radical departure from previous Fokker designs. It was meant to accommodate a heavy armament of two 23-mm (0.91-inch) Madsen cannon plus a pair

Fokker G.1 airborne. (*Courtesy of Thijs Postma*)

of 7.9-mm machine guns. This would later become a total of eight machine guns in the nose, with a ninth as a defensive machine gun. This much concentrated firepower caused quite a stir, and the G.1 was given the nickname 'le Faucheur' ('reaper'). This was, however, the least interesting aspect of the design.

The construction itself was a mixture, which was common to Fokker designs of the period. The central pod's front sections were constructed around a welded frame, which was then covered with aluminium plating. The rear of this pod, however, was wood. Unusually for the time, the wings, too, were made of wood. It was to be powered by a pair of Hispano-Suiza 14AB-02/03 engines, and it was with these that the prototype first flew in March 1937. The engines, however, were nearly catastrophic to the programme. In another test flight in September, one of the superchargers exploded, nearly causing the loss of the prototype—to say nothing of the loss of the pilot. The decision was made to re-equip the aircraft with Pratt & Whitney SB4-G Twin Wasp engines, which added significantly to the total horsepower (the production engines would produce significantly less than this, however).

At the time, the twin-boom design was relatively rare, and somewhat unusual for an aircraft. The rounded fuselage was meant for two or in some cases three crewmembers (the pilot, a navigator/radio operator/defensive gunner, and a bombardier). Even more amazingly, this radical departure from conventional design was conceived and created in an astonishingly short seven months. The X-2 prototype was introduced to the world at the Paris Air Show in November 1936 and caused an immediate sensation. It was apparently painted in a purple and yellow finish, both spectacular and evocative of Spanish Republican colours, making quite the statement.

Perhaps understandably, Spain was the first to order the aircraft. The Republican government placed an order for twenty-six of the export version of the aircraft, mounting the Pratt & Whitney engines. Fokker received payment for the order, but then the embargo on arms to the Spanish conflict was promulgated and the Dutch government blocked the sale. This did not stop the Germans, Italians, and Soviets from trying to influence the course of events, but it did mean that no Dutch fighters would ever reach Republican service. Fokker, perhaps hoping for a change in the prevailing wind, kept producing the aircraft as part of a mythical Finnish order, though the Finns did show interest in the G.1, but ultimately purchased Bristol Blenheim bombers instead.

Other foreign governments also showed interest in the design, including its capabilities as a dive bomber. Fitted with dive breaks, it was shown that the G.1 could dive at over 400 mph (644 kph) and also demonstrated aerobatic skills, to add to its already famed reputation. Ultimately the Swedes and Danes placed orders as well, with interest shown by Belgium, Finland, Turkey, Hungary, and Switzerland, though the latter nations never placed orders.

Closer to home, the *Luchtvaartafdeeling* (Dutch Air Force) placed orders for thirty-six aircraft, meant to equip three squadrons. These aircraft would be equipped with what was the standard Dutch aviation engine, the Bristol Mercury, which would simplify maintenance and the acquisition of spare parts. The first four of these aircraft were completed in the ground-attack configuration, with the rest finished as two-seaters. On the eve of war, twenty-six G.1s were available to the Dutch, spread across two squadrons. The first, the 3rd *Jachtvliegtuigafdeling* (JaVA), was based outside Rotterdam at the Waalhaven Airport. The other squadron, 4th JaVA, was at Bergen near Alkmaar. The aircraft were immediately put into use as border patrol aircraft, safeguarding Dutch neutrality as hostilities grew more and more likely. In one notable incident, a Royal Air Force Whitley bomber strayed into the airspace of the Netherlands, and a G.1 of 4th JaVA forced it down. This was on the 20 March 1940—with less than two months to go before Germany invaded. The G.1 defended neutrality to the last.

When the German onslaught came, and the Five Day War began, the G.1s suffered a mixed fate. The 4th JaVA was caught on the ground by an early morning Luftwaffe raid, and lost all but one of their aircraft, and thereafter the only aircraft it could field would be those that were made airworthy with parts stripped from other G.1s. However, 3rd JaVA was luckier, scrambling in time to engage its attackers. Primarily the G.1 was used in combat as ground-attack aircraft, strafing any advancing German columns they could find, putting the G.1s heavy concentrated firepower to good use.

They were also very successful in engaging Ju 52 transports, much like their stable mate, the Fokker D.XXI. The G.1 proved deadly against the Ju 52, stationed above The Hague and Rotterdam as an augmentation to anti-aircraft artillery. In this role, the G.1

A view of the early X-2 prototype of the Fokker G.1 (*Courtesy of the Ray Crupi Collection, 1000aircraftphotos.com*)

is known to have scored fourteen kills, though records are fragmentary. Unfortunately, much was lost in the chaos and short duration of the war, so that many incidents of the G.1's use are likely lost forever. The remaining G.1s were ground down by attrition in mission after mission, flying into the teeth of the German advance without hope of relief or replacement, a staggering feat given the circumstances.

The short duration, however, kept them from proving too effective on the battlefield. In the aftermath of the invasion, the Luftwaffe took over the remainder of Fokker's Spanish order of G.1s, still sitting unused as they had never received their armament. These, along with whatever G.1s the Germans could acquire, were sent to Wiener Neustadt where they became part of *Flugzeugführerschule (B) 8*, being used as advanced trainers for Messerschmitt Bf 110 pilots. These were kept in service for two years until attrition grounded them permanently.

This might be all there was to the story of the G.1, but the aircraft had one last memorable story to its credit. A sole G.1 made a daring flight that wrote itself into the history books as a brave attempt to escape the Nazis. On 5 May 1941, one of Fokker's test pilots, Hidde Leegstra, took up a G.1 with extra fuel and engineer Piet Vos, who also happened to be a part of Fokker's board of directors. The extra fuel had to be surreptitiously loaded, and, once in the air, the duo had to manoeuvre their G.1 into the clouds in order to slip their Luftwaffe minders. After a nerve-wracking flight, the pair landed safely in England, competing their daring coup.

The fate of their aircraft, however, was less heroic. The aircraft was conscripted by Phillips and Powis Aircraft, which would later become Miles Aircraft. The company was interested in the G.1's wooden structure, as they were working on an all-wood fighter bomber of their own. For the rest of the war, the G.1 was left to sit outdoors, to see the effect of British climate on its airframe, and it was scrapped sometime after 1945.

The Fokker G.1 was unlucky in many respects. While it did reach some countries in various export orders, it served its homeland in pitifully small numbers with which to oppose the might of the Germans. Still, it rose and struck back at the enemy, and one can imagine being German soldiers caught in the path of a concentrated blast of eight machine guns coming in at speed. The G.1 more than fulfilled its role, and despite bad luck and small numbers, still carved out its place in aviation history

No G.1 aircraft survive in their original condition. A replica, however, was built for the Netherlands Military Museum at Soesterberg. This replica was proudly on display until 2013, but as of the time of this writing it is apparently, and unfortunately, in storage at that museum.

18

Gloster Gladiator

It is difficult, sometimes, to remember that by the time the Second World War began, the biplane was still a major part of combatant air forces. Moreover, even as the major powers moved towards the first jet aircraft, many of these craft still performed a vital role in their respective air forces. Some, like the Polikarpov I-153 and Po-2, as well as the Henschel Hs 123, are discussed later in this book. Other air forces, such as the Regia Aeronautica, went into battle with biplanes as the mainstays of their air force—as in the case of the Fiat CR.42. Still another example would be the Fairey Swordfish, the beloved Stringbag of the British Navy, a biplane so useful it outlived its own intended replacement and achieved enduring fame. The Gloster Gladiator, however, is remarkable in the sheer variety of air forces in which it appeared. Not only that, it was to be found on both sides of the war, serving in myriad theatres for both the Allies and the Axis powers. In the process, the Gladiator would be seen across the world in combat and also inspire one of the most enduring legends of the Second World War.

These achievements are all the more remarkable, given that the opinion of some on the Gladiator was less than positive. As Roald Dahl noted in his short story *A Piece of Cake*:

> Those old Gladiators aren't made of stressed steel like a Hurricane or a Spit[fire]. They have taut canvas wings, covered with magnificently inflammable dope, and underneath there are hundreds of small thin sticks, the kind you put under the logs for kindling, only these are drier and thinner. If a clever man said, 'I am going to build a big thing that will burn better and quicker than anything else in the world,' and if he applied himself diligently to his task, he would probably finish up by building something very like a Gladiator.

> Dahl, p. 338

Despite Dahl's opinion, the Gladiator provides a fascinating example of the sheer variety of places the biplane still performed its duties, even in the age of monoplane fighters.

Specifications

First Flight: 1934
Powerplant: Bristol Mercury IX 9-cylinder radial-piston engine, 830 hp
Armament: Four 0.303-inch (7.7-mm) machine guns

Top Speed: 257 mph (414 kph)
Range/Service Ceiling: 440 miles (708 km), 33,500 feet (10,210 metres)
Dimensions: Length 27 feet 5 inches (8.36 metres), height 11 feet 9 inches (3.58 metres),
wingspan 32 feet 3 inches (9.83 metres)
Number Built: 747

The Gladiator had its origins in Britain's remarkably late development of biplanes as
frontline fighters. The Gladiator, or the Gloster SS.37, was the descendant of the Gloster
Gauntlet, which remained the fastest fighter in British service as late as 1937. The
Gladiator would prove to be the greatest and the last of the Royal Air Force's long line of
biplane fighters. The irony of the aircraft, magnified all the more by its extensive service,
is that it was obsolete even when it was on the drawing boards.

It came into existence to meet a new RAF fighter specification, Specification F.7/30.
This demanded a top speed for a new biplane fighter of 250 mph (400 kph), which could
mount four machine guns. Designers were also encouraged to use the then-new Rolls
Royce Goshawk engine. This evaporative-cooling engine, H. P. Folland's team clearly saw,
would prove unreliable, and the decision was made to extensively redesign the Gloster
Gauntlet into a new aircraft. The new project, labelled SS.37, would make a number of
changes to reach the specified top speed, and most of them had to do with reducing drag.

A line of pre-war Gloster Gladiators. (*Courtesy of the Vincent Jones Collection, 1000aircraftphotos.com*)

The pilot would receive an enclosed cockpit, a rarity for any biplane, and the wings would be changed too. The Gauntlet had featured two-bay wings, but the Gladiator would have single-bay wings. 'Bays' is a term for biplane design, meaning the compartments that are created by adding wing struts. The Gauntlet had featured two such bays on each wing, meaning the wing was braced twice. The Gladiator would require only one bracing on each wing, thus the designation 'single-bay'.

The first Gladiator prototype flew on 12 September 1934, with a Bristol Mercury VIS radial engine, but soon received a better engine, and by itself nearly reached the assigned speed with a full load of military equipment. The RAF began to evaluate the aircraft in April 1935, though the Gloster team was already hard at work improving the design further. The improved version would carry the Bristol Mercury IX engine that became standard, and had the fully enclosed cockpit that the original prototype had lacked.

The RAF evaluators were clearly impressed, for an order was placed within three months for the first 180 aircraft, which the RAF dubbed Gladiator. These would be the Mk I, but the Mk II was already on the way, with the better Mercury engine and also a three-bladed Fairey propeller to replace the two-bladed wooden one the Mk I came with. The Royal Navy had also taken an interest, and the Mk II was further modified— an arresting hook was added, as were catapult attachment points, a stronger overall airframe, and arrangement was made for an underbelly fairing for a dinghy lifeboat. The design was meant for the Royal Navy's aircraft carriers, and the Fleet Air Arm would still be operating fifty-four of its Sea Gladiators when war was declared. In fact, the aircraft carrier *Glorious* would shuttle Sea Gladiators to Norway in 1940 before being sunk, and the Norwegian campaign would prove just one of the many fronts in which the Gladiator would be employed.

The Gladiator began to roll off the production line even as far more advanced fighters were in the air. The Gladiator's varied service is all the more remarkable considering how extensively such aircraft already outclassed it. Both the Hawker Hurricane and Messerschmitt Bf 109 were already airborne, as was the Supermarine Spitfire. Nevertheless, Gloster not only sold a significant number to the RAF and Royal Navy, but made numerous foreign sales. The Gladiator was sold to Belgium, China, Egypt, Finland, Greece, Iraq, Ireland, Latvia, Lithuania, Norway, Portugal, South Africa, and Sweden, and after the fall of France some were sold to the Free French as well. As a result, the Gladiator would be used both against and by the Axis, and fight from Europe through all of Africa and into the Middle East and Asia. The agile, outdated, and obsolete from its birth Gloster Gladiator would be seen practically everywhere.

In terms of service, the Gladiator's worldwide appearances make for a complex story. Perhaps it is best to start with the Gladiator's service to its native land. On the outbreak of war, two squadrons of Gladiators were still in service with the RAF. As a result of the combat debut of the Bf 109 over Spain, and the resultant panic to get equivalent fighters in the air, very few Glosters were still on hand. This was not precisely aided by the fact that the Gladiator had proven accident-prone in the hands of inexperienced pilots, and so many Gladiators were lost in this manner that a replacement batch had to be ordered.

The reason for this was that the Gladiator had, in simplest terms, quite a lot of flaps. It had an extremely wide flap area, which made landings tricky for the inexperienced, and it also took great skill to pull a Gladiator out of a flat spin. In carrier operations, however, the Gladiator acquitted itself well, and was a mainstay of the Norwegian campaign. In Norway, the Gladiator was to be found both in British and Norwegian hands, jointly fighting the Germans. On the first day of the invasion, the Norwegian Gladiators managed to shoot down five German aircraft, losing only one of their own. Two, however, were strafed while refuelling and the remainder of Norway's seven Gladiators were ordered to land where they could, and were abandoned on the frozen lakes around Oslo, and subsequently were wrecked by civilians looking for souvenirs.

The RAF Gladiators, under 263 Squadron, fought hard for the remaining two months of the campaign, being re-equipped after burning through their aircraft. They were shuttled in on the carrier *Glorious* in late April 1940, and went to work from an improvised frozen landing field on Lake Lesjaskogsvatnet. It took a week for them to need replacement aircraft, as the harsh conditions, combat, and constant use wore down available aircraft. They returned again in May, flying from an airfield around Narvik. The Gladiators, reinforced by Hurricanes, fought hard and sharp engagements against the Luftwaffe before being ordered to evacuate at the start of June, as a German juggernaut was bringing about the Fall of France and little could be spared to save Norway in the face of such a catastrophe.

The Gladiators had flown 249 sorties, claiming a total of twenty-six aircraft destroyed. The remaining Gladiators of the squadron, however, were not destined to make it back to England. Once again embarking on HMS *Glorious*, they were on board when the German battlecruisers *Gneisenau* and *Scharnhorst* sprung upon *Glorious* and her escorting destroyers, HMS *Arcasta* and *Ardent*. All the British ships were sunk, and all the Gladiators lost along with many of the valiant Gladiator pilots.

While two squadrons of Gladiators were still on strength during the Battle of Britain (one with the RAF, one with the Royal Navy), these were mostly used as co-operation and liaison aircraft, taking part in no combat sorties. It is worth noting that Gladiators had also been successful patrol aircraft during the so-called 'Phoney War' that preceded the Norwegian campaign. Overall, this might all seem like a quiet end for the Gladiator, except that it had its greatest, and most storied, combat use still in store in the Mediterranean.

There is yet another irony to the Gladiator's story in that its Mediterranean service involved it in fights much like those that would have been fought in 1918—the last biplane to biplane dogfights in history. The opponent of the Gladiator would be the nimble and well-built Fiat CR.42 Falco, or Falcon. In whirling engagements over North Africa, the two contenders would clash for dominance of the skies as if it were another, older war. Both were superb aircraft for their type, possibly some of the finest ever made. The Gladiator would serve in three campaigns and in five air forces in those Mediterranean skies, and it would be over a speck in the middle of that ancient sea that it would create one of the most enduring legends of combat aviation.

In the end, the Gladiator would be operated by the RAF, but also by the Royal Hellenic Air Force (*Ellinikí Vasilikí Aeroporía*), the Royal Australian Air Force, and the South African Air Force, and also in the Iraqi Air Force. In both the Greek and North African campaigns, it proved the equal of the mainstay Italian fighters, both Fiat biplanes (the aforementioned CR.42 and the older CR.32). It also gave good account of itself against Luftwaffe bombers, and better account still against Italian fighters, and for the most part seems to have avoided tangling with the Messerschmitt Bf 109. It would also fly against the Vichy French in the skies over Syria, meaning that the Gladiator flew from almost one end of the Mediterranean to the other in combat.

It also served in the Anglo-Iraqi War of 1941, in which Britain sought to reoccupy Iraq after its puppet government had been ousted by rebels under Rashid Ali. The fear was that a pro-Axis government might entrench itself in a vital, oil-producing region. Indeed, the Germans sent a small group of bombers to support the rebels, becoming what was called *Fliegerführer Irak*—but in the main, the combat was between the Gloster Gladiator of the RAF—and the Gloster Gladiator of the Royal Iraqi Air Force on the other side. The clashes over Iraq were therefore matters of a pilot's skill as the aircraft were equal to each other. The result was a British victory, but it is yet another forgotten theatre of the Second World War.

It was over Malta, however, that the Gladiator would create its legend. Malta was a speck in the centre of the Mediterranean, but it had for centuries been a critical piece of strategic ground. By the Second World War, the nation that could control Malta could use aircraft or ships based there to interdict supply lines across to Africa, a fact the Italians were well aware of. In 1940, eighteen Sea Gladiators had arrived in Malta. Some had been shipped to Egypt, others were shipped out for service in Norway. Once the Italians declared war, however, it was decided to form a group for the air defence of Malta, and it would use the Gladiators that were on-hand and the spare parts to create a handful more. This is where the legend was born.

According to the legend, only three Gladiators were available to be un-crated, or cobbled together, and put into the early air defence of this vital little island. These three aircraft, named *Faith*, *Hope*, and *Charity*, were thrown into the fight and for a number of days formed the only air defence over the island, valiantly holding off the entire might of the Regia Aeronautica.

Much as one might want the story to be true, it is in, fact, a modern myth. There were always more than three aircraft in service, though Gladiators and a few Hurricanes formed the island's early fighter defence. The names *Faith*, *Hope*, and *Charity* were later adopted by aircraft in service, though by this point they had been reinforced.

Regardless of this, the outcome should by rights still have been an Italian victory. The Gladiators on Malta, however, were superbly employed. Through good tactics and agility, the Gladiators won engagement after engagement, frequently diving to attack Italian bombers from above, and being gone long before escorting fighters could engage. As the Gladiators held the line, and more and more Hawker Hurricanes were delivered, the advantage shifted to the British and stayed there. As a result, it was that, even without the myth, the Gloster Gladiator carried out sterling service for Britain at a vital moment in its military history, at an absolutely critical place.

Elsewhere, the Gladiator had further impressive service. In China, the Gladiator entered service in 1937—China's war began far sooner than any other combatant—and proved able to match the Mitsubishi A5M 'Claude' fighter then in frontline Japanese service. The problem for Chinese pilots, including Chinese-American volunteers such as Arthur Chin and John 'Buffalo' Wong, was that the A5M was nimble, but also faster than the Gladiator. That and problems in getting spare parts meant that the situation was increasingly dire. The arrival of A6M Zeros to the conflict rapidly drove the Gladiators from the skies. Even the story of how the Gladiator reached China was one rich in events. The British government officially prohibited the selling of surplus government material, but there was nothing to stop private firms from transporting Gloster Gladiators to Hong Kong. This was done with the full knowledge of the British government, and the unassembled Gladiators were then assembled by Chinese workers. The Gladiators were part of the very low surplus that the British had to spare as part of their own rearmament, as the Gladiators were then being phased out of domestic service. This way, the British could support China while avoiding both their official neutrality as part of the League of Nations and aggravating Japan. It was still support, even if the ultimate impact of the Gladiator in China was limited.

In Finland, the Gladiator was to serve again on the Axis side, in both the Winter War and the Continuation War. Like many aircraft used by the Finns, many of the Finnish Gladiators had their landing gear replaced with skis. By 1941, these aircraft were considered outmoded, and though they would soldier on until 1945, it was mostly as reconnaissance aircraft. Nevertheless, it was a Finnish aircraft that scored the last Gladiator kill in 1943. In a final twist of irony, it was a strange reversal. The Gladiator's first kill had been over China against a Japanese monoplane. Its last victory was against a Soviet biplane.

The Gladiator served as part of the Irish and Swedish air forces, busily defending neutrality in both cases. It also served in Latvia and Lithuania, albeit briefly before these countries were annexed by the Soviet Union. When the Germans annexed them in turn in 1941, it took over some Gladiators for use as target tugs. Thus it was that the Gladiator even served under the banner of the Luftwaffe, albeit in secondary duties.

How does one summarise such a career as that of the Gloster Gladiator? It was, simply, everywhere. Very few aircraft can be called ubiquitous—it takes an ability to work in nearly any condition to achieve that. The Gladiator was clearly able to do this, flying from chilly Norway to sun-baked North Africa. It flew under many colours, and everywhere it went it at least acquitted itself well. Unlike so many of the entries on this list, the Gladiator exercised influence out of all proportion to its numbers, mainly by having a handful of aircraft in a critical place at a critical time, which had a decisive impact on an entire theatre of war.

If anyone ever wishes to say that the biplane was merely an obsolete curiosity during the Second World War, one need only point to the Gloster Gladiator to prove that, obsolete or not, even old warbirds could still teach new tricks.

In a last noteworthy point, the Gladiator has, in fact, survived in decent numbers. In England, Gladiators can be found at the Cosford and Hendon branches of the Royal Air Force Museum, the Gloucestershire Aviation Collection in Bedfordshire (it is difficult to not happily say the Gloucestershire Gloster Gladiator), the IWM at Duxford, and the Shuttleworth Collection. The National War Museum in Malta also has a Gladiator fuselage, from an aircraft named *Faith*. Sweden also keeps one at the Swedish Air Force Museum in Malmen. Norway holds a Gladiator at the Norwegian Aviation Museum. This is, in the author's opinion, a rather fantastic showing for an aircraft that was obsolete even as it was built.

19

Grumman XF5F

The Grumman XF5F was part of a remarkable line of Grumman fighter aircraft. In its ranks were the American Navy's strong right arms—the F4F Wildcat and the F6F Hellcat. Added to these would be the F7F Tigercat and F8F Bearcat, which both arrived too late for combat in the Second World War, but would go on to lengthy service careers in the Korean War and other pacific conflicts, including Vietnam. The Bearcat is indeed still remarkably popular as an air racer to the present day.

However, in the middle of this wave of fighters is the black sheep—the XF5F Skyrocket. It was a strange aircraft, unlucky in that it never reached production. While it would inspire its more famous Tigercat cousin, the Skyrocket's unusual design would ensure that it served history in a different capacity—it became a part of popular culture, instead.

Specifications

First Flight: 1940
Powerplant: Two Wright XR-1820-40/-42 9-cylinder radial piston engines, 1,200 hp each.
Armament: Provision for two Madsen 23-mm cannon
Top Speed: 383 mph (616 kph)
Range/Service Ceiling: 1,200 miles (1,931 km), 33,000 feet (10,060 metres)
Dimensions: Length 28 feet 9 inches (8.76 metres), height 11 feet 4 inches (3.45 metres), wingspan 42 feet (12.8 metres)
Number Built: Single prototype

The impetus for the Grumman Skyrocket design came from the same place as the Focke-Wulf Fw 187 Falke. It was proposed at a time when high-speed medium bombers were still a relatively new threat, one that ultimately proved illusory yet still provoked a response. While the Fw 187 can be said to be the ground-based response to the problem, the XF5F was the carrier-based one, and it turned out to be a very unique solution, one of the stranger, more unconventional designs of the Second World War.

The XF5F was first proposed in 1938, that not only would be a response to the idea of quick bombers, but also was considered to be an extremely advanced proposal, some sources going so far as to call it 'revolutionary'. It anticipated the arrival of heavy carrier-borne fighter-bombers by many years, as the later Grumman F7F Tigercat was to demonstrate

A Grumman XF5F prototype in flight. (*Courtesy of the National Naval Aviation Museum*)

when it started to arrive in American naval use in 1944. The XF5F was to provide invaluable experience when designing this later aircraft, but was in its own right a fascinating design.

The XF5F was designed to be extremely lightweight, topping out at a maximum take-off weight of a mere 10,138 lb (4,599 kg). This was a necessity to get the craft off of carrier flight decks, but the aircraft was to have an absolutely outstanding rate of climb, and would be what a carrier pilot might dream of. The massively powerful Wright Cyclone engines would each drive a three-bladed propeller, and would be geared to counter-rotate, meaning a pilot would face no torque to either the left or right on take-off. The name Skyrocket was appropriate as the light aircraft would come with a huge amount of horsepower and could take-off like a rocket in a perfectly straight line.

The design only became more remarkable from there. It had a low monoplane wing that held both engines at their leading edge, but the fuselage nose did not even reach the front of the wing, let alone protrude beyond it, as did most designs. The tail unit was a twin as well, with matching endplate fins and rudders. While the nose would, after the first flight, be lengthened to a more conventional position, the aircraft that first took to the skies in April 1940 (designated XF5F-1) was destined to always have a place amongst the most unusual and fascinating of aircraft.

The initial flight, however, revealed a problem. All that power and performance came with a price—the Skyrocket was prone to overheating. Changes needed to be made in order to keep it flying. The oil cooling ducts were changed, the cockpit height was lowered, the engine nacelles were redesigned, and spinners were added to the propellers. The biggest change, however, was that the fuselage was extended forward of the wing, making it more conventional in design.

The Skyrocket would never be an easy aircraft to handle, requiring high rudder forces to keep the aircraft under control when one engine was turned off, though it still performed well when it was working on that single engine otherwise. It needed high elevator forces for recovery from spins. It was good at acrobatics, however, and pilot visibility, especially forward, was superb. In 1941, the Skyrocket was to be tested against numerous other aircraft—the Bell P-39 Airacobra, Bell XFL Airabonita, Brewster Buffalo, Curtiss P-40 Warhawk, Grumman F4F Wildcat, Hawker Hurricane, Supermarine Spitfire, and Vought F4U Corsair.

The Navy Lieutenant Commander in charge of the fly-off wrote glowingly after the fact to the President of Grumman, George Skurla, in 1985:

> I remember testing the XF5F against the XF4U on climb to the 10,000 foot level. I pulled away from the Corsair so fast I thought he was having engine trouble. The F5F was a carrier pilot's dream, as opposite rotating propellers eliminated all torque and you had no large engine up front to look around to see the LSO [landing signal officer] ... The analysis of all the data definitely favored the F5F, and the Spitfire came in a distant second. ... ADM Towers told me that securing spare parts ... and other particulars which compounded the difficulty of building the twin-engine fighter, had ruled out the Skyrocket and that the Bureau had settled on the Wildcat for mass production.

> Lucabaugh and Martin, p. 16

Despite all of this, the Skyrocket failed to generate much enthusiasm in the Navy. Further changes were made by January 1942, but in the meantime Grumman had begun work on the Tigercat, which meant that the Skyrocket was, unfortunately, now the backwater of Grumman's development. It also could never quite solve its problems with weak landing gear, given the unique configuration of the engines in relation to the rest of the aircraft. The airframe ended up being used extensively to test elements of the Tigercat programme. The XF5F-1 was struck from the list of active aircraft after the landing gear failed and it performed a belly-landing on 11 December 1944.

This should have been all for a strange, but remarkable aircraft. Yet the Skyrocket had a second life in pop culture, with its unique design providing a striking visual look that made it perfect for the comic books. It was created in an era that saw the creation of a slew of wartime comic book characters, ranging from the famous to the easily forgotten. Right at the top, however, was a fascinating character who would ride this fascinating plane into battle for decades to come.

The character of Blackhawk was created by Quality Comics and first appeared in *Military Comics No. 1* in August 1941. He was the creation of Chuck Cuidera, with input from Bob Powell and Will Eisner. The character was a Polish fighter pilot, fighting on at the head of an elite unit, known as the Blackhawks, hammering away at the Axis in adventure after adventure. The Blackhawks were a mixed crew, many coming from nations occupied by the Axis.

The Blackhawks flew from their based on Blackhawk Island, meeting an array of foes, from the standard comic-book Axis villains to femme fatales to unusual aircraft and other strange war machines. The character was so popular that he even made it to the movies in a 1952 serial. The comic adventures continued until 1956, when Quality Comics folded. This might have been the end of a character and group that, at its peak, sold at a rate second only to Superman. DC Comics (the brand of Superman and Batman) bought the character, and the adventures of Blackhawk and his crew continue to this day with the group operating in many different time periods.

The XF5F Skyrocket was the most famous mount of the character throughout their history, making it even to the animated cartoon *Justice League* in 2002. Visually, the long-lasting success of the Skyrocket in fiction can be attributed to the unique look of the aircraft, almost a hot rod for the skies.

In an interview for DC Comics, Will Eisner explained the reasons why the Skyrocket was chosen as Blackhawk's mount:

> So we came up with the idea of using a certain model Grumman airplane, which had a very strange configuration. It had tailfins coming out from under a wing. It also apparently had the capacity to make a rapid take-off from the deck of an aircraft carrier. It was a Navy plane, as I remember, not an Army Air Force plane. Actually, in real life, it turned out not to be as good a plane as everybody thought it would be, but it sure looked sexy!

The XF5F Skyrocket was one of those unique designs that never quite made it to the production floor. It was strange and a little bit fantastical, with potential that was never quite realised. It was a fascinating might-have-been as an aircraft, but it had a second life that its designers could never have expected. It has lived on in popular culture, painted in vibrant, brilliant colours and splashed across pages ever since the aircraft itself took to the skies. The Skyrocket lives on, having adventures in fiction that it never could have had in reality.

While the character Blackhawk and his pilots most often flew the XF5F, Blackhawk's original mount in the comics was a native Polish fighter, the PZL P.50 Jastrząb ('Hawk'). The P.50 was only in prototype stage by the time Poland fell, but it was an advanced fighter set to replace all the others of the Polish air force. Only two prototypes were completed, but anybody with an interest in researching Polish fighters, or interested in the fictional character Blackhawk, may be interested in knowing more about this aircraft.

When asked about the Grumman Skyrocket, Mark Evannier (one of the writers of the Blackhawk comic) said:

> I'm not really an expert on planes, I'm afraid. I just always thought it was a neat-looking craft and it always looked great when the artists I worked with got to draw it. Several of them asked me to make sure I gave them plenty of opportunities in my scripts to do so.

Brief, but definitely to the point; the Skyrocket just had—and, indeed, has—the right 'look' for popular culture, and it seems likely that this little-known hot rod of the skies will linger in popular culture for some time to come. One would certainly hope that it will continue in the future to be the mount of choice for a remarkable character who has lasted for decades.

20

Heinkel He 177 Greif

The Luftwaffe's heavy bomber programme was terminally delayed, and Germany was well behind the times and facing increasingly vast numbers of Allied heavy bombers, with no real response. Ultimately, they would place their main hopes in an aircraft that, because of a combination of poor design choices and political pressure, could have been remarkable, but instead was remarkably badly designed.

The He 177 Greif ('Griffin') was meant to be an answer to American and British heavy bombers, and in a sense it was; however, it arrived far too late and was stymied by its inherent flaws, meaning that for the course of the war Germany would never have any substantial fleet of heavy bombers.

Specifications

First Flight: 1939
Powerplant: (He 177A-5/R-2) Two Daimler Benz DB 610A/B 24-cylinder double-inverted Vee piston engines, 2,950 hp each.
Armament: Three MG 81 0.31-inch (7.92-mm) machine guns, three MG 131 0.51-inch (13-mm) machine guns and one MG 151/20 20-mm cannon, plus a maximum of 2,205 lb (1,000 kg) of bombs, plus two Henschel Hs 293 missiles, one under each wing.
Top Speed: 304 mph (490 kph)
Range/Service Ceiling: 3,417 miles (5,500 km)—with missiles, 26,245 feet (8,000 m)
Dimensions: Length 72 feet 2 inches (22 metres), height 21 feet 10 inches (6.67 metres), wingspan 103 feet 1.75 inches (31.44 metres)
Number Built: 1,169

After the death of *Generalleutnant* Wever and the cancellation of all existing German heavy bomber designs, the RLM specification that resulted in the Heinkel 177 was the only one for a heavy bomber for the Luftwaffe. It was a programme that would proceed without any benefit of experience, either technical or operational. Nevertheless, superb engineering work, while never fully countering the type's problems, produced an aircraft with some excellent characteristics. However, the Heinkel 177, Germany's Griffin, would suffer from officialdom's heavy hand and would never quite get the chance to live up to its potential.

Captured Heinkel He 177 in RAF markings, for evaluation. (*Courtesy of the Bill Pippin Collection, 1000aircraftphotos.com*)

The design specification that brought the Heinkel 177 to life was Wever's final dream. As previously stated, it was promulgated on the day of his death, and was the one piece of his strategic vision to survive his demise. The specification called for a craft then identified as 'Bomber A'—a formidable vision that Wever had safeguarded that called for an aircraft that could carry at least 2,200 lb (1,000 kg) of bombs for at least 3,100 miles at a speed of 311 mph (500 kph), and that was to be the speed at altitude, as well. This was a formidable specification for any project, let alone one proceeding in a climate of official disinterest and with little experience of the concept in any practical sense.

Given the design expertise at Heinkel's command, these demanding statistics might still have been easily achieved, but, as initial work was set to begin on a prototype, a second command came down from the RLM insisting that the design should have sufficient strength in its structure to carry out at least medium-degree dive-bombing operations. This requirement would make the two-nacelle design for Heinkel's heavy bomber an absolute necessity. A four-engined design would mean much more drag, which was unsuitable for a diving attack. A two-nacelle design would have significantly less drag, would also be more stable in any dive it performed, and was likely to be significantly more manoeuvrable. Yet there were no aircraft engines that could, in a pair, create the performance requirements.

The solution, such as it was, was the Daimler-Benz DB606, which was really two paired DB 601 engines, the same as those that powered the Messerschmitt Bf 109. Heinkel had previously placed one of these paired engines in the high-speed He 119, but this was an order of complexity unto itself. These engines featured a common gear housing, which in turn meant that both engines could drive a single propeller shaft. The engine would eventually evolve into the DB610, and could produce a monstrous amount of horsepower, but they would also be plagued with difficulties in the testing phase and indeed into their service life as well.

Everything else about the design was chosen to reduce its drag. This would be necessary just to meet the exacting requirements of the programme, but also would be necessary if it were to ever fulfil the medium dive-bombing role. As a result, the engine nacelles were designed for evaporative cooling, to dispense with drag-increasing radiators as on more conventional designs. Ultimately, these were never fitted to production aircraft since the system proved utterly unable to cope with the vast amounts of heat the He 177's engines would actually end up producing. The initial design also called for a remotely operated defensive armament, plus a more conventional tail gunner's position, meaning a further streamlining of the fuselage and thus reducing drag further. This, too, never came to pass with the development of such remotely operated mountings simply not keeping up with progress of the bomber programme.

If all this makes the project sound dubious from the start, there was worse to come when prototypes were actually finished and took to the air. After the first flight of the prototype in November 1939, it became obvious that there was a structural problem in the wing itself, which was proving incapable of surviving even relatively low-angle diving runs without damage. This problem persisted into the production version, the A-1. It would take multiple versions and major revisions to fix this, and it wasn't until the A-5 variant began to go into production that the problem was fully solved. The dive-bombing requirement was proving an intractable nightmare for Heinkel, as Ernst Heinkel had always known it would. When Ernst Udet had mentioned it to him as early as 1937, Heinkel had replied that the Greif would never be able to achieve it. He was right, but all of this paled in comparison to the problems caused by fire.

If the difficulty of diving and wing design were a nightmare for Heinkel's designers and test crews, then the paired-up engines would be almost an unholy plague. It took a grand total of twelve minutes in the air for the He 177V1's engines to overheat to the point that the flight needed to be cancelled. While it had some excellent handling characteristics, modifications were immediately made to improve some of its issues with instability and fluttering. Then the wing problem reared its ugly head, as the V2 prototype simply came apart in the air when attempting a dive trial. The V3 ended up being set aside for trials with a traditional four-engined arrangement, but the V4 was also lost, failing to recover from a dive and crashing into the sea.

The plague was merely getting warmed up. The V5 prototype, in testing in 1941, had both engines burst into flame, upon which the airplane crashed into the ground and exploded. The trouble was that there were just so many theoretical reasons that the engines might catch fire, or at the very least overheat. The theoretical concept of the paired engines was sound, true, and it offered advantages, but the teething problems were legion, and each one of them could lead to a potentially fatal accident. Even Hermann Goering, a man not renowned by history for possessing much in the way of insight and wisdom, understood there was a serious issue with the concept. Angry at the slow pace with which the powerplant problems were being dealt with, Goering wrote:

Why has this silly engine suddenly turned up, which is so idiotically welded together? They told me then, there would be two engines connected behind each other, and suddenly there appears this misbegotten monster of welded-together engines one cannot get at!

Griehl and Dressel, p. 52

As a result of all of these issues, the early A-model Greifs were unhappy, accident-prone aircraft that were very quickly withdrawn from service.

From late 1942, production centred on the much improved A-5, which constituted the vast bulk of the bomber's production, totalling 826 aircraft. There were also 170 of the A-3 version, which was also significantly improved. While the programme was devolving into variant after variant incorporating small changes or adaptations for other roles, the first Greifs went into combat usage.

These still untested, problematic bombers were immediately employed in ways that it was unsuited for, namely for the airlift at Stalingrad. Utilised as a supply transport, it could carry little more than a Heinkel 111, and proved utterly unsuited to evacuating the wounded. The aircraft was then thrown into bombing and flak-suppression missions, the former of which it was still not fully operational for, and the latter of which it had never been designed to do. Unsurprisingly, it made little impact on the outcome of the campaign.

Heinkel He 177s preparing for launch. (*Courtesy of the Bill Pippin Collection, 1000aircraftphotos.com*)

This use on the Eastern Front had the side effect of angering the German navy. By early 1943, production of guided weapons was progressing, with bomber aircraft using them to good effect, such as when Dornier Do 217s sank the Italian flagship *Roma* as it sailed to surrender to the Allied fleet. The weapon used was the Fritz X radio-controlled bomb, and this weapon, along with the Henschel Hs 293 guided missile, were being built in larger and larger numbers even with production limited by the priority by then given to fighters.

With these weapons, and a good service bomber, the Luftwaffe could remain a lethal anti-ship weapon. For this purpose, the Navy's commander, Karl Dönitz, wanted the Greif to replace the medium bombers he had, which he had already found significant success with. He lobbied Hitler directly to get first priority for the He 177, but Hitler instead decided to send them to the Eastern Front to relatively little effect. Dönitz was left with less capable aircraft in small numbers that could not protect his U-boats that were in the Atlantic and North Sea. Dönitz eventually got his aircraft, but it was late 1943 before they went into operation carrying the advanced guided weapons. While successful, the operations cost the Grand Admiral dearly in He 177s as well. In a single attack on 26 November, German aircraft sank a British transport carrying American soldiers, causing heavy loss of life; however, German losses included six of the He 177s, including their commander.

These naval Greifs served as part of KG 100, with a mixture of other types—though from February 1944, most of its units upgraded to the He 177. By this point, however, the weight of ordnance and the bomber's performance (when it worked) was mitigated by new Allied developments in radar-jamming, which ensured that losses were never catastrophic. Nevertheless, the He 177s with their deadly weapons did take their toll, even if their bolder operations (such as raiding Plymouth harbour at the end of April 1944) failed to cause the intended damage.

When the Normandy landings came, the 177s were to suffer badly. The Allies knew they would be coming, and the concentration of defensive measures ensured that the Germans suffered heavy losses for every ship they damaged or sunk. By September, there were not enough aircraft left to continue serious operations. Overall, the naval usage of the Greif was successful, if limited, and it remained to be seen how it would do in its original design roles.

As it began to serve over water, the aircraft did do some good service on the Eastern Front, however, carrying out the bulk of what little strategic bombing the Luftwaffe did in the latter stages of the war. It had the significant advantage there that the Soviet air force was designed for low-level operations, and had little with which to challenge a strategic bomber at altitude, at least in the way of fighter opposition.

On the Western Front, there was less success to be had. The Greif, true to Heinkel's prediction, never fulfilled the role of a large dive bomber, and the still unsolved engine problems ensured that its service life would continue to be rocky. It participated in the disastrous Operation Steinbock, a night-time strategic bombing campaign against England from January to May 1944. For very little result, at very high cost, the Luftwaffe once again hammered away at Britain. The Greif's role in the operation was relatively minor, but indicative of its history. Fourteen of the craft were available, but only four reached their target, which was London. Eight had returned with overheating engines or, once again, their engines had caught fire. Another had suffered a burst tire, and one was lost to British night fighters.

The type also was used extensively as a weapons platform, carrying many varied and sometimes fascinating armaments that only ever saw limited use at best. The Greif could carry bombs, torpedoes, or guided missiles, and was being constantly modified for tests and special missions. One, for instance, was mounting a pair of power Mk 101 30-mm cannon mounted in a gondola that went beyond the already far-extended nose-glazing that was termed a fishbowl. These guns had a limited traverse and were intended for a train-busting, ground attack, or possibly an anti-shipping role. Aside from experimental use, as was the case in so many He 177 modifications, it was never put into major use.

The Greif would participate, however, in what was perhaps the last major Luftwaffe victory on the Eastern Front. Late in 1943, the United States had requested permission from the Soviets to use air bases in their territory as landing and take-off points for bombing missions. The idea was that a plane leaving Britain and landing in the Soviet Union would not have to make the long return flight from its target back to Britain, exposed to a second round of German defences. It took until early 1944 for Stalin to approve the plan, but three air bases were set up at Poltava, Myrhorod, and Priyatin. They operated under very strict controls, which was the norm with Stalinist paranoia. The main point was that Soviet fighters would be responsible for protection of the bomber bases.

By 21 June, three raids had been carried out, with 114 B-17 Flying Fortresses and their escorting P-51 fighters heading for Russia. They were shadowed by a Junkers Ju 88, watching the bombers land at Poltava and the fighters at Priyatin. That night, as celebrations were occurring in the mess at Poltava, warnings began to arrive that there were German bombers in the area. Perhaps owing to complacency at this stage of the war with German capabilities, they were ignored. It was not until a third warning message arrived that the Americans and Soviets took cover. It was just in time—a fleet of eighty He 177s and Ju 88s roared over the airfields, cruising back and forth and dropping 110 tons of bombs, with some of the Ju 88s dropping low to lace the field with antipersonnel bombs and conduct strafing runs. All told, they were there for an hour and a half, and the P-51s were not allowed to take-off from Priyatin on Soviet orders. The Red Air force never appeared, and the Germans lost not a single plane, while leaving forty-seven B-17s destroyed. Proof positive that when the Greif worked, it was a very capable aircraft.

Despite being technologically innovative in many ways, the end for the Greif came as it did for every other German bomber aircraft—the fleet was grounded owing to fuel shortages as 1944 progressed, and the Luftwaffe dedicated all of its efforts to keeping its defensive fighters in the air. It was an ignominious end for a daring, if troubled, programme. In essence, despite the limited uses the He 177 could be put to, Germany never had a heavy bomber that would fulfil a strategic purpose adequately. Wever's dream was never realised, and a combination of time, inexperience, and the unending teething troubles of the He 177 ensured that German capabilities would always include this major gap.

As for the He 177, it is difficult to assess the aircraft as a whole. On the one hand it was technologically innovative and an extremely daring design, but on the other hand it was so plagued by technical problems that its actual use was permanently hamstrung. That and the deteriorating war situation played against it, and it seems unlikely the aircraft could have exercised a decisive role. Yet, when it flew without catching fire, it could carry out its purpose as well as any strategic bomber. In the end, it might be better to say that it was an attempt to be too clever, and that technical innovation simply could not make up for foolhardy official requirements that ultimately kept the programme from ever surpassing its shortcomings.

Some years ago, the author had the honour of having an e-mail conversation with the grandson of one of the test pilots of the Heinkel 177, confirming much of what was said about the aircraft and its fire-prone nature. It should also be noted that the ultimate solution to the problem was the Heinkel 277, a design that was mostly the same, except it featured four engines in conventional nacelles. The 177 was also the starting point for the Heinkel 274, a high-altitude bomber with pressurised compartments, of which only two were ever built. Thus, the 177 was the start of a family of projects for heavy bombers, all of them too late in the war to fulfil much of a role for the Luftwaffe, or be built in any significant numbers.

21

Heinkel He 280

The Messerschmitt Me 262 Schwalbe is, rightly, one of the most famed fighter aircraft in the history of aviation. It was a revolution in technology, vastly influential and holding the potential—squandered—to transform the air war in Germany's favour. The Me 262 was a world-beater, arriving too late and in too few numbers to alter the conflict, but posing the 'what if?' that has become a standard—what if the Me 262 had been available earlier in greater numbers?

The debate over such a question is at best speculative, since in the event Allied airmen proved equal to the task of defending against even a technological marvel. Yet the history of the Me 262 points to something else: it was certainly not the first jet fighter, nor even the first jet. Those honours go to Messerschmitt's competitor Heinkel, which not only produced the first ever jet aircraft to fly, but also produced the world's first jet fighter— the Heinkel He 280. Though it would ultimately lose out to the Me 262, the He 280 is an interesting part of the history of jet development.

Specifications

First Flight: 1940 (unpowered), 1941 (powered)
Powerplant: (V3) Two Heinkel HeS 8 turbojets, 1,320 pounds of thrust each.
Armament: Three MG 151/20 20-mm cannon
Top Speed: 512 mph (820 kph)
Range/Service Ceiling: 230 miles (370 km), 32,000 feet (10,000 metres)
Dimensions: Length 34 feet 1 inch (10.4 metres), height 10 feet (3.06 metres), wingspan 40 feet (12.2 metres)
Number Built: 9

The jet age came quickly, and was a closer competition than many people realise. Despite the legends of German scientific prowess, it was a very close-run thing as to which nation would take the lead in the race. Germany achieved a narrow, but important lead in this race through government support of a brilliant mind, Hans von Ohain. The only close competition was Great Britain, owing to the genius of Frank Whittle, but the outcomes were majorly different. While Whittle would place the first patent for a jet engine, von Ohain's would be the first built and the first to power an aircraft. As *The Times* of London put it in von Ohain's obituary:

Heinkel He 280 V1 in an airborne test. (*Courtesy of Thijs Postma*)

The experiences of the pioneering von Ohain as he worked to give Germany the lead in jet technology had been radically different from those of Whittle. Whereas the British scientist had been balked at every turn, and was forced to found his own company, working—often with reclaimed scrap metal—in a shed near Rugby with funds raised from a merchant bank by himself and his two fellow directors, von Ohain was given every encouragement by the aircraft manufacturer Ernst Heinkel for whom he worked from March 1936. Lavish funding and first-class facilities were placed at his disposal…. Even at this late stage, having been ignored since 1930, Whittle was actually still just ahead of the game, despite the handicaps under which he laboured. He had successfully run his gas turbine engine under control in April 1937, but he had still failed to secure the adoption of his invention by the Air Ministry, which was at that time absorbed in its struggle to modernise its conventional aircraft to meet the belatedly perceived threat from Germany. But from that point, von Ohain and the Heinkel company forged ahead. By March 1938, his new petrol-fuelled HeW3 jet engine was delivering 1,100lb static thrust under test conditions, and Heinkel were at work on the airframe.

The Times, 6 April 1998

The story of the Heinkel 280 rightly begins with the aircraft that was designed to carry that pioneering engine, the Heinkel He 178. The He 178 was the world's first turbojet aircraft, built at the same time as Heinkel also was working on the He 176 rocket aircraft. The diminutive test aircraft was powered by Heinkel's own HeS 3b engine, which developed 750 pounds (340 kg) of thrust. On 27 August 1939, mere days before the start of the war, it became the first jet aircraft to fly. Pilot Erich Warsitz made a small circle of the factory airfield at Rostock-Marienehe, and one must wonder if he understood just what his flight heralded.

Heinkel had worked in complete secrecy, and unveiled his jet to officials in November, to little effect. Ernst Udet and Erhard Milch witnessed the flight and were thoroughly unimpressed, which was undoubtedly a huge disappointment for Heinkel. What he could not know was that the RLM had been working on jets on its own, so his demonstration did not come as much of a surprise. The prototype was ultimately placed in the Berlin Air Museum, where an air raid destroyed it in 1943. The lessons of the He 178, however, would go into Heinkel's next project, to build a proper jet fighter.

Heinkel plunged into the new project in late 1939, as part of a private venture since he had met with indifference from official channels. The project's chief designer was to be Robert Lusser, who immediately set to work on what would end up being a strangely conventional design, given the revolutionary nature of the powerplant.

The fuselage was rounded, but in many ways resembled previous Heinkel fuselages. The wings would stick out at straight from the fuselage, though they had rounded edges. The tail assembly had twin fins and rudders, though the later prototypes would mount a more forward-thinking dihedral tail structure. The landing gear was situated in a tricycle configuration. This, at least, was unusual, and it was considered too fragile for any soft fields. This would, however, become a standard configuration for other jet fighters, especially the Messerschmitt Me 262.

The He 280 was the first aircraft to come equipped with an ejection seat, powered by compressed air. This was years in advance of ejection seats becoming commonly used, let alone standard issue. In this, at least, Heinkel anticipated the course of design over history to come.

The prototype was mostly ready by the summer of 1940, but then engine trouble began to plague the project. The intended engine at that point was the HeS 8, but it was having significant trouble in development, so the first flights of the prototype occurred without engines on 22 September 1940. The weight difference was made up for with ballasted pods to simulate the presence of the engines. The prototype was towed aloft behind a Heinkel He 111, and then released to its own devices. The prototype performed well, and no fault could be found with its design or handling. It would take another six months before the problems with the engines were ironed out enough for the second prototype to go aloft under its own power. There is little indication of any interest from the RLM at this point, or anyone outside of Heinkel and his company. Interestingly, the engines could burn kerosene, which would have been a significant advantage as the Reich's fuel situation began to deteriorate.

The V1 prototype continued to fly, making numerous glide tests, both powered and unpowered. The V2 prototype was demonstrated for the RLM on 5 April 1941, before

Ernst Udet and other officials. It performed well enough to garner some interest as it was convincing proof that the project was sound, and its continued development would be important to future jet development.

The main weakness of the Heinkel He 280 programme would always be in the engines, however. Development of German jet engines was still relatively in its infancy, and the efforts of Heinkel's own designers were slowly being overtaken by those of Junkers as the HeS 8 engine continued to lag in its development process. The HeS 8 would not be ready to fly with the airframe until 1943, and when it did it was not producing as much thrust as envisioned.

Development in the meantime consisted of testing the airframes and trying to find a replacement for the HeS 8. One interesting proposal that was considered was using the Argus As 04 pulsejet, which would later power the well-known V-1 flying bomb. The idea in that case was to use as many of eight pulsejets, in what would have been a very interesting design. This was never fully implemented, however, and the engine troubles continually dogged the project. In 1942, the RLM passed on the official order to abandon the HeS 8 and the other design Heinkel was trying, the HeS 30. The engine specified instead was the HeS 011, which was brand new and came with the teething problems inherent in all new jet engines in this period.

Meanwhile, re-equipped with pulsejet engines, the V3 airframe was towed aloft to test them. The aircraft iced up before the jets could be tested, and the aircraft crash-landed, but the pilot did use the ejection seat for the first time in aviation history, and did so successfully. At this point, however, it was becoming clear that the Heinkel turbojets

A crash-landed Heinkel He 280—specifically the V2 prototype. (*Courtesy of Thijs Postma*)

were not coming for some time, and the Heinkel team were forced to look at competitors' engines, a move that might have been particularly galling.

Heinkel selected the BMW 003 engine, but this too proved to be unready for the task, at which point Heinkel went with the only other available engine, the Junkers Jumo 004. The trouble was that the engine weight of the Jumo was significantly higher than the other choices, which meant a corresponding drop in overall performance. It flew well enough, but it flew in May 1943, by which point the Messerschmitt Me 262 project was already well advanced. The situation, then, would have likely seemed very simple to the RLM. The Heinkel 280 was plagued with engine troubles and was a conventional design based on 1939-era design principles, from an era that had little knowledge of the jet. By 1943, the more advanced Me 262 design offered better performance and as a result the project was passed over in favour of the Messerschmitt design.

The decision may have had some political overtones, but in the main it was the result of the He 280's technical limitations and the constant, nagging problems in developing adequate engines to fit the airframe. Interestingly, however, Heinkel had proposed a much more advanced version, tentatively named the He 280B-1. It would have featured a longer fuselage in order to accommodate fuel—to compensate for the very limited range of the prototypes—and to increase its armament to a grand total of six MG 151 20-mm cannon, which would have constituted a wicked punch. An improved tail was also specified, as were bomb racks, which conformed to the confused RLM idea that these revolutionary fighters should be used as fighter-bombers. That decision would haunt the Me 262 programme as well. There was likely to be a decrease in performance, however, as the wing area was also be increased. Despite all of this, the Me 262 was simply a superior aircraft in the final analysis. It was aerodynamically superior and in the early stages had a third more range, as Heinkel's design consumed fuel prodigiously. This was the downside to von Ohain's pioneering work. In addition, the He 280's engines simply were not powerful enough to keep up with the Me 262. The solution was to add bigger engines, but what this would mainly accomplish was more fuel consumed and a negative impact on handling. All of these factors weighed down the project, and as a result no production order was forthcoming.

Thus, the chance of the He 280 ever seeing combat disappeared forever. In spite of this, development and testing of the airframe continued. This was done in order to enhance Germany's knowledge of jet aircraft, still a radical concept. These tests involved checking on aerodynamic principles of the machine and also checking on how the high speeds affected wing design. In this capacity, the He 280 V7 achieved the type's fastest ever speed. In a dive, the V7 reached a maximum speed of 578 mph (930 kph), with no bad effects. These tests ran through into 1944, with a grand total of nine prototypes being completed.

The He 280 was never destined to be the world-beater that Ernst Heinkel wanted it to be. It was, however, a glimpse into what would happen in the future. The design had a foot in two worlds, which would ultimately prevent it from becoming a combat fighter. The design was advanced, especially for when it was conceived, but on the other hand it was a design conceived in an older world of piston-driven fighters. This is an interesting point and singular to the He 280. It carried the production version of the first jet engines to fly, carrying all the strengths (and indeed weaknesses) of being an early producer of a technology. The Messerschmitt Me 262 was destined to be the first operational jet fighter and a superb machine, but the He 280 was the first jet fighter and it was also a valuable font of information to aid in the creation of the jet age. It was a testament to the technical prowess of von Ohain and Heinkel's engineering team, and above all is a reminder of the contribution of men like von Ohain and Whittle to creating the modern world of aviation—even if it was first used for war.

22

Henschel Hs 123

Henschel is not amongst the most easily recognised names in the history of German aviation. Popular culture is already full of Messerschmitts, Heinkels, and Junkers—many times, in popular perception, it is difficult to find room for a more expansive view. Yet outside this mainstream, there was a vast and complicated world of aircraft designs, firms, and competition. Henschel, ultimately, focused its production efforts outside of the standard categories of fighter and bomber, and instead focused on a role that frequently is forgotten by film and fiction, but proved crucial to the conduct of the war—ground attack.

Henschel's superb Hs 123 would serve the Luftwaffe until there were literally none left, being used up by hard service and slow attrition. In this process, it would once again demonstrate the remarkable durability, and indeed versatility, of the biplane as a design form.

Specifications

First Flight: 1938
Powerplant: BMW 132Dc 9-cylinder radial-piston engine, 880 hp.
Armament: Two MG 17 0.31-inch (7.92-mm) machine guns, and up to four 110-lb (50-kg) bombs under the wings, and one 550-lb (250-kg) bomb beneath the fuselage.
Top Speed: 211 mph (340 kph)
Range/Service Ceiling: 531 miles (855 km), 29,530 feet (9,000 metres)
Dimensions: Length 27 feet 4 inches (8.33 metres), height 10 feet 6 inches (3.2 metres), wingspan 34 feet 5.5 inches (10.5 metres)
Number Built: 245

The tough little Henschel design that commenced in 1933 was destined to be the Luftwaffe's last operational biplane, aside from a handful that would serve with the *Nachtschlachtstaffeln* in the late stages of the war. Henschel had, until recently, been a builder of trains and only got into the aircraft business upon Hitler's rise to power, when the sudden re-emergence of a public German military air arm meant large opportunities for many companies. Henschel's first chance came when Ernst Udet handed down a specification for a dive-bomber in 1933. Udet was a firm believer in the power of the

Pre-war Henschel Hs 123. (*Courtesy of the Jacques Trempe Collection, 1000aircraftphotos.com*)

dive-bomber, and indeed in the 1930s the concept was in considerable vogue. Henschel moved to seize the chance.

There was, however, to be opposition. The main rival for the contract was Fieseler, who had a competing design designated Fi 98. Both planes met the basic requirement, that of a single-seat biplane that could be used as a dive bomber, and indeed there were many similarities in the two eventual prototypes, at least visually. Henschel, however, had designed a much more modern biplane. Fieseler's design had too many struts and guide wires, while Henschel's had single, streamlined struts between its wings. This feature alone would have possibly been enough to secure the Hs 123's dominance, but it had other features that made it superior. The landing gear was, like on most biplanes, fixed, but it was also streamlined with spats. Moreover, the fuselage and all the fixed tail surfaces were metal, with a light alloy covering. Forward of the main spars, the wings were metal-skinned, though all the control surfaces were still fabric covered.

Both of the duelling prototypes emerged from their respective factories in 1935, and it was immediately apparent that the Henschel was the superior design. The Hs 123V-1 flew in May of that year, and, as a consequence, all work on the Hs 123's Fieseler rival was ordered stopped. From here, however, the doughty biplane was destined to have a significantly rougher ride.

The first three prototypes were fitted with the BMW 132A-3, which delivered significantly less horsepower than the engine that would eventually be fitted to production models, coming in at 650 hp—as compared to a later production-model output of 880 hp. Also of some minor note, the V3 was the first of the prototypes to be given her weapons, with the two machine guns that would become standard.

These prototypes were handed over to the RLM for testing, which is when disaster struck. In testing in August 1935, two of the prototypes entered into their dives and the wings ripped off in the process. This catastrophic defect was found to be owing to the fact that the wings ripped off from the centre-section struts, which indicated a significant weakness there. As a result, the V4 prototype incorporated much more structural toughness in the wings, which luckily for the Henschel design team solved the problem. As a result, the Hs 123 was ordered into production in the summer of 1936, and the first Hs 123A-1 rolled off the assembly lines at Johannisthal and Schönefeld soon thereafter.

These aircraft were put into immediate service, though their life as the most advanced Luftwaffe dive bomber was to be short-lived. In the short run, they replaced older aircraft such as the Arado Ar 65 and Heinkel He 50 and 51. By October 1935, Hs 123s equipped three *Gruppes* of the newly formed dive-bomber units, and were put to use training pilots in the concept and execution of dive bombing.

Events soon pushed the Hs 123 into combat far earlier than might have been anticipated. When Spain descended into Civil War, five of these biplanes were sent to aid the Nationalists as part of the Condor Legion. Henschel's biplane went into combat in early 1937, and soon after that found itself serving in an unintended role. It served less as a dive bomber and more of a close support aircraft, acting in a tactical capacity rather than being employed in pinpoint bombing of strategic targets.

Back home in Germany, the situation had taken a grim turn for the Henschel. The first of the legendary Junkers Ju 87 Stuka (a shortened form of the German *Sturzkampfflugzeug*, or 'dive bomber') aircraft had begun to arrive in service. This aircraft was far more modern, and fitted with a dive siren it achieved a psychological effect that the Henschel could not match. Even today, the Ju 87 looks intimidating, with sharp wings and pointed snout. It would be only a little stretch of the imagination to imagine what it would have been like to be on the receiving end of a screaming, diving attack from such an aircraft.

As far as Henschel was concerned, however, the Ju 87's arrival signalled the immediate demise of the Hs 123 programme. Production was phased out in 1938, despite Henschel's best efforts. The V6 prototype had been up-engined to feature a 950-hp BMW 132K, and came with an enclosed cockpit. This was supposed to form the genesis of an Hs 123B programme, but no order was forthcoming and this never came to pass.

It should be noted at this point that Germany was not the only operator of the Hs 123. A handful were exported to the Spanish, where it received the nickname Angelito, or little angel. The Nationalists had come to love the aircraft during the Civil War, when its durability had been well remarked upon, withstanding direct hits to the airframe and engine and shrugging them off. At least one of these aircraft was believed to still be in service with the Spanish Air Force as late as 1945.

China was another buyer for the Hs 123. It may surprise many to know that Germany exported a good deal of arms to China before Japan became a signatory to the Tripartite

Pact. In fact, in some pictures one can see members of the Chinese military in the familiar helmet that has since been universally associated as 'German'. Part of this was a shipment of twelve Hs 123s, which carried out extensive bombing attacks on Japanese warships on the Yangtze River in 1938.

In her native Germany, by the time the war came, only a single *Gruppe*, II. (S)/LG 2, still operated the Henschel. The biplane's combat career, however, was destined to be far more interesting than anyone might have thought at that stage. The Henschel was used to terrorise troops and horses alike, given the very loud roar of its engine, and caused significant effect that far exceeded the physical damage it caused, since after it dropped its bombload it had only a light armament of two machine guns with which to carry out strafing runs.

The Hs 123 would also play a critical role in smashing a Polish counterattack that might have been problematic for the German offensive. The thirty-six Henschels fighting in Poland were a core component of the ground attack aircraft under General von Richthofen's command as part of Luftflotte 4. They had already been attacking the Poles with bombs, guns and small incendiary devices to great effect, and were ready for Polish attempts at a counterattack. On 9 September 1939, the Germans had bypassed 170,000 Poles under General Tadeusz Kutrzeba. This force had remained intact despite the initial shocks, and mounted a major counterattack that sent a German division reeling and threatened the northern flank of the German Army Group South. It was an impending catastrophe, and the Luftwaffe went into the fray. The Ju 87s carried out dive bombing, but the thirty remaining Henschels took on the dangerous work of low-level bombing and strafing, hitting the Poles with their incendiaries (called flambos) and anti-personnel fragmentation bombs. The Poles had never experienced concentrated aerial bombardment, let alone dive bombing or ground attack of such ferocity. The horses that moved their equipment and cavalry was also very easily panicked. This and the air attacks that followed by the rest of the air fleet defeated the Poles, who retreated back to their starting lines. Interestingly, one of these pioneering Henschel pilots was Adolf Galland, destined to become one of Germany's most famous fighter aces. By the close of the campaign, the Henschel had definitely made its mark on events, despite the operation of only a small number of the aircraft.

When 1940 came and it was time for Germany to smash westwards, the *Gruppe* was ready again, with even better results than in the Polish campaign. The aircraft were used to hammer back Belgian troops holding bridges over the Albert Canal, and then were employed to great effect in crushing two French divisions. While proving superb against ground forces, however, the aircraft proved vulnerable to fighters, and so a *Jagdgruppe*, I. /JG 21 was assigned to keep enemy fighters at bay. One remarkable achievement of these paired *Gruppes* came on 22 May 1940, when they held off an assault of nearly forty enemy tanks on their own advanced air base.

After the conclusion of this campaign, II. (S)/LG 2 was re-equipped with Bf 109E fighter-bombers, but some Henschels remained in service. After the Balkan campaign— in which the remaining Hs 123s participated—the formation was reorganised as

Schlachtgeschwader I, and thrown into combat during the invasion of the Soviet Union. The Hs 123 was, by this point, thoroughly obsolete in a technical sense, but it gave sterling service over Russia, having fully matured into its unexpected role as a ground-attack and close support aircraft. It developed a reputation for durability and also for being able to operate from the most *ad hoc* of airfields. Some of them were given a pair of 20-mm cannon, and still others would fly carrying a deadly crop of ninety-two anti-personnel bombs.

The Henschel was so successful in its role that it very nearly came back into manufacture. In January 1943, General von Richthofen actually demanded that the Henschel go back into production, owing to urgent need for such a durable and versatile aircraft. The proposal was ultimately ruled impractical, since unfortunately for the Luftwaffe all the tools and jigs related to the project had been scrapped. By this point, the Henschel was considered so useful that aircraft were scrounged up from training schools and even derelict dumps to be returned to service. The Hs 123 seemed to be ideally suited to combat in Russia, operating from dirt strips and shrugging off weather conditions that ranged from snow to mud to ice and rain that had taken a toll on more advanced aircraft.

Therefore, it was that the Hs 123 continued on without reinforcement and a slowly dwindling supply of spare parts. The aircraft was so useful that it was essentially used up. The numbers slowly dwindled through normal attrition until there were not enough left to equip an operational unit. The last use of them was likely as anti-partisan aircraft in 1945, a role for which the Henschel was once again apparently ideally suited.

While this might be called a rather anticlimactic end, it is also proof that the biplane really was a durable concept, even when the intended role for it had long been filled by a more modern aircraft. The Henschel was never withdrawn from combat, as most other Second World War biplanes ultimately were. Whatever last aircraft could be scraped together—after there were too few for operational use—were only relegated to training duties in 1945. The Henschel had served as long as it was capable, and its dwindling presence was much lamented at a stage in the war when the first jet fighters were preparing for combat. In the final analysis, however, the greatest compliment to the Hs 123 must remain that it was so lamented that it was almost called back into production, years after the famed Stuka had supposedly replaced it.

23

IAR 80

Romania's contribution to aviation during the war is infrequently mentioned, but it is one that deserves greater evaluation and respect. Romania was forced to practically throw together an aviation industry to supply its needs in a theoretical time of war, a rare and fairly impressive feat. When war came it would not be reliant on the outside world to supply it with air defence. In the midst of the war, the Royal Romanian Air Force possessed a native-built aircraft to ensure Romanian air power was a viable force during the war. The fighter would be oddly both modern and archaic in some respects, but the most important feature is that it would fully Romanian. It would also be the first domestically produced Romanian fighter in history. The IAR 80 would serve both domestically against the American air force, as well as on the Eastern Front against the Soviet Union.

Specifications

First Flight: 1939
Powerplant: IAR K14-1000A radial piston engine, 1,025 hp
Armament: IAR 80A—six machine guns. IAR 80B—four 0.31-inch (7.92-mm) machine guns, two 0.52-inch (13.2-mm) Brownings.
Top Speed: 342 mph (550 kph)
Range/Service Ceiling: 584 miles (940 km), 34,450 feet (10,500 metres)
Dimensions: Length 29 feet 5 inches (8.97 metres), height 11 feet 7 inches (3.535 metres), wingspan 36 feet 1 inch (11 metres)
Number Built: 346

The Romanian aviation industry was hastily created in the 1920s on the orders of the Romanian government. The logic behind the move was obvious. In the first place, who knew what parts and aircraft would be available in the constantly shifting political climate? It was better to have a solid, reliable source of materiel. Secondly, the best foreign types were very seldom for sale. If Romania wanted a state of the art aircraft, the only solution was to build it themselves. This would, naturally, make sure that the *Forțele Aeriene Regale ale României*, the Royal Air Force (FARR), would be able to adequately defend Romanian airspace in the event of war.

An IAR 80 in Bucharest. (*Courtesy of Alex Trandafir*)

The government subsidised three separate companies over the coming years. The first was Societatii pentru Exploatari Tehnice (SET), which opened its doors in Bucharest in 1923. Next came Industria Aeronautică Română (IAR), opening up its factory in 1925 at Brasov. The last was Întreprinderea de Construcții Aeronautice Românești (ICAR), which opened up in Bucharest in 1932. The situation, however, was not ideal. The three subsidised companies were a magnet for corruption and bribery, all of which outweighed any actual construction. In 1935, the Romanian government responded by cutting all subsidies and nationalising IAR, leaving SET and ICAR to compete for a handful of contracts. IAR had been chosen above the others since it had proved it could construct fighter planes in the past, and the Romanian government was hopeful it would produce excellent ones in the future.

As a result, when the FARR produced a specification for a new fighter in 1930, IAR was ready to compete. Not much was expected of a company still in its infancy, and it appeared as if a choice was already clear: the PZL P.11B. IAR had a prototype ready to challenge it, but it ultimately lost out because the Poles had the ability to mass-produce their plane, where IAR was still several years away from matching that capacity. The P.11B was selected, and IAR went back to the drawing board, certain that there was potential to their designs.

Realising that the Polish design could give them much-needed experience, they extensively examined the PZL P.11, and responded with prototypes to challenge it, labelled the IAR 15 and 16. Many of these fighters' features were derived from the

PZL, and both prototypes ended up being faster than the plane that inspired it. The government, however, decided to upgrade the engine of the P.11B, using one of IAR's own engines, the K9. This produced a version of the P.11B that was faster than both of IAR's prototypes and also much easier to produce. This was designated the PZL P.11F. IAR had to make do with getting the contract to license build the P-11F, in essence putting their engines in a foreign fighter.

IAR went back to the drawing board and built on their experience, continuing to design fighters. Time and the course of events played into their hands. In 1936, when Hungary began to rearm, Romania cast a wary eye at a country that had always been a rival. The FARR decided they needed a new fighter, preferably a domestically produced one—Europe was obviously in an unstable position, and as events descended towards chaos the chances of getting a good supply of fighters seemed minimal.

IAR was more than ready to take advantage of this consideration. They were certain that they had developed something really good—the design work they had was for a low-wing monoplane that IAR was certain was superior to the 'Polish wing'—the high gull-wing used by PZL. Once again, however, PZL was quicker off the mark; they had created the PZL P.24 in 1933, which was the ultimate export evolution of the PZL P.11, and Romania once again opted to purchase the PZL product, and once again equipped with IAR-built engines (in this case the Gnome-Rhone 14 Kmc/36).

One would imagine such a situation was frustrating in the extreme. Yet IAR only responded by going back to the drawing board, determined to supersede the Poles once and for all. The design team was led by Dr Ion Grosu, and the result was a revolutionary step forward for Romanian design. From the tail forward, the design was entirely that of IAR, while the tail was taken from the PZL P.24. The engine, mounting, and cowling were also from the PZL. The initial version featured an open cockpit (still fairly common at the time) and also the old-fashioned tail skid that was a strange juxtaposition to the fully retractable landing gear. The design was also exceedingly light, coming in at only 5,040 lb (2,286 kg). It was initially armed with two Browning machine guns, but heavier armament was planned.

The first prototype would take to the air in April 1939, with pilot Dumitru Popescu at the controls. The Romanian government was suitably impressed, and ordered 100 fighters in December 1939. The wisdom of Romania's strategy soon became apparent, however. The Browning machine guns were to come from Belgium, and the 600 guns they had on order had their manufacture disrupted by the German invasion in May 1940.

It took until November 1940 for the Germans to authorise the order and get the first guns into the first machines, and those first machines finally came off the production line, ready to go in early 1941. They made certain changes from the prototype, installing more powerful IAR engines and a fully enclosed cockpit, complete with oxygen for the pilot at high altitudes. This craft was a vast improvement over the PZL P.24 and comparable to any fighter then in the skies.

Romanian pilots were thrilled by their new mount, but made several recommendations to improve the aircraft, all of which IAR incorporated into the fighter. To counter the pilot's belief that that it was underpowered, IAR upgraded the engine to a 960-hp IAR engine, and IAR interrupted production to include the new engine on the twenty-first plane off the line, and continued with it until the fiftieth. At the moment, they were unable to upgrade the armaments package, which still consisted of a weak Browning machine guns—IAR simply did not have the weapons to equip the planes. Romania's foreign policy helped IAR significantly, however. Romania had by this point officially moved into the Axis sphere, which meant that there were no longer any delays or road blocks on receiving their guns. As a result, IAR was able to add the Brownings to the IAR 80A. This featured yet another engine, the 1,025-hp IAR 14K 1000 engine, which would remain standard.

The 80A was altogether a more lethal craft, mounting six of the Browning machine guns, as opposed to the light two of its predecessors. It also came with significantly more armour. All of this led to a slight reduction in speed, but with the benefit of being a much more capable fighter plane.

The combat debut of the IAR 80A, however, would come far away from Romanian skies. As one of the states aiding the German invasion of Russia, Romania lent fighter strength to the effort. By the end of 1941, a total of three squadrons in Russia were equipped with the type. It did spectacularly well early on and all the way through 1942. Famed Romanian aces like Lieutenant Dan Vizante racked up numerous kills against the Red Air Force, with Vizante scoring most of his thirty-two confirmed kills in the type.

As 1943 dawned, however, the increasing proficiency of the Soviet pilots, in their superb new aircraft, meant that the tide was shifting against the IAR 80 on the Eastern Front. The planes were withdrawn, and Romanian units on the Eastern Front were hastily re-equipped with German aircraft that were somewhat more capable of engaging the Soviets. The IARs were returned to home defence, the role they had been originally designed to fulfil.

By this time, the United States Army Air Force had taken square aim at Romania itself. The Ploiești oilfields were the main source of Germany's oil, and the USAAF wanted to deny it to the Germans by grinding it into dust with the full weight of their Consolidated B-24 Liberator bombers.

At this point, the main version of the IAR fighter in service was the IAR 80B, which had been the first response to the evolution of Soviet fighters. Two of the Brownings were now of a larger calibre, and radios were fitted to improve communication and coordination. It was these planes that rose to challenge the might of the American bombers over Romanian skies.

On 1 August 1943, the IAR 80 went to war against the Americans. As part of Operation Tidal Wave, 178 B-24s made an attack on Ploiești. Three squadrons of IAR 80s rose to meet them with assistance from a squadron of Bf 109s and Bf 110s drafted in from the Romanian night fighter units. The result was a significant tactical defeat for the Americans who lost fifty-one bombers in combat or on the way back; only eighty-nine American bombers returned to base, with most of them too damaged to be immediately used again. Romanian losses were a grand total of two aircraft, one of them an IAR 80.

A replica Avia B-534. The landing gear spats were removed as they interfered with landing on dirt airstrips. (*Courtesy of Slovenské Technicke Museum of Košice*)

A rear view of the B-534 Replica. Note the streamlining.
(*Courtesy of Slovenské Technicke Museum of Košice*)

An underside view of the XP-59 Airacomet. Note the clearance for her turbojet engines. (*Courtesy of Richard L. Kitterman*)

A replica Boeing Peashooter in flight. (*Courtesy of Mervin Austin Photography*)

A preserved Boulton Paul Defiant. (*Courtesy of Alan Wilson*)

Above: A replica Brewster Buffalo in Dutch markings. (*Courtesy of Robert Kremer*)

Below: A Buffalo preserved as it was recovered, decades after being shot down. (*Courtesy of Ville Ruusunen*)

A surviving Caudron C.714 in flight. (*Courtesy of Thierry Deutsch*)

Above: A surviving Dewoitine D.520. (*Courtesy of Pierre Clément Got*)

Below: A production Fisher P-75 today. (*Courtesy of Richard L. Kitterman*)

A replica Fokker D.XXI. (*Courtesy of Alan Wilson*)

A replica Fokker G.1. Note single tail wheel and nose armament. (*Courtesy of Alan Wilson*)

A preserved Mk I Gloster Gladiator in flight. Note original two-bladed propeller. (*Courtesy of Alan Wilson*)

A close-up image of a surviving IAR 80. (*Courtesy of Alex Trandafir*)

A preserved Kawasaki Ki-100. (*Courtesy of Arjun Sarap*)

A view of a preserved Macchi Veltro. (*Courtesy of Davide Olivati*)

A preserved Macchi M.C.205. (*Courtesy of Martin Stephen*)

The Martin Mars, specifically *Hawaii Mars II*, in her role as a firefighter.
(*Courtesy of Tom Harnish*)

Hawaii Mars II in action. (*Courtesy of Coulson Flying Tankers*)

The remains of the original Me 209 prototype, which was captured by the Poles. (*Courtesy of Piotr Biskupski*)

A surviving Messerschmitt Me 410 on display.
(*Courtesy of the Colin Urry Collection, 1000aircraftphotos.com*)

A side view of the Nakajima Ki-84. (*Courtesy of R. A. Scholefield*)

A close-up view of the Ki-84. (*Courtesy of Arjun Sarap*)

A preserved Polikarpov I-153. (*Courtesy of Alain Picollet*)

A Polikarpov I-15bis replica. (*Courtesy of Alan Wilson*)

A Polikarpov Po-2 in flight today. (*Courtesy of the Jim Larsen and the Flying Heritage Collection*)

A preserved Polikarpov Po-2. (*Courtesy of Alan Wilson*)

A preserved PZL P.11c. (*Courtesy of Alan Wilson*)

A close view of the PZL P.11c. Note external gunsight, open cockpit, and the beautiful gull wing. (*Courtesy of Alan Wilson*)

A replica PZL.37 at Mielec, Poland. (*Courtesy of PZL Mielec*)

A side view of the same PZL.37 at the factory that used to manufacture the type. (*Courtesy of PZL Mielec*)

A view of a preserved Vought Kingfisher. (*Courtesy of Thierry Deutsch*)

A preserved Westland Lysander in Ottawa, Canada. (*Author's Collection*)

A preserved Lysander in flight, showing off her night colours. (*Courtesy of Alan Wilson*)

As the Americans continued to try to achieve their objective, the IAR 80 received its final combat evolution. The IAR 81C was a development of the airframe that had allowed for bombing missions, though this was never popular. The 81C removed the bomb rack, and upgraded the Browning guns to the far superior MG 151/20. This better punch, along with the extraordinary agility of the light airframe, meant that even superb American escort fighters such as the P-38 Lightning faced a significant challenge in engaging Romania's pilots.

On 10 June, Lightnings tangled with the enemy again and out of twenty-two P-38s lost that day, the IAR aircraft claimed eight. Though American claims were much higher, Romania lost only a single IAR 81C that day. It was, perhaps, a high-water mark for Romanian combat aviation. From that point on, the Americans started to appear in larger and larger numbers, and Romanian losses started to climb, with the IAR airframes being lost and replaced instead by the Bf 109G. The losses accelerated so fast that in four months the Romanians lost thirty-two IAR pilots killed in combat, eleven of these being aces (these losses were higher than the previous two years of fighting against the Soviets). It was these increasing losses and the easy availability of Messerschmitts that caused the IAR 80s and 81s to be withdrawn from combat.

The IAR 80 series was, ultimately, outdated if not outclassed. The IAR machines were, even in 1944, capable aircraft, all the more remarkable given that it was designed as a replacement for a monoplane that came from a generation before. Outdated or not, it did sterling service for Romania both in foreign skies and over its home. It was created as Romania's first, operational, domestically produced fighter plane, and it was an excellent one. It fought well against two air forces, and was the sleek, agile mount of numerous Romanian aces. Above all, the IAR 80 series is most definitely worthy of remembrance.

No IAR 80s survived the immediate post-war period, but one was constructed after the fall of Communism and is currently on display at the National Military Museum in Bucharest. This example was rebuilt from parts meant for the IAR 80DC two-seater trainer variant. The author has also seen photographs of what appears to be a replica IAR 80 painted in the 1941–44 colour scheme, but has found no further information as of the time of this writing.

24

Ikarus IK-2

When speaking of combat aviation in the Second World War, the first word on everyone's mind is rarely Yugoslavia. The role assigned to Yugoslavia during the war is generally confined strictly to the narrow view of a brief conquest followed by a long uprising and civil war against the Germans, followed by the emergence of a Communist state in the post-war years. This is, perhaps naturally enough, a gross understatement. In truth, the story of Yugoslavia during the war is an immensely complicated one, pitting various nationalities and ethnicities against each other in a vicious internecine conflict whilst still fighting against the German and Italian occupiers of the country.

Beyond this, there is still the role—albeit a brief one—Yugoslavia played when invaded by the German army. In this expanded view, there is a definite place for Yugoslav aviation. Although the small Royal Yugoslav Air Force did use foreign designs, it also boasted native-designed aircraft. Most notable amongst these is the Ikarus IK-2, Yugoslavia's own fighter.

Specifications

First Flight: 1935
Powerplant: Hispano-Suiza 12Ycrs V-12 liquid-cooled piston engine, 860 hp
Armament: Two Darne 0.3-inch (7.92-mm) machine guns, one Hispano-Suiza HS 404 20-mm cannon.
Top Speed: 270 mph (435 kph)
Range/Service Ceiling: 435 miles (700 km), 39,730 feet (12,000 metres)
Dimensions: Length 25 feet 10 inches (7.88 metres), height 11 feet 3 inches (3.42 metres), wingspan 37 feet 5 inches (11.4 metres)
Number Built: 12

In the late 1930s, Yugoslavia found itself in a similar position to Romania. Its neighbours were in some cases rearming and war clouds were gathering. Moreover, Yugoslavia was very far down the line of priority for arms from other nations, either by license or by sale. Critically, the air force of Yugoslavia was catastrophically out of date, with its stable of aircraft dating to the 1920s. Something clearly had to be done, and the Yugoslavians adopted an aggressive approach that, had time permitted it to take its course, would have made Yugoslavia an air power that was not to be trifled with.

A photo of the Ikarus IK-2. Note the high wing and open cockpit. (*Courtesy of Thijs Postma*)

In late 1937, the *Jugoslovensko Kraljevsko Ratno Vazduhoplovstvo*, or the Royal Yugoslav Air Forces (JKRV) began to embark on their ambitious plan to modernise and expand the air force, and completely reorganise it. The plan was to terminate in 1943, by which time Yugoslavia would possess an estimated total of 1,068 aircraft, with a further reserve of 396. This was to be organised into nine air regiments, which would each break down into three squadrons, called *Grupa*. These *Grupa* would then further break down into three flights, or *Eskadrila*, each. To stock these ambitious plans, the most modern fighters available would be purchased from abroad. In the end, Yugoslavia would be forced to take what licenses they could get for domestic production.

The bag of aircraft licenses and purchases was varied. From England, Yugoslavia received Bristol Blenheims and Hawker Hurricanes, both of them Mk I models. From Germany, they got Dornier Do 17Ks, Bf 109E fighters, and from Italy obtained Savoia-Marchetti SM.79 bombers. The domestic aviation industry was also nurtured in a process that would birth the IK-2. The result, however, was a nightmare of logistics.

When the JKRV went to war in 1941, they would be flying a total of thirty aircraft types, between bombers, fighters, trainers, and auxiliary aircraft. There would be between them twenty-two engines, four machine guns, and two cannon. In the details the nightmare became even more prevalent. An aircraft might be a German airframe, but mount French engines. They might also have weaponry from Belgium, with instruments made domestically in Yugoslavia.

The reorganisation would not start until 1939, and would be complete mere days before war began, though the numbers had yet to be produced to match this achievement. When the Germans struck, the JKRV possessed around 340 front-line aircraft with which to face the full onslaught of the Luftwaffe, with further assistance from the Regia Aeronautica.

In the midst of this chaos, and then the onslaught of what was then still one of the mightiest aerial weapons ever created, was a smattering of domestically produced aircraft, with one in particular being the focus here: the Ikarus IK-2. When the Ikarus Company was asked to construct a new fighter in 1934, it readily complied. Previously, Ikarus had been building licensed Potez 25 reconnaissance planes and Avia BH-33E fighters. The fighter that Ikarus designed would be a significant improvement over these designs, especially the aged Potez.

The resulting design was a high-winged, all-metal monoplane fighter, a considerable leap in sophistication both in construction and design for the company. The designers were Kosta Sivčev and Ljubomir Ilić, and they equipped their gull-winged fighter initially with an 860-hp Hispano-Suiza 12Ycrs engine. The IK-L1 prototype first flew on the 22 April 1935. It unfortunately crashed very soon thereafter, and a second prototype was constructed: the IK-02. It was discovered soon after the crash of the original prototype that the fault was some negligent sewing of a seam on one of the fabric covered wings, and thus the IK-02 would have metal wings and also a shallower cooling radiator. It was from this version that a series of twelve, indigenously designed and produced fighters was ordered.

The IK-2 had, in some ways, the misfortune to be designed and built in the transitory period between the arrival of all-metal monoplanes in service and the arrival of the next generation of these designs, which would include aircraft like the Spitfire and the Bf 109. They were, however, good aircraft. The high gull wing meant that the pilot had superb visibility, and the spatting on both the forward landing gear and the tail wheel, as well as struts kept close to the fuselage, meant that the aircraft was relatively well streamlined and had a variable-pitch propeller that was manually adjusted.

All of this was still fairly new when it was designed and proposed, and, as in many nations, it had to swim upstream against conservative design opinion from those who still believed that the agility offered by biplane designs was critical. The IK-02, as such, was put into mock combat in 1936 as part of its initial flight tests. Its opponent was a Hawker Fury biplane, flown by Captain Leonid Bajdak. Bajdak had been the pilot in the unfortunate IK-L1, and had been forced to bale out from the descending aircraft and thus survived the accident. A staunch advocate of the biplane, Bajdak had felt Ikarus' design was unsuitable as a fighter. The improved IK-02, however, was to prove him extensively wrong. The designers must have felt a surge of pride as the IK-02 outperformed the Hawker in every single measure, and the production contract was soon forthcoming for the Yugoslavian air force.

The twelve that had been ordered were all completed and in service by 1937, and there they remained until the Germans invaded on 6 April 1941. The aircraft were operational with the 4th Fighter Regiment, made up of the 33rd and 34th Air Force

Groups, which were stationed at Bosanski Aleksandrovac airfield in Bosnia. Though it would occasionally meet enemy fighters in combat, the IK-2 did the most work as a ground-attack aircraft, strafing advancing German troop columns despite the enemy's ever-increasing air superiority. Though agile and a good design, the IK-2 could not hope to compete against the might of German aviation, especially as it started the war with a mere dozen examples in existence—no more were forthcoming—and attrition meant that by the end of the brief campaign only four aircraft were left.

The Germans handed over the aircraft to the puppet government of Croatia, the Ustaše. As such they became part of the *Zrakoplovstvo Nezavisne Države Hrvatske*, or the Air Force of the Independent State of Croatia, abbreviated as the ZNDH. Every aircraft remaining to Yugoslavia was lumped into the ZNDH, from the old to the modern. It was tasked with helping to suppress the guerrilla movements that were springing up to resist German—and Ustaše—domination in the Yugoslavian territories. Ustaše methods were brutal in the extreme, so much so that the Germans were worried about the reflection it would have on their troops. Even the SS, the most brutal, cruel, and extensive organisation behind the Holocaust and Nazi Germany's other war crimes, considered Ustaše war crimes to be bestial. Small wonder that the precise opposite result occurred. Rather than being cowed into submission, more and more joined the ranks of the guerrillas, especially the Communist Partisans under Josip Broz Tito.

In Croatian service, the handful of remaining IK-2s were pressed into anti-Partisan missions as resistance in Yugoslavia mounted in both size and complexity. The original four IK-2s were kept at these missions until late 1944, and proved well-suited to them. Although slow, they were a stable and reliable platform and were kept in service until each was destroyed by Allied interceptors.

Despites its later service in what might be properly termed a civil war, the Ikarus IK-2 represented the complexity and fairly advanced state of Yugoslavian aircraft design as war clouds descended. Had more been built, it is possible this agile monoplane may have made a larger impact on the war, but with a mere dozen in service this was, naturally, impossible. It demonstrated not only that Yugoslavia was capable of producing good and indeed excellent domestic designs, but is also evidence of a comprehensive rearmament plan that never made it to where it needed to be in order to put up a strong fight against much larger rivals.

For those interested in learning more about Yugoslavia's domestic aircraft industry during the war, the Ikarus IK-2 was not the only domestically designed and produced fighter to see service. Another was the Rogožarski IK-3, which first flew in 1938. The IK-3 was meant to be the replacement of the IK-2, but was a completely new aircraft, comparable to the Hawker Hurricane and even similar in terms of look. Only twelve were built by the time Yugoslavia fell, and only six were operational during the conflict. The IK-3s are believed to have given good account of themselves, though the brevity of the conflict was hardly conducive to any aircraft performing well. If any reader of this book is interested in further study of Yugoslavian aviation, both planes would be interesting sources of further research.

25

Kawasaki Ki-100

By the latter stages of the war, it seemed as if Japanese aviation was on its last legs. The types with which it had entered the war were badly outclassed by swarms of superior American aircraft. Moreover, as the new Boeing B-29 Superfortress arrived in larger and larger numbers over Japan itself, the industry producing Japan's aircraft was being steadily reduced. Thousands of planes, both new and outmoded, were being expended in sporadically effective, and horrifying, Kamikaze attacks.

The overall picture was grim. Yet as the war progressed, new types began to arrive in service that seriously challenged American technical superiority, often matching or exceeding their opponents. Universally, however, these craft arrived too late and in numbers that were unable to crack American domination of the air.

For the Japanese Army, which for so long had soldiered on with the outmoded Nakajima Ki-43 Hayabusa, the solution to the problem of inferior performance came in the form of two aircraft: the Nakajima Ki-84 Hayate, discussed later, and the Kawasaki Ki-100—a rare bird indeed. Remarkably for the Japanese, the fighter was never assigned a true name and was known only as the 'Type 5 Fighter'. Still, it rose to challenge the might of American air power, and proved a formidable weapon that, once again, came too late.

Specifications

First Flight: 1945
Powerplant: One Mitsubishi Ha-112-II radial engine, 1,500 hp
Armament: Two Ho-103 0.5-inch (12.7-mm) machine guns, two Ho-5 20-mm cannon
Top Speed: 360 mph (580 kph)
Range/Service Ceiling: 1,367 miles (2,220 km), 36,090 feet (11,000 metres)
Dimensions: Length 28 feet 11 inches (8.82 metres), height 12 feet 4 inches (3.75 metres), wingspan 39 feet 4 inches (12 metres)
Number Built: 395

Perhaps the greatest deficiency to Japan's military aviation was that it could not effectively challenge the B-29 Superfortress that was beginning to arrive over Japan in 1944. Far more Superfortresses would be lost to fuel issues and mechanical failures than Japanese fighters, especially in the early stages of the type's use. It was a matter of Japan's fighters

War time photograph of a Kawasaki Ki-100. (*Courtesy of the Bill Pippin Collection, 1000aircraftphotos.com*)

simply not being designed to effectively operate at the altitude the B-29 occupied, a problem Japan was desperate to solve.

The Ki-100 was developed from an already superb fighter. Its immediate ancestor was the Kawasaki Ki-61 Hien or 'Flying Swallow'. This fighter had first debuted in 1942 and by 1944 had evolved into the Ki-61-II (later designated the Ki-61-II-KAI), which mounted a Kawasaki Ha-140 engine and performed superbly. Unfortunately, the engine suffered from reliability issues as the assembly line quality was degrading. Both in numbers and in quality, production was utterly insufficient to meet the needs of the Imperial Japanese Army Air Force (IJAAF). The IJAAF ordered the aircraft to be fitted with a different engine, the new Mitsubishi Ha-112-II Kinsei ('Venus') engine. This was a significantly bigger aviation engine, but it was believed critical to adapt the airframe to mount it. This was made all the more critical when a B-29 raid annihilated the production plant for the type's engine on 19 January 1945. This left over 275 Ki-61s without engines, further exacerbating an already bad situation.

The Japanese had by this point imported examples of the Focke-Wulf Fw 190, which demonstrated that wide engines could indeed be successfully mounted in thin fuselages. Three Ki-61-II-KAI airframes were ordered modified, and three engineers, Takeo Doi, Makato Owada, and Tomio Oguchi, went to work modifying the airframe. After several ideas, the final concept called for the fuselage to have a second skin fairing riveted to it, in order to smooth out the airflow behind the cooling flaps, and the many exhaust stubs that were part of the design as a result of the engine's new cowling. Initially, the design had the problem of being significantly tail-heavy, but once a lead counterbalance that had been part of the Ki-61 was removed, the centre of gravity was restored. The lead counter weight had been in place to counter the Ha-140 engine's increasingly heavy weight. The new engine was lighter, yet provided more reliable power.

The first of the new aircraft took to the air on 1 February 1945. The new airplane was lighter, with far superior take-off and landing characteristics, and also added more manoeuvrability to an already agile fighter. The turning circle was better too, though the top speed was a little slower—a total of 18 mph (29 kph) slower than the Ki-61-II. This was not considered a problematic loss as the agility and increased ceiling was impressive—all this in an aircraft that was 725 lb (329 kg) heavier.

The construction of the aircraft was mostly metal, with all-metal parts aside from the fabric-covered control surfaces a fairly common feature at the time. The aircraft also came with a significant punch, with two cannon and two machine guns, a decent armament with which to take on the heavily armoured B-29 bombers.

Perhaps most importantly, it could rise to combat quickly. It had a superb ability to climb, and could rise to over 16,000 feet (4,800 metres) in a mere six minutes and it could be at 32,000 feet (9,700 metres) within twenty minutes. This rate of climb made it perhaps the best available choice for a bomber interceptor, as the Japanese frequently had relatively little warning of B-29 raids over the homeland. The suitability of the aircraft as a bomber interceptor was also enhanced by the fact that it had excellent visibility for the pilot.

Production was immediately ordered, with the new aircraft being designated the Ki-100, or in IJAAF parlance the Goshikisen (the Army Type 5 Fighter). Since initial production would be using converted Ki-61-II and III airframes, Japanese industry would not have to entirely convert to new equipment. The airframes were so unchanged, in fact, that some of the redundant engine fittings from the Ki-61 were retained. As a result of this, the first 200 Ki-100-Ko aircraft had rolled off the assembly line by June 1945. This hurried conversion, bereft even of an auspicious name as were other Japanese aircraft, was thrown into combat nearly immediately, though a follow-on version was planned. The Ki-100-II, which would never see combat, was planned to have a turbocharged engine to be better suited still to fighting the B-29. Only three examples of this improved version were ever built.

During March and April 1945, training began in the type, and experienced instructors at the Akeno Army Flying School vigorously tested the type against what was then considered the finest fighter in Imperial Army service: the Nakajima Ki-84. The expert's verdict was that the Ki-100, if given an equal pilot to the Ki-84, would always prove victorious. There was significant importance placed on the new fighter, and this is demonstrated by the fact that it was ordered to equip nine Sentai along with an Independent Fighter Company.

It is a sign of how critical the introduction of this new craft was that it first flew in combat on 9 March 1945—a mere month after it first flew. It would suffer its first combat loss on 7 April, when a Ki-100 of the 18th Sentai with Yasuo Hiema at the controls was shot down by defensive fire from B-29s.

The new type proved to be not without its flaws. While it could effectively reach the B-29s, the Mitsubishi's engine performance did drop off at that altitude. As a result, the best way to attack the B-29s was considered to be making head-on attacks. With a sluggish altitude performance, a missed attack would be deadly, since failing to down the bomber left the pilot exposed to the defensive fire from not only that bomber, but the nearby ones as well—and the heavily armed B-29 could make short work of opposing fighters. It was not the best sort of fighter for this type of strategy, and was considered inferior to the Mitsubishi J2M fighter in that respect.

When B-29 missions began to descend to low-level, this was not a problem and American airmen realised they were facing a new and capable foe. By July 1945, the Ki-100 was in heavy combat against American fighters. By this point, Japan's defensive situation had deteriorated so much that US Navy carriers were operating within range of the coast with near-impunity. In combat with Grumman Hellcat fighters, the Ki-100 proved the equal of its enemy. In a hotly debated encounter on 18 July, a major fight between Hellcats and Ki-100s resulted in a claimed twelve kills by the Ki-100, opposed to the loss of two. The US Navy, however, claimed an equal loss of 2:2—one on each side being the result of a collision.

Then production was badly delayed by the bombing of the Kakamigahara plant, and between May and July a total of only twelve Ki-100s were completed. The bombing was a wound that ultimately proved fatal, as the plant never recovered and production ultimately ceased. Aside from the pre-completed Ki-61 airframes, only 118 examples of this remarkable fighter were produced.

The Ki-100, at low and medium altitudes, proved equal and indeed superior to every American fighter in service in terms of manoeuvrability, including the P-47 and P-51 fighters, which were by then escorting the B-29s over Japan. The type proved easily one of the finest Japanese types produced, and once again it was a matter of too little and too late for the Japanese. This superb type, never even given a name, rose to challenge the unstoppable might of American arms. It was a product of desperation, which somehow worked superbly. A testament to the work of good engineering and ingenious solutions to nearly insoluble problems.

A single example of the Ki-100 survives today, found at the RAF Museum at Hendon.

26

Macchi C.205 Veltro

Italian fighter design was forced to hurriedly draw up and adopt new aircraft as the war progressed, its mainstay fighters proving obsolescent against Allied aircraft, being both underpowered and, usually, under-armed. The ultimate result was a triumvirate of excellent fighter aircraft as part of the 'Serie 5' programme—the Regianne Re.2005, Fiat G.55, and the superlative Macchi C.205 Veltro ('Greyhound').

Built around the powerful Daimler-Benz DB 605 engine, the Veltro was perhaps the best of Italy's fighters, a formidable craft respected by friends and enemies alike. While it was limited by the small—and indeed diminishing—industrial capacity of Italy, the Veltro nevertheless created for itself a remarkable reputation.

Specifications

First Flight: 1943
Powerplant: One Fiat RA.1050 R.C.58 Tifon liquid-cooled, supercharged inverted V12 engine, 1,475 hp.
Armament: Two Breda-SAFAT 0.5-inch (12.7-mm) machine guns, two MG 151 20-mm cannon, plus two 350-lb (160-kg) bombs.
Top Speed: 400 mph (640 kph)
Range/Service Ceiling: 590 miles (950 km), 37,730 feet (11,500 metres)
Dimensions: Length 29 feet (8.85 metres), height 10 feet (3.05 metres), wingspan 34 feet 9 inches (10.58 metres)
Number Built: 262

Macchi was perhaps the greatest contributor of aircraft to the Regia Aeronautica. Fighters bearing the Macchi name were, in fact, the mainstay of Italian fighter forces during the war, and the C.205 Veltro was the finest of the lot. Far from being a dilapidated institution filled with obsolete planes and obsolete thinking, the Veltro demonstrated that Italian arms could be superb.

Aeronautica Macchi had already provided Italy with its main wartime fighter, the Macchi C.200 Saetta ('Arrow'). The Saetta proved to be an exceptionally manoeuvrable fighter, well suited to dogfights and ground attack, but ultimately proved to be underpowered and under-armed against the newest Allied fighters. The initial solution was a major upgrade, which birthed the Macchi C.202 Folgore ('Thunderbolt'). The Folgore rebuilt the old Saetta design around a powerful Daimler-Benz engine, and what emerged was a superb aircraft. It retained the nimbleness of its predecessor with better power, and was well-regarded.

The Folgore served wherever Italy did, and Allied airmen appreciated it as one of the most deadly and undervalued opponents they faced. It was a superior dogfighter, but it retained some its predecessor's problems. Like the Saetta, it could easily enter a dangerous spin, and was badly under-armed. Also problematic was the fact that the radios were very unreliable, meaning that pilots often had to communicate via the waggling of wings. The worst sin of the Folgore, however, was a faulty oxygen system. It is estimated that up to 60 per cent of pilots were forced to break off missions as a result—with often fatal consequences.

The need for further improvement therefore rather plainly existed, and Macchi would be given the chance to do so. In 1941, the Regia Aeronautica sought to improve the quality of its fighters across the board. Much of the problem had to do with armament, but the biggest problem were the engines available. The decision was made to import and build under license the Daimler-Benz DB605 engine, developing 1,475 hp. For comparison, a Saetta was powered by a Fiat engine that developed a total of 870 hp. The DB605 went into production as the Fiat RA.1050 RC.58, and the usage of this specific engine was built into Italy's next fighter specification. The specification called for designs to be submitted to be the military's new *caccia della serie 5* ('series-5 fighter').

Three designs were ultimately submitted and went into varying degrees of service, and each were superb in their own right. The aircraft were the Fiat G.55, the Macchi C.205, and the Reggiane Re.2005, each design vaguely similar to each other. Macchi held an advantage in terms of development, in that its previous aircraft had already been using a Daimler-Benz engine, so the fuselage required far less modification than its competitors. The resulting aircraft, initially designated the C.202bis before receiving its separate identification, first flew on 19 April 1942—a fairly quick turnaround from the specification to the first flight.

It was a vast improvement over the Saetta, and it was also a good increase in performance over the Folgore. The Veltro would come with an armament of two 20-mm MG cannon, as well as two machine guns, creating a much heavier punch than its predecessors. Behind this already critical improvement would be the vast power of a superb powerplant, but there were other improvements. The tail was larger than that of the Folgore, and the cockpit and 'hump' of the rear fuselage were redesigned, featuring a bigger antenna for the radio equipment. The wings were also improved, and they were made of steel and light alloys. The rest of the plane was all metal, with the exception of most of the control surfaces (aside from the inner wing flaps, they were all fabric covered).

The Veltro was also designed to be a well-protected aircraft. The fuel tanks were self-sealing, there was an armoured seat for the pilot, as well as an armoured windscreen. Overall, this was a design that could take hits, deliver much heavier ones itself, and perform as well as most fighters then in service, if not better.

The Veltro was also ready faster than its competition, so it was ordered into immediate production. Macchi continued to work on what they felt was a superior version, the C.205N Orione, the 'n' standing for 'new'. Unfortunately, when it finally flew in early November 1942, it proved to have inferior performance—but a higher altitude—to the main-line C.205. As an added 'bonus', the C.205N also was found to experience overheating when climbing. Further improvement may have saved the type, but since 1943 was already dawning, with Italian surrender not far off, there was little time in which to do so. Only a single prototype of the C.205N, which might have developed into a decent high-altitude fighter, was ever completed.

The C.205's main drawback, in terms of design, was poor rearward vision for the pilot. In later examples, a rear-view mirror was fitted to correct this. As it stood, there were very few flaws to the design; after evaluation tests by the air force, production was ordered, with the first production model Veltros beginning to leave the factory in September 1942. At this point, however, production difficulties intervened to significantly delay the project. Macchi found itself short of engines and strategic materials, and, besides this, the Veltro was a slow aircraft to construct (it took about a month to complete twelve of them, for instance). The initial order for 100 fighters was not completed until June 1943, and by September only seventy-seven had been added to this total. What fighters there were, however, were put into service as quickly as possible.

The service history of the Macchi C.205 under the Regia Aeronautica was to prove successful, but there were as ever simply too few of these superb fighters to make a critical difference against overwhelming opposition. It would never fully equip any unit in Italian service during wartime, simply because there were too few Veltros available. They were instead parcelled out Italian *Stormos* in bits and pieces, with the rest of their numbers made up of Folgores. The speed of getting the C.205 to frontline service was commendable however; a mere five months had elapsed between its first flight and production, and the type went into combat by April 1943. This, too, happened very quickly; the first Veltros had only equipped 1° *Stormo* a mere two months previously. This unit, based at Pantelleria, an island in the Strait of Sicily, found itself testing the type immediately in combat. On its very first sortie, the unit's C.205s ran into superior numbers of Curtiss P-40 Warhawks and Supermarine Spitfires. According to all accounts, the Veltros gave excellent account of themselves, despite being outnumbered significantly.

This single wing ended up fielding a total of a tenth of all the Veltros produced, having a total of twenty-four aircraft. It became difficult to get a truly good assessment of combat usage as the aircraft operated at such a significant disadvantage of numbers. This is demonstrated by a single battle on 20 April 1943 when thirty-three Macchis of the *Stormo* were ambushed by Polish pilots and eventually faced sixty Spitfires. Bearing in mind that only a portion of the Italian numbers in the engagement were C.205s as opposed to C.202s, one gets a sense of the problem facing the type.

The 1° *Stormo* fought on until it quite literally ran out of serviceable Veltros, depleting their stock of them by the end of June. In this period they had been forced to relocate as the Allied tide advanced, and this would affect every unit that equipped the type.

The 3° *Stormo* was equipped with a total of only three C.205s, with the rest of their strength made up of other types. The main use of note for this group would be the Defence of Rome, with the Veltros rising to harass American bombers. Its aircraft were parcelled out to the best pilots, owing to the paucity of numbers available. This was a beneficial practice, but it reflected the difficulties facing the Italians at this stage of the war, with the enemy soon to land on Italian home soil.

The 4° *Stormo* fared slightly better. They received a total of ten aircraft, and would eventually receive another ten. This group was based at Catania, in eastern Sicily, when the Allied landings began. The Italian pilots flew with energy and bravery, flying up to six sorties per day. However, by the middle of July 1943, with enemy paratroopers in the valley of Catania itself, the unit had to retreat to Calabria, the toe of Italy's 'boot'. They left behind whatever units could not be made ready in time, setting them on fire.

The picture of use for the C.205 in Italian service thus far is of an aircraft arriving too late in pitifully few numbers to even attempt making an impact. Yet, with courage, the pilots tried anyways. One other group, 51° *Stormo*, received decent numbers of the type. This unit fought bravely over Sardinia, but by August their losses were increasing as more and more Allied aircraft became operational and, in essence, swamped whatever brave defence the Italians could put up.

Then came the Armistice. When Italy surrendered and then subsequently switched sides on 8 September 1943, the C.205 had been slow to production and badly used up in service. In the chaos of the Armistice, the machines went to both sides, and two *Gruppos* in service to Mussolini's puppet state in Northern Italy would use the type as part of the *Aeronautica Nazionale Repubblicana,* the ANR, or the Italian Social Republic Air Force. Initially, these planes flew in German markings, so new was the ANR. Not much might be expected of units operating from a rump state, but the Veltros were unique. They were, after all, still mostly in the hands of the best pilots, and as a result they were still deadly and capable opponents in the right circumstances. The 1° *Gruppo* would go into combat in February 1944, against B-17 bombers and the fabled P-51 Mustang as its escort; at heavy cost, the Veltros would extract their price, claiming fifty-eight Mustangs and lancing repeatedly into the heavy bomber formations, though with little practical success. Macchi would manage to produce a total of seventy-two more aircraft for the ANR before their factory was shut down permanently by bombing in May 1944.

The type would also see brief service with the Croatians, part of the collaborationist air force, the ZNDH. These would be rather badly handled by the vastly superior flights of Allied aircraft then swarming over Yugoslavian skies, and the type would see no real success. Beyond this, the last Axis use of the C.205 came in the guise of the Luftwaffe. JG 77's II *Gruppe* used requisitioned C.205s until the end of 1943, and they were none too impressed with the type. They liked the flying characteristics, but their assessment revealed that Macchi had never managed to fix the problems with the aircraft's ability to lose control in a tight sharp turns, nor had they produced a sufficiently reliable radio to meet German needs. The Germans, unfamiliar with the type, had a slow time of it refuelling and rearming the craft, and the unit re-equipped with Bf 109s as soon as possible.

The C.205s were sent back to ANR hands, and essentially used up. After the bombing of what remained of Italy's aircraft industry, Italian units were forced to re-equip with 109s, as domestic production had stopped. The Italian Co-Belligerent Air Force, or the ICAF, had much the same problem. They, however, were operating not as a long-standing ally of their bigger partner, but as a recently defected, and certainly not trusted, rump force. As a result, when the ICAF used up their C.205s, they were left to re-equip with whatever old P-39 Airacobras and Spitfires the Allies handed over.

This was, perhaps, an ignominious end to combat service in the war, though the C.205 would have a post-war career as well. After hostilities ceased in 1945, the type resumed production and indeed picked up foreign orders. Egypt purchased a total of sixty-two refurbished C.205s, and the type did see combat during the Israeli War of Independence. The last Veltros lingered in Italian service into the 1950s, when they were replaced by jet fighters.

Perhaps the best way to assess the Macchi C.205 Veltro is in the words of one of its opponents. One captured C.205 was evaluated by Captain Eric Brown of the British Royal Navy:

> One of the finest aircraft I ever flew was the Macchi MC. 205. Oh, beautiful. And here you had the perfect combination of Italian styling and German engineering. I believe it was powered by a Daimler Benz DB 605. It was really a delight to fly, and up to anything on the Allied programme. But again, it came just before the Italians capitulated so it was never used extensively. And we did tests on it and were most impressed. The cockpit was smallish but not as bad as the Me 109.

Thompson and Smith, p. 231

The Macchi C.205 was, in simplest terms, one of the best Italian designs. It was a sleek shape powered by a superb engine, and as is becoming almost a refrain in this work, it suffered the same fate as all the other superb Axis aircraft types—too few were made or they came far too late to make a real dent in the opposition. Nevertheless, this superb Macchi fighter was employed with bravery and skill, and it made its mark on those who fought against it, if not on the history of the Italian campaign.

There are a few C.205s on display, all of them in Italy. Given the close nature of the C.202 and C.205, many of the parts are interchangeable, and the surviving C.205s are a hybrid of both. One can be seen at National Museum of Science and Technology in Milan. Another can be seen at the *Museo storico dell'Aeronautica Militare* in Vigna di Valle, along with a restored C.202—though both use each other's parts. Perhaps most remarkably, there is a third, partial survivor. Parts of a crashed Veltro were discovered by the Romagna Air Finders, and can be viewed with permission at the museum in Fusignano, Ravenna. One might also be seen at the Volandia Park and Museum in Somma Lombardo.

27

Martin JRM Mars

The Martin JRM Mars was one of the greatest of a group of aircraft that had their heyday in the 1930s and 1940s: the flying boats. The flying boats were the first aircraft that could reliably travel the globe, using any decent body of water as their landing strip. This specific flying boat was the largest in the world when it arrived in service, made for one purpose then used for another. Yet, remarkably, the Martin Mars would survive in strange ways and places, and alone of all the aircraft in this book, is still in service as of 2015. Despite the passage of decades, the Martin JRM Mars has been so successful that it has managed to survive everything that time has thrown at it. A tough airplane, built for tough jobs, which still lives on.

Specifications

(Note: Specifications are for the final production example, the JRM-3, which became the upgrade standard for the production aircraft.)

First Flight: 1942.
Powerplant: Four Pratt & Whitney R-4360-5 Twin Wasp 28-cylinder air-cooled engines, 3,000 hp each.
Armament: None.
Top Speed: 238 mph (383 kph)
Range/Service Ceiling: 6,750 miles (10,863 km), 14,600 feet (4,450 metres)
Dimensions: Length 120 feet 3 inches (36.66 metres), height 38 feet 5 inches (11.71 metres), wingspan 200 feet (60.96 metres)
Number Built: 7

The impetus for the Martin Mars came in 1935. In that year, the Navy gave the Martin Corporation a contract for an experimental flying boat, designated XPBM-1R. What would result would be one of the biggest flying boats in history, and the plane would be the last in the long line of Martin aircraft until the company re-emerged as one half of Lockheed-Martin in 1994. The aircraft that came off the drawing boards was a true leviathan; on its first flight it would be the largest flying boat in the world. A long, high wing mounted four engines, and a huge all-metal fuselage terminated in a twin tail configuration. It was originally conceived of as a long-range maritime patrol bomber, but the programme got off to a rocky start. The prototype caught fire and had to be extensively repaired. It finally flew in on 2 July 1942, by which point the original purpose behind it had been supplanted. The United States Navy had planned on a fleet of 'Sky Dreadnoughts', but the decision was made to acquire large numbers of smaller flying boats such as the famed PBY Catalina or Martin's own PBM Mariner.

Rather than simply cancel the design, the Navy decided to hand the prototype over for testing as a potential long-range, heavy transport. Thus it was that the prototype was re-engineered for this task, all the combat equipment being stripped out of the design. The prototype was extensively modified and emerged as the XPB2M-1R, which was in many respects a partially new aircraft. Though the original wing and engines were retained, the hull was lengthened 6-feet forward, with the aft fuselage being shortened, and a huge single tail took over from the old twinned version.

Internally, the design was shifted around for its new cargo-carrying mission. An overhead hoist was installed, and many of the bulkheads that had previously separated compartments (much like a ship) were removed for ease of loading and storage. At this point Martin also began to work on a civilian version of the aircraft for potential post-war use, dubbed the 170-24A, but in the event the post-war world had increasingly less place for large flying boats as land-based aircraft matched and surpassed their range, and the concept was apparently not pursued.

The new prototype finished her service trials in late 1943, and was handed over to VM-2, one of the Naval Air Transportation Service (NATS) units. The aircraft was immediately put to use making cargo runs from its home base in California to Hawaii. The Navy subsequently decided to order a small number of large flying boat transports, intended to support an invasion of Japan. This decision came in June 1944 and resulted in Martin receiving a contract to build twenty improved transports under the designation of JRM-1 Mars.

In the event, each Mars received an individual name, much like a ship (which, really, they were—just one that could fly). The first was *Hawaii Mars*, delivered to the Navy in late July 1945, but after a mere two weeks in service was destroyed in a landing accident in Chesapeake Bay. The next aircraft to follow were given names of other Pacific destinations: *Philippine Mars*, *Marianas Mars*, *Marshall Mars*, *Hawaii Mars II*, and *Caroline Mars*. In the end, with Japan's surrender, the need for a large number of massive transports evaporated and the order was suspended after these six aircraft. The last of these, *Caroline Mars*, was built as a JRM-2 Mars, meaning it mounted the Pratt & Whitney engines intended for the never-built civilian version. These engines were fully reversible, meaning that *Caroline Mars* could back up on the water, and the increase in power upped her useful lifting weight by 10,000 pounds (4,535 kg), bringing the maximum take-off weight to a staggering 165,000 lb (74,842 kg). All the Mars aircraft in service before her were then retrofitted with these engines to become JRM-3s.

The Mars that went into service was more than capable of colossal feats and, indeed, still is. The prototype was used to train crews in operating the Mars, until it was finally scrapped in 1949. All five production Mars aircraft were assigned to squadron VR-2, located in San Francisco Bay. Their main duty was to haul cargo from the American mainland to Hawaii, but they sometimes deviated from these standard runs. In 1949, for example, *Caroline Mars* carried a payload of 68,282 lb (30,972 kg) from Baltimore to Cleveland, landing on Lake Erie. This load represented double what the normal rated load for a Mars was.

Also in 1949, *Marshall Mars* carried a whopping 301 troops, plus her crew, from San Diego to Honolulu, Hawaii, and the next year *Caroline Mars* ferried 144 marines along the same route. In another notable incident, a Mars flew from the Philippines to California carrying a cargo of monkeys—160 of them, to be precise, destined for Polio research. Though twenty were stolen along the way, the plane still hauled 140 of them to California in what must be a very unique flight for any transport aircraft.

The Mars also proved extremely durable. In one case in 1946, *Philippine Mars* shed an engine on approach for landing, the engine literally tearing away from the wing. The aircraft landed with no particular problems. A more serious accident, however, consumed *Marshall Mars* in 1950, when the number three engine caught fire and the on-board firefighting gear failed. After valiant efforts to extinguish the blaze, the aircraft exploded and the remains continued to burn fiercely for the better part of an hour before sinking.

The Navy decided to retire the Mars in 1956, but not before VR-2 had racked up some astonishing numbers. Between 1946 and 1949, they had flown for 32,997 hours, with only those two incidents worth mentioning, and transported 76,403 people. Then, between 1950 and their retirement, they carried 108,198 people, plus large amounts of cargo and mail, in 1,940 flights across the vast reaches of the Pacific. They did so with an absolutely astounding 87,000 accident-free hours. The Navy made the decision to sell the aircraft for scrap in 1959, and here their remarkable story would have ended save for one man.

Dan McIvor was a pilot for a Canadian timber company, an early pioneer in using aircraft as firefighters. Fires were destroying large amounts of potential stock, and McIvor's suggested remedy was to find flying boats that had the speed, capacity, range, and turnaround capability to fight them. The search was fruitless as the era of the flying boat had already passed, but a friend alerted him to the sale of the Mars aircraft. They had unfortunately been sold for scrap, but McIvor was able to negotiate a deal to purchase them, their entire stock of spare parts, and the entire documentation archive.

Fairey Aviation of Canada modified the planes into water bombers, installing 7,200-gallon water tanks in each, and modifying some of the fuel tanks to carry additional water. A secondary tank was added to hold a foam-concentrate thickener that allowed the water to adhere to the trees. In their original firefighting service, two of the Mars aircraft were lost. One, *Marianas Mars*, suffered a tragic accident and crashed into a mountain in 1961, killing the crew. *Caroline Mars* took the brunt of a hurricane in 1962, and was damaged beyond repair.

The last two Mars aircraft, however, went on to a remarkable career. In 2007, still in service, they were sold to Coulson Forest Products, who still owns them today. After a long life, *Philippine Mars* was finally retired in 2012 to become a museum plane at the National Naval Aviation Museum in Florida, in her original Navy colours. This has not, as of the writing of this book, occurred. The aircraft's huge payload and sheer durability have given them long careers indeed. It seemed like the end had finally been reached when the government of British Columbia decided to stop using *Hawaii Mars II* in 2013. Yet the last of the Martin Mars flying boats was not so easily dispensed with. With new fires raging, and the number of more modern aircraft insufficient to stopping them, the government recalled *Hawaii Mars II* to service in the summer of 2015. As such, she is still fully engaged in her firefighting duties and it remains to be seen whether this is a last hurrah or, indeed, the start of continued service for this remarkable aircraft.

Though the Martin Mars flying boats never fulfilled the original purpose they were designed for, their career has been all the most astonishing as a result of it. For aircraft that came into service in 1945, to find even one still performing active duties in 2015 almost beggars belief. It is a tremendous testament both to the era of the flying boat and also to the remarkably durable and capable design of the Martin Mars.

28

Messerschmitt Me 209

The Messerschmitt Bf 109 is, rightly, one of the most famed aircraft of history. It formed the backbone of the Luftwaffe throughout the war, even after it was rendered technologically inferior. German engineers refined the design as much as possible, adding to it in hopes of keeping the basic airframe a match to its opponents.

Messerschmitt's engineers would strive to replace the Bf 109 with superior versions of piston-engined fighters, some of which were never completed and others barely reaching a handful of examples. They were successively named Me 309, 409, 509, and 609—each bearing little resemblance to the others—but what of the logical missing link in that change, the Me 209? The answer to that question would prove the exception to the rule, and an aircraft built for a single purpose: to be a record-breaker.

While it would never see combat, the Messerschmitt Me 209 would nevertheless serve Germany in two unique capacities: to try to enhance the aura of invincibility given to the Bf 109, and also to set unparalleled speed records.

Specifications

First Flight: 1938
Powerplant: (V1) One Daimler-Benz DB601ARJ inverted V-12 liquid-cooled piston engine, 1,775 hp.
Armament: None.
Top Speed: 423 mph (678 kph)
Range/Service Ceiling: Unknown, 36,080 feet (11,000 metres)
Dimensions: Length 23 feet 9 inches (7.24 metres), height 10 feet 6 inches (3.2 metres), wingspan 25 feet 7 inches (7.8 metres)
Number Built: 4

The entire programme that resulted in the Me 209 came from a singular desire: to beat the land speed record. It was almost a personal project of Willy Messerschmitt, starting in 1937. It was, like many record breakers, designed around its engine. In this case, the engine was a 12-cylinder Daimler Benz, with the cockpit set far back just in front of a unique tail shape. In a major departure from Messerschmitt's previous design, the Bf 109, the landing gear was mounted in the wing rather than in the fuselage. It was a design

Messerschmitt Me 209 V1 prototype. (*Courtesy of the Nico Braas Collection, 1000aircraftphotos.com*)

entirely devoted to achieving a single purpose, and it did just that. On 26 April 1939, test pilot Fritz Wendel took the aircraft aloft and it hit a speed of 470 mph (756 kph).

This scored the Germans a bit of a propaganda victory and caused the British, who had also been pursuing the absolute land speed record, to decide not to use a modified Speed Spitfire in their own attempt, as the Speed Spitfire was only expected to make 419 mph (675 kph). As a result, Germany was able to demonstrate a technical mastery—at least, in a propaganda sense—and upstage a rival on the world stage. Beyond that, it was an enduring record that stood until 1969.

Interestingly, though the Speed Spitfire never flew, the Me 209 did have to defeat a rival, and it was another German aircraft. Before it flew, the record had initially and briefly been claimed by a variant of the Heinkel He 100 (itself a fascinating aircraft), which had hit 463.92 mph. The record stood for a mere twenty-two days before the Me 209 took the title for Messerschmitt and held it.

This might have been the end of things, but events took a hand in the history of this little plane. The Battle of Britain convinced some that it was high time to equip the Luftwaffe with a new fighter, and it was suggested that a plane with such lightning speed would be suitable for the job. Examination, however, quickly put this notion to rest. The engine's liquid cooling system took up most of the wings, which meant that installing any sort of military hardware was impractical—there simply wasn't enough room for the cooling system, which the engine required, and guns. In addition to this, the plane was very difficult to control in the air and especially on the ground.

The speedy test aircraft was so difficult to control that Fritz Wendel stated:

With its tiny wing and ... horrifying wing loading, the 209 was a brute. It had a dangerous tendency to nose down without any reason or warning, and it touched down on the runway like a ton of bricks. Even on the ground its tendencies were no more ladylike, as it would suddenly swerve off the runway without any provocation.

Jackson, p. 28

As for its actual performance with Wendel himself at the controls:

On 4 April 1939, I took off for a training flight in preparation for the speed record attempt in the second prototype, the Me 209 V2. After a few tiring minutes of heaving the unwieldly controls, I turned in for a landing approach. I was accustomed to lowering the undercarriage when I reached the Siebentischwald, a forest near the airfield of Haunstetten, but on that day, without warning [everything happened without warning in the Me 209] the lubricating system packed up, and immediately the pistons were grinding in the cylinders and the airscrew was standing as stiff as a poker. With a hell of a jolt, the plane virtually pulled up in mid-air, the result of the combined drag of the lowered undercarriage and the unfeathered airscrew. The vicious little brute started dropping like a stone, and below me was that damned forest. I strained on the stick with all I had and, to my surprise, the plane responded. I screamed over the last row of trees bordering the Haunstetterstrasse, and was even more surprised to find myself staggering away, relatively unhurt, from the heap of twisted metal that [had seconds before been] an Me 209.

Jackson, pp. 28–30

Those passages say much about the talents of the pilot that he was able to walk away from such a crash, and even more about the unpredictable nature of the aircraft. They also speak to what should have been a fairly obvious choice that the aircraft could not possibly have made a good fighter. Nevertheless, efforts were made. The wings were lengthened, and the tail plane was made taller to make the plane more controllable. The V4 prototype took to the skies and it was found that, with all the changes to make it into any sort of flyable fighter plane, the resulting aircraft had no advantage whatsoever over the existing Bf 109.

In the end, the plane's only practical value beyond claiming the record was in propaganda. The aircraft was referred to as the Bf 109R (the 'R' designation was never used in any model of the actual 109) in an attempt to infer that it was merely a development of the existing fighter aircraft, in order to enhance the then fearsome reputation of the type. This reputation would last until the Luftwaffe was checked in the Battle of Britain, though it is difficult to assess if the Me 209 played any real role in strengthening this reputation.

In essence, the Me 209 is something of a short story; an aside in aviation history that says more about the determination of human beings to go faster than ever before, rather than about anything having to do with combat aviation in the Second World War. Yet it is still instructive, both as to the technical prowess of Messerschmitt in the late 1930s, but also to what was becoming an increasingly complex battlefield. Even before the war began, there was value to propaganda about certain aircraft, and in attempting to portray the Me 209 as some sort of super plane, and indeed as merely an enhancement of the 109, this can be amply demonstrated.

The history of the Me 209 also demonstrates that (much like the Breda Ba.88) no matter how spectacular performance can be it does not necessarily translate into any sort of military usefulness. Engineering has certain rules and limitations, and in aircraft design as in all other things, one thing cannot simply become another.

If anybody is feeling confused by the Messerschmitt 209, they have good reason for this. There were, in fact, two aircraft with the designation. The first is the plane described above, the racer that served as a propaganda tool. The second Me 209 bore no relation to its predecessor, and was instead an attempt to upgrade the famed 109 to compete against the new high-performance Focke-Wulf 190 D and Ta 152. Like those designs, the same airframe was used (in this case the 109 G), but was meant for an upgraded engine. The project was also meant to be developed quickly, but ran into difficulties with parts and the intended engine was unavailable, and thus a Jumo 213A had to be used, which required further modification and lost time. When the V5 prototype finally flew, it had no superior handling characteristics to the Fw 190 D, and was 31 mph slower. Ironically, both attempts to create a fighter called Me 209 had much the same result. The project was cancelled, ending Messerschmitt's piston-engined fighter programmes. Messerschmitt thereafter concentrated exclusively on jet designs until the end of the war.

The record-breaking prototype of the Me 209 itself still exists and can be visited by aviation enthusiasts. The engine and wings are missing, but the rest was seized by the Poles in 1945 and can be seen in the Polish National Aircraft Museum in Krakow.

The second aircraft to bear the designation Messerschmitt Me 209. (*Courtesy of the Nico Braas Collection, 1000aircraftphotos.com*)

29

Messerschmitt Me 410 Hornisse

Alongside its more famous stablemate, the Bf 109, the Messerschmitt Bf 110 was meant to be a heavy fighter, or 'Zerstörer', to annihilate enemy bombers. In the event, it enjoyed some limited success as a day fighter until faced by solid fighter opposition that ultimately relegated it to the role of night fighter, where it was more successful. This left a gap that Messerschmitt sought to fill with a more advanced vision for a heavy fighter.

Specifications

First Flight: (Me 410) 1942
Powerplant: Two Daimler-Benz DB 603A liquid-cooled V12 engine, 1,726 hp each.
Armament: Two MG 17 0.312-inch (7.92-mm) machine guns, two MG 151/20 20-mm cannon, two MG 131 0.51-inch (13-mm) machine guns on each side of the fuselage, firing rearwards in remote-operated turrets, up to 2,204 lb (1,000 kg) of bombs, or four Werfer-Granate 21 8-inch (21-cm) rockets.
Top Speed: 388 mph (624 kph)
Range/Service Ceiling: 1,400 miles (2,300 km), 32,800 feet (10,000 metres)
Dimensions: Length 40 feet 8.187 inches (12.4 metres), height 12 feet 2.625 inches (12.4 metres), wingspan 53 feet 9.25 inches (16.39 metres)
Number Built: 1,189

The Hornisse (Hornet) suffered through a major redesign before it could make any impact whatsoever, but the ultimate result was a sleek and deadly heavy fighter that is frequently forgotten in the annals of history. The story of the Messerschmitt Hornisse is, in fact, the story of two siblings. The first would be the Me 210, which would evolve into the 410.

The genesis of the Me 210 was in the perceived need to replace the Bf 110 long-range heavy fighter, which was then the Luftwaffe's main and only such design. The Zerstörer concept would face tremendous difficulties in the face of single-engined fighter opposition. In the end, the Bf 110 would find its niche as a night fighter, whereas day time usage produced often appalling results when it met the enemy. Nevertheless, in 1937 all of this was unknown, and the Luftwaffe decreed that there needed to be a replacement for the type even before it had seen combat.

Wartime shot of a Messerschmitt Me 410. (*Courtesy of the Bill Pippin Collection, 1000aircraftphotos. com*)

The new design was certainly a beautiful one. It was designed to have twin engines and a twin rudder like its predecessor, but, instead of the Bf 110's cut-off wings, would have tapering wings. The engine nacelles were lengthened too, with a rounded cockpit. Interestingly, the bomb bay was internal and under the cockpit, which would provide a significant reduction in drag.

Interestingly, the RLM's specification for the aircraft had called for remote-controlled defensive armament and rearward facing remote barbettes would be installed, one on either side of the fuselage. It was an interesting, if ultimately difficult to operate, defensive scheme.

At this point, Willy Messerschmitt's stock was riding high in Germany and the Luftwaffe made the remarkable decision to order 1,000 examples of the untested aircraft directly off the drawing board. At the time, it made sense. The Bf 109 was a superb fighter and the Bf 110, while not stellar, still was being put to good use. However, presuming future performance was a catastrophic mistake, and Hermann Goering would be heard to remark that his epitaph would say that he would have lived longer had the Me 210 never been produced.

The Me 210 V1 first flew on 2 September 1939 and immediately there were obvious problems. The longitudinal instability in the air was such that the twin tail was immediately replaced by a large, single vertical tail. Other changes such as a different canopy were installed, but none of this prevented the V2 from crashing during flutter trials on 5 September 1940.

Despite these results that might, with an understatement, be described as merely unsatisfactory, production Me 210A-1 aircraft were already being sent out to be prepared for combat, as well as A-2 fighter-bomber variants. Despite its flaws, it was decided to send it into combat anyways.

Its first use came during the invasion of the Soviet Union as part of II. /ZG 1. Late in 1941, they started to use the Me 210 and quickly discovered that the test flights had not resulted in necessary improvements. The aircraft would enter a spin for little apparent reason, especially when trying to make high-angle attacks. This propensity, naturally, led to numerous accidents and crashes, and all of Messerschmitt's attempts to introduce improvements on the factory floor failed to overcome the problems faced.

The Me 210's contract was cancelled after over 300 examples had been produced, at a high cost to the state. The furore over the aircraft was so bad that there were calls for Messerschmitt himself to resign from the company. Determined to save both his position and reputation, Messerschmitt went back to the drawing board and, ultimately, a solution was discovered.

By fitting leading-edge automatic wing slots, much of the instability was solved, and this upgrade was fitted to as many aircraft as possible. The Me 210 would go on to be used in intruder raids over England into 1942, with minor success. The aircraft could, at least, be said to be in working order. There had been other improvements, too. Besides the improved wing slots, the last 210s produced featured a new rear fuselage and parallel-bar airbrakes, all in attempts to improve the type's performance.

Messerschmitt, however, was certainly not finished. The idea to improve and reintroduce the type gained momentum, and ultimately the Me 410 Hornisse would be the result. The 410 incorporated the improved wing slots, but also had the lengthened fuselage and nacelles that had been part of early attempts at improving the type. It also featured more powerful engines, and, best of all, from the point of view of the RLM, Me 210s could be upgraded into Me 410s. The first Me 410 flew towards the end of 1942, and an immediate large order was placed as the improvements finally solved the problems that had plagued the Me 210.

The first Me 410s off the line were meant to be light bombers, designated Me 410A-1. These aircraft came with two machine guns and two 20-mm cannon that were forward firing, along with two in the rearward facing barbettes for defence. It could also carry two 2,205-lb (1,000-kg) bombs internally, but for intruder raids over England the type more usually carried eight 110-lb (50-kg) bombs internally, with an additional four under the wing-centre section.

It was this aircraft that returned to British skies, and proved to be a tough adversary for British night fighters. It was a fast aircraft, and the methods used by the intruder raids hardly helped the defenders. The bombers would enter British airspace at high altitude, then dive onto their objective, drop their payload, and make a high-speed exit. The problem for the aircraft chasing them, such as the Bristol Beaufighter or de Havilland Mosquito, was that in the pursuing dive, their own radar would lose contact frequently as the ground returned false readings. The ultimate solution to this was to patrol far out to sea and trap the intruders there. The Me 410A-1 would be used as part of the bombing of London in early 1944 as well, though with limited results.

Most of the aforementioned intruder raids were carried out by Me 410s belonging to V. /KG 2, though I./KG 51 also operated the A-1 in this capacity to a limited degree over England. The type was used more by this unit, however, against the Normandy landings, though the unit was withdrawn for re-equipment to the Me 262 jet in the late autumn of 1944.

The other main variants of the type were used as bomber destroyers against the USAAF bombers that were pounding Germany. These were fitted with a bewildering array of armaments, some of which worked and others that merely had a deleterious effect on the aircraft's performance. One of the latter was the armament fitted to the A-1/U-4 variant: a 1,984-lb (900-kg) 50-mm gun. It carried twenty-one rounds and its weight severely restricted manoeuvrability. According to some sources, the gun may have had a recoil pressure of around 7 tons.

In more standard configurations, the Me 410 as a bomber destroyer often had its machine guns replaced by additional 20-mm cannon, and this heavy armament could cause havoc on a bomber formation. The problem for the Hornisse was that it was always going to be vulnerable to enemy fighters, which accounted for most of the type's losses in daylight attacks. There were many other bomber-destroyer configurations, some of them exceedingly lethal. Many of the aircraft produced carried *Rüstsatz* field-modification kits, while others were modified in the field itself with them. One was a pair of external packs that would add either two MG 151 or two MK 108 cannon. Some experienced Hornisse pilots went aloft with an extremely lethal total of eight MG 151 cannon, all of them firing forward. Another common fitting were underwing tubes for 210-mm rockets, in common usage by 1944. Some Me 410s had a remarkable mounting in the bomb bay of a rotating pack of six of these tubes, making the entire aircraft into something like a giant rocket revolver, flying at high speed into bomber formations. Small wonder that these aircraft could prove highly lethal to bombers, when they got past the escorting fighters.

Another notable use of the type was a photo-reconnaissance aircraft, designated the A-3. This one mounted cameras in the bomb bays and proved to be excellent at this work, as the camera installation was considered to be superior to many of the more *ad hoc* arrangements then in use.

The Me 410 ultimately evolved into the Me 410B, which upgraded the engines again, this time with a pair of 1,900-hp Daimler-Benz DB603G. These new 410s took on most of the same roles, but had other specialised variants built. One was a torpedo-bomber variant, the Me 410B-5, which carried two 882-lb (400-kg) or 441-lb (200-kg) torpedoes. With the weapons-bay fuel tank removed, this type could carry a 1,984-lb (900-kg) torpedo, making it a potentially lethal ship-killer; although, by this late stage in the war, the opportunities for the aircraft were becoming more limited. The B-6 variant was also meant as an anti-shipping aircraft, being radar-equipped with the Hohentwiel search radar, plus a pair of 20-mm and 30-mm cannon, along with the standard defensive machine guns.

Further high-altitude versions of the aircraft were planned, but never implemented, using a special wing that had been developed for the never-built Me 310. Development of all of these aircraft was abandoned when production of all the varieties of Me 410 was halted in September 1944, to concentrate on the best fighter designs in the final defence of the Reich.

The Messerschmitt Me 410 Hornisse could be said to have had an unlikely service history, given its less than illustrious predecessor. Once significant improvements were made to the dismal Me 210, it re-emerged as an excellent design that finally reached its potential. It gave the Luftwaffe excellent service, and in many ways did achieve its original purpose of replacing the Bf 110 in combat usage. It proved a versatile airframe with many uses, and a dizzying array of potential weapon loads that testifies to this fact.

There was indeed a Me 310 design, and it was in fact Messerschmitt's initial idea to replace the Me 210. It was ultimately rejected in favour of the Me 410, which was a far less ambitious design, but also more readily producible. The Me 310 was designed with a specialised high-altitude wing, a pressurised cockpit, and a pair of Daimler-Benz DB 603A engines driving four-bladed propellers. The wingspan would have been just over 59 feet (18 metres), with a maximum speed of 419 mph (675 kph) at high altitude. Only the prototype was built, and it offered not enough of a performance increase over the 210 to warrant production over the easier 410—to which, it must be remembered, 210s could be converted more readily. The other high-altitude variants of the Me 410 were conceived from this starting point.

As for surviving Me 410s, there are two. One is awaiting restoration at the Gerber Facility of the Smithsonian in Washington, D.C., and the other is on display at the Royal Air Force Museum in Cosford, England.

30

Nakajima Ki-84 Hayate

Of all the later-war aircraft in the Japanese armoury, one has in recent years started to receive some major notoriety. The Nakajima Ki-84 has become a legendary part of flight simulators and Second World War video games of all varieties, a fighter with a reputation attached. It was easily one of the most superb Japanese fighter of the war, and certainly the best to see large-scale service. It was a radical departure from everything that had come before in the Japanese arsenal, an airplane built specifically to counter the deficiencies of its forebears and to successfully challenge the best that Japan's enemies could field. It achieved all of these ambitious objectives, and did so with apparent ease.

The legend of the Hayate is of a plane that corrected all the failings of the previous generation of Japanese warplanes: better powered, armoured, and more heavily armed—a deadly mount for Japan's airborne warriors. The actual history of the Hayate provides one of the rare instances in which the legend is closely matched by the reality.

Specifications

First Flight: 1943
Powerplant: Nakajima Ha-45-21 Homare 18-cylinder radial engine, 1,970 hp.
Armament: Two Ho-103 0.5-inch (12.7-mm) machine guns, two Ho-5 20-mm cannon, and either two 220-lb (100-kg) bombs, or two 551-lb (250-kg) bombs.
Top Speed: 426 mph (686 kph)
Range/Service Ceiling: 1,347 miles (2,168 km), 38,800 feet (11,826 metres)
Dimensions: Length 32 feet 7 inches (11.238 metres), height 11 feet 1 inch (3.385 metres), wingspan 36 feet 11 inches (11.238 metres)
Number Built: 3,514

The legend of the Ki-84 begins with Nakajima's previous fighter, the Ki-43 Hayabusa ('Peregrine Falcon'). The Hayabusa had been the army's main fighter in the early stages of the war, and followed the then-standard design paradigm in Japanese service that called for range, speed, and manoeuvrability at the cost of all else. In combat, the Hayabusa, known as 'Oscar' to the Allies, proved to be under-gunned and its lack of armour put it at a huge disadvantage against the newest enemy aircraft. These aircraft were starting to suffer appalling losses, and their survivability rate was poor. This caused the Japanese to re-evaluate their entire fighter philosophy, and the call for a new Type 4 Army Fighter would privilege high performance over manoeuvrability.

The specification to replace the Hayabusa was handed down in early 1942, and Nakajima quickly went to work. The design was fairly conventional, but it featured all the structural and power improvements that could be added. Perhaps most importantly, it featured a much heavier armament than its predecessor. The armament would continue to grow in calibre as the design was improved through various marks, but the aircraft that first flew in March 1943 was already excellent. To the surprise and, undoubtedly, delight of those aware of the programme, the design would combine excellent necessary improvements with no major decrease in manoeuvrability. In essence, the Ki-84 Hayate ('Gale') would cover everything a designer could possibly have wished.

Nakajima's factory at Ota began production the next month, in April 1943, and the production model addressed all of the problems that the Ki-43 had possessed. It fixed the poor rate of climb, lack of defensive armour, and as previously stated had already fixed the firepower problem. The design was all metal, aside from fabric-covered control surfaces.

The type's Achilles' heel would prove to be the same thing that gave it strength: its engine. The engine was superb, but it was also difficult to build, and it required significant maintenance to keep it fully functional. In addition, the type proved to have fragile landing gear, which would be a continuous problem. Far and away, however, the greatest limitation on the Hayate was the quality of pilots it received. By the time it entered combat in the latter stages of 1944, the cadre of experienced veteran pilots that had once characterised the Imperial Japanese Army Air Force was mostly gone. In the hands of a good pilot, the Hayate was a deadly weapon. In the hands of an expert veteran, the Hayate was able to outperform any Allied aircraft.

The first Hayates went into combat in China, and they proved an unwelcome surprise for American air crews. The type was at least marginally superior to the P-47s and P-51s then in service, which were the American military's highest performance fighters. These first fighters were organised initially in the 22nd Sentai, under Major Jozo Iwahashi, the chief test pilot of the programme. There was nobody better to lead the first Ki-84s into combat.

The unit took to the skies with a total of thirty Hayates, and, starting on 28 August 1944, the type went into near constant combat. The Hayate allowed the 22nd to immediately go on the offensive, though this came with a heavy cost. Though they claimed forty aircraft destroyed, the cost was high. By September 1944 Major Iwahashi had been killed, and the unit was withdrawn for recuperation, leaving behind twenty Hayates still intact.

In service in China, results deteriorated from there. The increasing death of experienced pilots coupled with ever-rising numbers of Allied aircraft precluded the Ki-84 from exercising its full potential. In addition, the high-maintenance engine kept the aircraft on the ground far more often than its pilots would have liked. This situation was not helped by a declining production quality, as what materials that still managed to reach Japan were of a lower grade than they previously had been.

The Hayate was also rushed to the Philippines, anticipating the American landings there. The effort would be led by the 200th Sentai, under Lt Col. Takahashi. This unit would receive reinforcements of more Ki-84s, including some in service to the 24th Sentai. After the catastrophic Japanese naval defeat at Leyte Gulf, the Ki-84s went into combat against the enemy, strafing the landing grounds and engaging in air-to-air combat. As it turned out, the Ki-84 was well suited to the ground attack role given its speed and far higher durability than previous Japanese aircraft.

One daring attack, undertaken by Ki-84s of the 51st and 52nd Sentais, involved attacking a US airfield at Tacloban with over 100 planes using phosphorous bombs. Though this action and others met with at least some success, they were costly. In this case, seven Ki-84s were lost. In another attack on the same airfield as well as one at Burauen later in the struggle for the Philippines, the Ki-84s encountered B-24 Liberator bombers and shot two down and damaged three others for no loss to themselves.

All the units using the Hayate in these battles fought on against overwhelming odds, giving good account of the type and giving it a reputation amongst the American pilots who opposed it as a deadly aircraft. Moreover, attempts were made to continue to improve the type. The first production run had been labelled the Ki-84-Ia, which had maintained the two machine guns and two cannon of the prototypes. The next model, the Ki-84-Ib, replaced the two machine guns with a second pair of 20-mm cannon. Then, in the Ki-84-Ic, the armament was upgraded again so there were two 20-mm cannon and two lethal 30-mm cannon.

The next development in design had everything to with Japan's rapidly deteriorating position. The Ki-84-II had wood introduced into its airframe, saving as much of the light alloys that made up the construction as possible without sacrificing performance. This type was given the armament of either the Ib or Ic models.

The Ki-84 would fight on to the end, but the reliability and maintenance problems of its engine, combined with insufficient production of declining quality, kept it from exercising a bigger role than it did. As it stood, over 3,000 of this exceptional fighter were produced, making it numerically the most important of Japan's late-war aircraft.

So often with the aircraft of the Axis powers it can be said that it was a lack of numbers that prevented a larger success. In the case of the Hayate, it was not so much numbers that did this—though facing a vastly superior number of enemy aircraft at any time did not help much—but the problems of producing a complicated engine with increasingly inferior materials. That the Japanese still managed to make as many aircraft as they did, and that they managed to make the mark they did despite all the limiting factors the type faced, point to the superior nature and great power of the Ki-84 Hayate.

Only one Ki-84 survives today. It was captured and shipped to North America after the war, after which it was sold off and restored by the Planes of Fame Museum in Ontario, before eventually being given back to Japan. It currently resides at the Chiran Tokkō-Heiwa-Kaikan Museum, otherwise known as the Chiran Peace Museum, in Kagoshima, Japan. It should be noted that the airbase there once served as the launching point for hundreds of kamikaze sorties, and the museum commemorates their sacrifice and documents their lives.

31

Petlyakov Pe-8

The Red Air Force's speciality was always close co-operation with the ground forces. It carried this out in a spectacularly effective fashion as the war on the Eastern Front progressed. In this case, however, strategic bombing barely enters the picture. In point of fact, the Soviet Union did almost no strategic bombing during the war, despite a vast array of pre-war heavy bombers. During the war, however, the Soviet Union did produce one heavy bomber, which tells an interesting story: the Petlyakov Pe-8.

Specifications

First Flight: 1936
Powerplant: Four Mikulin AM-35A liquid-cooled V-12 engines, 1,340 hp each
Armament: Two 20-mm ShVAK cannon, two 0.5-inch (12.7-mm) UBT machine guns, two 0.300-inch (7.62-mm) machine guns, up to 11,000 lb (5,000 kg) of bombs
Top Speed: 275.2 mph (443 kph)
Range/Service Ceiling: 2,299 miles (3,700 km), 30,504 feet (9,300 metres)
Dimensions: Length 76 feet 2.5 inches (23.2 metres), height 20 feet 4 inches (6.2 metres), wingspan 128 feet 4 inches (39.13 metres)
Number Built: Less than 100

There was a long history of heavy bombers in Russian and then Soviet aviation that had started with the Ilya Muromets during the First World War. From here, Soviet designs had proliferated and grown into a considerable corps of aircraft. By the mid-1930s, however, doctrine had shifted away from the heavy bomber and relatively few were still in service, with new designs being even scarcer. The mainstay of Soviet heavy bombing had been the Tupolev TB-3, and it was considered time for a replacement. The new specification called for a bomber that could heft a load of bombs totalling 4,400 lb (2,000 kg) for a distance of 2,800 miles (4,500 km) and at a speed greater than 270 mph (440 kph).

The Tupolev Design Bureau was given the task of fulfilling this, given their previous experience. The chief of the bureau, Andrei Tupolev, gave control of the project to Vladimir Petlyakov. The initial design was given the name TB-7, short for *Tyazholy Bombardirovschik* ('heavy bomber'). It would prove to be a major departure from its

Petlyakov Pe-8, often labeled as the Tupolev TB-7. (*Courtesy of the Al Zeig Collection, 1000aircraftphotos. com*)

predecessor, the TB-3. The design was far more modern in all respects. The final result was a streamlined, cantilever monoplane design. The main problem for the plane, initially called the ANT-42, would be in terms of its engines. The Mikulin engines did not deliver the power that the designers wanted. In a strange yet innovative solution, a fifth Klimov engine was mounted in the fuselage to power a fuel injection system to turbocharge the engines. Sources disagree as to whether or not the plane ever solved its power problems, but given the satisfactory service it gave, it can be concluded that performance was, at the least, good enough to keep it in service.

In any event, the first prototype's maiden flight went well enough, and the aircraft was passed on for state acceptance trials in August 1937. While the aircraft performed well, there were a number of minor problems. The outer engines were found to be prone to overheating, and the rudder was proven ineffective. This and wind tunnel testing revealed an aerodynamic problem around the nacelles and radiators. A redesign of the engine nacelles and a movement of radiators solved the major problems with the engines.

The second prototype was redesigned to fix all of these issues, but at this point the design's progress was hampered significantly by the fact that Stalin's paranoia reached deeply into the aviation industry as well. As part of his purges of the armed forces, both Tupolev and Petlyakov were arrested and imprisoned. Though by this point the prototype was complete, and had flown for the first time at the end of 1936, the production model had to wait until Petlyakov was released—or 'rehabilitated'—upon which he was actually rewarded with his own design bureau (Tupolev was also rehabilitated).

The second prototype, and later the production model, dispensed with the fifth engine, using better superchargers that were mounted more conventionally with the engines themselves. It finally flew in 1938, but the damage was done. The order to begin production was not given until 1939, and the first production aircraft did not arrive until 1940.

What came of this, however, was a capable aircraft that is frequently compared to American heavy bombers, and compared favourably at that. It could carry a higher tonnage of bombs than a B-17, although at a slightly lesser range. One strange feature was the defensive armament, far less than that of a B-17, but installed less conventionally. There was a retractable machine gun in a dorsal turret, another in a tail turret, but also a machine gun in barbettes in each inner engine's nacelle. The first prototypes had had a gondola, called a 'beard', beneath the cockpit with another gunner's position—this was removed in the production models. Furthermore, the addition of another fuel tank increased the production aircraft's range.

Production, however, was sluggish at best. Part of the reason had to do with bureaucratic confusion in the wake of the Great Purge, but it was also owing to a shortage of workers paired to a shortage of materials. The bomber, then, suffered from a combination of factors that slowed its design and implementation ranging from technical glitches to a lack of required materials and labour to official paranoia and the arrest of its chief designers. This combination was a rather unique one, to say the least.

The production model suffered from a plethora of engines being used as they became available. Soviet priorities were for fighter and lighter bombers, so the Pe-8 went through

Another view of the Petlyakov Pe-8 at the same event. (*Courtesy of Thijs Postma*)

a number of engines in early production. Production, as a result, was slow, and this was paired to a low level of official interest in the project. One source reasons that this was because, in addition to the priority of Soviet thought for combat aviation, geography played a hand. After the Germans and Soviets divided Poland, Soviet arms were a mere 350 miles from Berlin, making a long-range strategic bomber of little use. In short, the Soviets short-changed a programme owing to the circumstances of 1940, which by the end of 1941 would be radically different. This may be part of the reason for the bomber's slow development, but it is likely a combination of all the factors previously discussed.

When war came, however, the aircraft was ready to perform its mission in defence of the Soviet Union. It should be noted here that the designation Pe-8 was not made official until 1942, owing to Petlyakov's death in an air accident in 1942, but the Pe-8 designation will be used from here on.

As the German Operation Barbarossa stormed into the Soviet Union at extreme cost to the Soviets, only one unit had been equipped with the type. This unit, the 2nd Squadron of the 14th Bomber Regiment, was not ready to go into operation and a few were lost in German raids and the bombers were withdrawn past Kazan, deeper in Soviet territory. This regiment was reformed as first the 412th *Tyazholy Bombardirovochnyy Avia Polk* (Heavy Bomber Regiment (TBAP)), then as the 432nd TBAP.

This group was ordered to carry out the first Soviet air raid on Berlin. The Pe-8s that were chosen were given the Charomskiy M-40 diesel engines, which were unreliable. The raid took off on 10 August 1941, and was something of a disaster. Of eight bombers that took off, only four managed to reach Berlin, and only two made it back to base—all but one of the bombers that didn't make it back were lost owing to the unreliable M-40.

However, the point was made, that Berlin itself could be attacked by Soviet bombers. The bombers that came into service thereafter were equipped, finally, with the reliable Mikulin AM-35 engines, and all surviving aircraft not mounting the AM-35 were modified. These engines cut down the total range of the aircraft, but the benefit was a much better operational reliability. The unit went back into operation against both German and captured Soviet targets for the rest of the year.

In the spring of 1942, the Pe-8 took on another role: that of long range transport. It was in this plane that the Soviet Foreign Minister Molotov flew to Britain for talks with the British government, and then on to Washington, D.C., across the Atlantic. It would be used in this capacity until the end of the war, being a favourite for high officials.

In mid-June 1942, another group was formed; this was the 890th *Avia Polk Dahl'nevo Deystviya* (Long-Range Aviation Regiment (APDD)). This and the other unit started an increased tempo of bombing German strategic targets, very often at night. The two regiments carried out as many missions in August as they had in the first ten months of war. Thereafter, efforts shifted to hitting important transport centres, airfields, troop concentrations, and railroad yards through into mid-1943. One of these raids was on the German-held city of Königsberg, and it involved dropping a special bomb, the FAB-5000; this was an 11,000-lb (5,000-kg) bomb that the Pe-8's bomb bay had been modified to carry before it entered production.

By the summer, however, losses started to mount as German night fighters were tasked with stopping them. Losses to all causes had increased from one aircraft every 102 flights in 1942 to 1:46 by 1944, a fairly heavy increase. The relatively light defensive armament may have made it a little bit easier for the German night fighters. Nevertheless, the bombers continued to fly. There is a good deal of debate as to when the bombers were withdrawn, or indeed if they were withdrawn. The Statistical Digest of the Soviet Air Force shows bombers still on-hand to operation units at the end of the war, though it may not have been a primary combat aircraft.

The bomber served on into the post-war world in different ways. It was used extensively to test a Soviet version of the V-1 flying bomb, as well as serving as the mothership for a rocket-powered supersonic research aircraft, the Bisnovat 5, in 1948–49. Others had their military equipment removed and were used for polar exploration, with one Pe-8 landing at the North Pole in 1954.

Very few Pe-8s were ever built, certainly no more than 100, though specific numbers differ from source to source. For a plane built in such small numbers, it exercised an effective presence for most of the war, and its value in terms of propaganda was perhaps even higher than its actual effect. It remained, however, the only Soviet bomber that could drop a large tonnage of bombs on a long-range strategic target, and in this regard was the equal of any Allied heavy bomber. It was a break with the standard strategy of the Soviet Red Air Force of its day, and a continuation of a long tradition of strategic bombers.

32

Piaggio P.108

As previously discussed, the Axis powers possessed relatively few heavy bombers in their arsenal. Germany had turned away from four-engined designs and would not return to them until later in the war. Japan, too, had different priorities; her military needs privileged range and seaborne capabilities. In Europe, however, Italy had produced a heavy bomber that would be used in a variety of roles, her impact lessened by the Italian armistice and by slow production and development. The Piaggio P.108 would prove to be a rarity—an effective Axis heavy bomber, though in such limited numbers as to never exercise a potential effect on the strategic battlefield.

Specifications

First Flight: 1939
Powerplant: (P.108B) Four Piaggio P.XII RC.35 radial engines, 1,500 hp each.
Armament: Five Breda-SAFAT 0.5-inch (12.7-mm) machine guns, two Breda-SAFAT 0.303-inch (7.7-mm), 7,700-lb (3,500-kg) of bombs
Top Speed: 267 mph (430 kph)
Range/Service Ceiling: 2,157 miles (3,520 km), 27,187 feet (8,500 metres)
Dimensions: Length 73 feet 2 inches (22.3 metres), height 20 feet (6 metres), wingspan 105 feet (32 metres)
Number Built: 50

The Piaggio P.108 evolved from an earlier Piaggio design, the P.50-II. The P.50 was also a four-engined bomber, with the engines unusually mounted so there were two nacelles, with one engine facing forward and the other backwards, on each side of the fuselage. The P.50-II was essentially the same plane with the engines mounted more conventionally. Neither version was ordered for production, but Piaggio continued to develop the concept.

When the Italian air ministry handed down a new specification for a heavy bomber in 1939, Piaggio was already well equipped to produce a design. There were competing designs from Cant and Caproni, but these two companies only had aircraft on paper. Piaggio had already constructed heavy bombers in the past, and when the requirement arrived Piaggio had, in fact, already constructed a prototype for what would become the

View of a production-model Piaggio P.108B. (*Courtesy of the Bernhard Klein Collection, 1000aircraftphotos.com*)

P.108. It had been built as a private venture in 1939, and the very fact that it existed was a heavy advantage—though it certainly did not hurt that Piaggio ultimately underbid its competitors significantly. There was also a practical consideration to the decision—the Cant and Caproni designs would not begin to produce meaningful numbers of aircrafts until well into the 1940s. With war less than a year away, the Piaggio prototype would at least be entering production as Italy's war needs grew.

The aircraft was modern too. It was an all-metal, low-wing monoplane, with retractable landing gear. The design also featured a very large tail because of the need to stabilise the aircraft on take-off; it was a very powerful and heavy design, rating 6,000 hp at take-off with a weight that was 20 per cent heavier than early model B-17 bombers. Another interesting feature was part of the P.108's defensive armament. The bomber had wing armament, which consisted of two hydraulically powered and radio-controlled Breda 'Z' turrets, located in the outer-engine nacelles, each linked to an operator back in the fuselage. This was an innovative arrangement, though not designed for sustained combat. Piaggio was also rare in that they built their own engines like, in the case of the P.108, the P.XII engine. The P.XII, however, was a very unreliable engine, and this would lead to fatal consequences.

The prototype flew for the first time on 24 November 1939, and after the usual testing production examples began to arrive for familiarisation. The P.108s were assigned to 274a *Squadriglia*, which is where the accidents began. This was, after all, a big and heavy aircraft, and it was easy enough to make a fatal error, even if the engines were fully reliable. These accidents culminated on 7 August 1941 in the death of the *Squadriglia* commander, Bruno Mussolini, son of the dictator. The younger Mussolini flew too low and the heavy plane crashed into a house, the cockpit section separating from the rest of the airframe, fatally injuring Mussolini's favourite son. Mussolini was, for all his many sins, close to his children and suffered tremendous grief and shock when he learned of the event.

Despite these problems, the P.108 went to war as Italy's only production heavy bomber. The type's main limitation would be lacklustre altitude performance. The combination of weight and powerful engines meant high fuel consumption, with a service ceiling of, at best, 26,300 feet (8,000 metres), which was comparable to British aircraft of the time, but American bombers such as the B-17 left it far behind. There was, of course, the other consequence of its fuel consumption—a reduced range. Whatever the type's limitations, however, there remained the critical fact that it was the only aircraft Italy had that could fulfil the need for a heavy bomber.

Three basic types were constructed, each with separate mission profiles. The P.108A was meant as an anti-shipping weapon, with the 'A' standing for Artigliere, or gunship. It came equipped with a massive Ansaldo 90-mm (3.5-inch) gun mounted in the nose, firing at a depressed angle. The heavy recoil action was absorbed by the strong, heavy airframe, and the P.108A could also carry torpedoes. Only one of the handful of P.108s produced was modified to carry this weaponry, and it was never used in combat owing to the arrival of the Armistice.

Another version was the P.108C transport, which had a wider fuselage and a pressurised cockpit, but no armament. This further strained the already slow production of the P.108 bomber version, but the P.108C was ordered in small numbers, a total of six aircraft being produced. This evolved into the P.108T, which was a dedicated military transport that could carry sixty soldiers, eight torpedoes, or 13 tons of cargo. It could also hold two Macchi C.200 fighters, with the wings removed. Of the cargo P.108s produced, many of the 'C' and 'T' examples were taken over by the Luftwaffe and served on the Eastern Front, most notably in the evacuation of soldiers from the Crimea.

Piaggio had ambitious plans for the P.108C. The aircraft was meant to pioneer air routes to South America as part of a massive Italian plan for post-war air routes all over the world, including new Piaggio aircraft to reach North America. It goes without saying that none of these particular plans came to pass.

The main version, however, was the P.108B, the original bomber concept. The greatest weakness of the design in combat would prove to be the fact that there simply were never enough P.108s. The attacks the plane carried out were in small groups, less defensible than large numbers of bombers. Moreover, the handful of bombers employed at any time ensured that too small a tonnage of bombs was dropped on any target to properly saturate it, and thus the P.108 tended to do relatively little damage with rather appalling losses.

The aircraft went into combat in June 1942, and was employed against ships and land targets. The first attack was at Gibraltar on 28 June, and it was a disaster. Five aircraft launched the attack, though one turned back because of engine trouble, and three suffered forced landings in Spain, two of them being written-off.

This pattern followed it through the rest of its operational service until Italy's surrender. Too few bombers were ever employed to produce results, and these bombers were vulnerable to large amounts of enemy fighters, both by day and by night. Aside from the transport versions taken over by the Luftwaffe, only one P.108 appears to have remained flyable after the Armistice—the remaining aircraft were probably sabotaged to keep them out of German hands. This last P.108 met an untimely end. Members of the Allied 57th Fighter Group found the P.108 at Taranto, and flew the aircraft to the 57th's base at Gioia Del Colle. The aircraft received a quick paintjob and was meant to be part of the ferrying equipment for the group. To repay the ground crew for a good and speedy job, pilot Benedict Leaf took them all up for a joyride. Leaf was unused to the heavy machine, and predictable things went wrong. The landing gear collapsed as he brought the plane in to land, cartwheeling the aircraft. While nobody was injured, the last flyable P.108 in Italy was reduced to a pile of metal.

It might seem simple to write the P.108 bomber off as a failure, though it was never used in sufficient numbers or under optimal conditions, making it difficult to assess its operational capabilities. Simply too few were built to use the aircraft properly as a heavy bomber, either by day or night, and the craft was frittered away in small numbers and never concentrated. It was an interesting aircraft that had it been further developed and produced in greater numbers, might have given the Italians a fearsome strategic weapon.

33

Polikarpov I-15/I-153

The Polikarpov family of combat biplanes gave truly sterling service to the Soviet Union, evolving into a plethora of forms and missions. Though obsolete by 1941, they would give good account of themselves against both the Japanese and Germans, even being a critical part of a defeat the Japanese would suffer at Soviet hands in Mongolia as part of the Khalkhin Gol border conflicts of 1939. The family line that would begin with the I-15 would travel through the I-15bis and finally arrive at the I-153, one of history's most unusual, and capable, biplane fighters. One of the only biplanes fitted with retractable landing gear, the I-153 would continue a tradition of agility and durability, and, in one memorable test case, was even fitted with rocket engines, likely the only rocket-propelled biplane fighter ever tested.

Specifications (I-15)

First Flight: 1933
Powerplant: M-22 radial engine, 472 hp.
Armament: Four PV-1 0.3-inch (7.62-mm) machine guns, up to 220 lb (100 kg) of bombs, or six RS-82 rockets.
Top Speed: 220 mph (350 kph)
Range/Service Ceiling: 310 miles (500 km), 23,800 feet (7,250 metres)
Dimensions: Length 20 feet (6.1 metres), height 7 feet 3 inches (2.2 metres), wingspan 32 feet (9.75 metres)
Number Built: 3,313

Specifications (I-153)

First Flight: 1938
Powerplant: Shvetsov M-62 radial engine, 800 hp.
Armament: Four ShKAS 0.3-inch (7.62-mm) machine guns.
Top Speed: 280 mph (444 kph)
Range/Service Ceiling: 292 miles (470 km), 35,105 feet (10,700 metres)
Dimensions: Length 20.3 feet (6.1 metres), height 9 feet 8 inches (2.95 metres), wingspan 33 feet 3 inches (10.2 metres)
Number Built: 3,437

The Polikarpov I-15 had its genesis in Nikolai Polikarpov's earlier I-5 biplane, which was to be the standard Soviet fighter until 1936. The new I-15 was meant to be an upgrade to this previous nimble biplane. The Soviet Union believed in the necessity of the project, so the design and testing process was extraordinarily rapid. The main differences from the I-5 were the gulled upper wing to improve pilot visibility and spatted-landing gear to reduce drag. Other than that, it was a fairly standard biplane design for the era.

The prototype, designated TsKB-3, first flew in October 1933, and, after abbreviated testing, it was already in production by the start of 1934—a frankly astonishing turnaround. The first 400 aircraft were built around the insufficient M-22 radial engine, which limited top speed to 199 mph (320 kph). Both the prototype and some of the aircraft that followed had Wright Cyclone engines, which were far better engines. The prototype of the later batch of Cyclone-powered aircraft, called the TsKB-3bis, soon set a record for the Soviet Union. Stripped down to the bare minimum of components, it was flown to a record height of 47,818 feet (14,575 metres)—a feat for any aircraft of the time, let alone a biplane.

Once the Soviet M-25 engine was developed, all further production switched to this engine, and some of the M-22 equipped I-15s were upgraded, with the last of the over 3,000 aircraft produced by 1937. The I-15 proved to be an exceptionally manoeuvrable and effective gun platform, surprising its enemies in the skies over both Spain and Manchuria. It would be best remembered, however, for the service to Spain's Republican Government during the Civil War.

The first I-15s arrived in Spain in October 1936, where its remarkable performance made it a fearful opponent. It was not only fast for a biplane, but it climbed extremely quickly, able to reach 16,250 feet (4,953 metres) in just over six minutes. It could out-turn almost anything it was going to face, and it did so with four machine guns, double the firepower of more traditional biplane designs.

In service both in Spain and in the Soviet Union itself, the type had problems. The first was generally poor quality in manufacturing, which led to frequent breakdowns and mechanical failures. The big radial engines were mounted without any dampeners, which meant a lot of vibration on the airframe that led to further damage. Pilots came to know the plane as Chaika (Seagull) owing its wing, and despite its many problems it was used hard in combat.

Early on, it was the most powerful aircraft in the Spanish Republican arsenal, until the arrival of the more modern Polikarpov I-16. The I-16 had been developed in tandem with the I-15, and it was ultimately deemed a more modern aircraft, supplanting it in production and service. For the moment, however, the I-15 went into action mainly against the Fiat CR.32 biplane, and for the last time in European skies, biplane duels formed the core of fighter-to-fighter action.

The I-15, and its major improvement, the I-15bis, would also see combat in China and over Mongolia. By 1939, 347 I-15s and I-15bis fighters had been delivered to the Chinese, with many Soviet volunteer pilots. It would prove a capable opponent in either Chinese or Soviet hands until it was confronted with newer Japanese monoplanes. A similar story applies to its use in the Khalkhin Gol border war in Mongolia, also against the Japanese. Although the I-15 once again proved a nimble opponent when it began to face Japanese monoplanes, the I-15 pilots were no match for experienced Japanese veterans.

It should be noted that the main differences in the I-15bis model was that the famed gull wing was straightened, and it also received the more powerful Shvetsov M-25V engine. Many of them had their wheel spats removed, since the design meant that grass could accumulate and become an unexpected and fairly severe brake, which could do heavy damage to the airplane.

By this point, with the I-16 already in service, it might seem that the I-15 and I-15bis had a rather imminent destiny with the scrap heap, but there was one last trick up Polikarpov's sleeve for his remarkable biplane. That 'trick' was the I-153, quite possibly the finest biplane fighter ever produced and flown in combat. Though it was definitely obsolete even by the time it flew, it was a remarkable achievement nonetheless.

Design work on the I-153 commenced in late 1937. Polikarpov had been ordered to improve the biplane, as results of early combat in Spain were believed to vindicate the continuing usefulness of biplane fighters. The project leader was Aleksai Shcherbakov, and the project involved keeping the fuselage and tail plane of the I-15bis, but refining and strengthening both. In addition, the gulled wing was restored, with staggered, single-bay wings. Uniquely, the landing gear retracted backwards and the type would eventually be equipped with the powerful M-62 supercharged engine.

Thousands of I-15, I-15bis, and I-153 fighters served both in the Winter War against Finland, and were still on-hand when the Germans invaded in 1941. Most of these aircraft had been transferred to secondary duties, but they still made up a major portion of Soviet losses, which would have been apocalyptic for any other air force. Soviet production more than made these losses good, however. Pilot inexperience also meant that losses for newer types were nearly the same as those for the older types, so serious thought was given to restarting I-153 and I-16 production, though the idea was ultimately dismissed.

Polikarpov's last series of biplanes was doomed, much like the Gloster Gladiator, to emerge at a time when they were already obsolete by any measure of aviation design. Much like that aircraft, they soldiered on regardless. Some of the last I-153s were rocket-equipped ground attack aircraft, still valiantly serving the Soviet Union despite being hopelessly outclassed by the enemy. In addition, the I-153 may well represent the pinnacle of combat biplane design, a superior plane for an earlier age. Regardless of whether or not they were obsolete, they gave sterling service, and this is worth remembering more than time passing them by.

There are several surviving examples of the I-15, I-15bis, and I-153. A replica I-15 sits in Madrid's Museum del Aire. The Avia Restoration Company in Russia completed a restoration on an I-15 in 2002, which was likely sold on privately thereafter, though there was mention of a second airframe being recovered. An I-152DT trainer survives in flying condition, seen at air shows. At least two I-153s survive today. The first is at the Armée de l'Air Museum in Paris, and may be the only completely authentic I-153. The other is a rebuild, which still flies, located at the National Air Museum in New Zealand. Another flying I-153 is held by *Fundació Parc Aeronàutic de Catalunya* (FPAC) collection, in Spain. This may only be a partial list of restorations currently ongoing or completed.

Lastly, it is worth mentioning that the I-153 received one other noteworthy sub-type, the I-153DM. It had a pair of auxiliary ramjets mounted under the lower wings, first of the 15.75-inch (400-mm) diameter variety, then later 19.68-inch (500-mm) variety, which was tested in 1940. One can only imagine what the experience was like of taking a superb biplane up with extra rocket propulsion, but as far as is known only one was completed and tested in 1940. Apparently the ramjets did not add much more than 30 mph (48 kph), but it remains the only biplane equipped as far as the author knows with ramjet engines.

34

Polikarpov Po-2

Polikarpov produced another remarkable biplane, in this case long before the war. The Polikarpov Po-2 first entered production in 1928 and continued there until 1952. In its long life, the Po-2 would serve as a crop duster, a trainer, a reconnaissance aircraft, a liaison aircraft, and as a ground-attack aircraft, it would even help carry out psychological warfare operations. The design would feature the rugged durability that made it, and many Soviet designs, legendary. The Po-2 would be best known, however, as the mount given to the Night Witches, the all-female unit that harried the Germans in the dark of night. Officially, the designation Po-2 was not added until the death of her designer, but she would go down in history with his name attached.

Specifications

First Flight: 1928
Powerplant: Shvetsov M-11D 5-cylinder radial engine, 125 hp.
Armament: One ShKAS 0.3-inch (7.62-mm) machine gun, and up to six 110-lb (50-kg) bombs.
Top Speed: 94 mph (152 kph)
Range/Service Ceiling: 391 miles (630 km), 9,843 feet (3,000 metres)
Dimensions: Length 26 feet 10 inches (8.17 metres), height 10 feet 2 inches (3.1 metres), wingspan 37 feet 5 inches (11.4 metres)
Number Built: 20,000–30,000

The aircraft originally designated the U-2 (but hereafter referred to as the Po-2) started its long career owing to a 1927 Soviet requirement for a new general purpose biplane. The original intended purpose for the aircraft was to be the Soviet Union's new trainer, so it would be necessary for the design to be durable and extremely easy to fly, easy to maintain, and to be operable from almost any condition of airfield. Polikarpov's design bureau set right to work, but the first prototype did not work out as intended. It was a very rectangular craft, with very simple surfaces. It actually failed to take-off when it first tried, and the designers went back to the drawing boards. The revisions included single-bay wings, as well as rounded wingtips. The resulting aircraft would be one of the most successful aircraft in Soviet history.

The aircraft immediately went into production, and would continue in production until 1952, when over 40,000 were built. Outwardly, it might not look like one of the most versatile aircraft in history. It had most of the standard biplane features, such as an open cockpit and fixed landing gear, as well as a wooden propeller. The aircraft was skinned with plywood or metal, which meant it was a highly durable design. Some parts, such as the undercarriage and some of the bracing, were fully metal. All of this meant that the Po-2 was a design that put a premium on ruggedness.

It rapidly moved into one job after another, becoming the basic general trainer for the Soviet military, and also for the civilian agencies of the country. In addition, it became a crop duster, scout, liaison aircraft, passenger plane, air ambulance, patrol aircraft, and a photography platform. In the cold and remote regions of the Soviet Union, many were fitted with skis or floats, meaning it could operate anywhere that an airplane could manage it. One notable incident was when the Po-2, in 1938, located a team of Soviet scientists who had been stranded on an iceberg for nine months.

When war came in 1941, the Po-2 was in near universal Red Army service as an observer and liaison aircraft. Wartime weaponry was added, including a rearward mounted machine gun for the observer, a machine gun firing through the propeller, and bomb racks underneath the wings. On first glance, the Po-2 might seem to be an aircraft that was destined for destruction in the skies over Russia, as the Luftwaffe rampaged in the early months of the war. This would technically be true, as the Po-2 was vulnerable to gunfire. The saving grace was that the Po-2 was actually so slow in the air that a skilled pilot could escape an enemy Messerschmitt by staying low to the ground and swerving, as the Po-2 was able to fly so slowly that its flight speed was beneath the 109's stall speed. The German pilot would only have a few moments in which to attack, moments in which the light, swerving Po-2 would be very difficult to score hits against.

The Po-2 found its best service, however, as a night bomber. In fulfilling this kind of mission, it turned out to be ideally suited to the task. In the course of the war, entire regiments were formed around the Po-2, attacking the German soldiers on every possible night for the psychological value, as well as its actual value in terms of causing casualties and damage. Soviet flyers would cruise over the front lines, looking for fires that indicated the presence of German troops. The aircraft would dodge flak batteries, search lights, and German night fighters, denying the Germans sleep—this would have had more of a mental effect than any physical damage the Po-2 could have given. The aircraft carried the message that the Soviet Union would fight around the clock, giving the Germans no rest and no quarter. It was a potent message, carried out with astonishing bravery.

The most daring Po-2 tactic was to actually shut its engine off and dive towards the target, with a steadiness that had made it such a superb trainer in its earlier days. Then, silently, the bombs would be released, and the engine would roar back to life as the rear gunner opened fire with the machine gun and escape hurriedly. The distinctive putter of the Po-2's small and durable five-cylinder engine became a hated sound amongst the Germans.

The most famous amongst the night regiments were the ones that the Germans called the *Nachthexen*, the Night Witches. The Germans meant the name to be one of contempt, but it was taken up with pride by the Soviet women. These were the all-female regiments of the Soviet Air Force, some of the more than 800,000 women who served the Soviet Union in combat during the Second World War. In October 1941, Stalin issued secret order No. 0099, calling for three all-female aviation regiments. These women would receive sporadic official press during the war, which reflected Stalin's belief that women should be kept from combat. The Soviet government carried the same view of women having defined, non-masculine roles as other governments of the time, after all. In the event, however, the emergency overwhelmed Stalin's reticence and deeply entrenched perceptions of gender in the Soviet government. It was well that it did, for the Soviet women who served in combat gave sterling, courageous service to the USSR.

One unit of women, specifically, would use the Po-2: the 588th Regiment, which would later become the 46th Bomber Regiment. All the women were to be volunteers, and their successes would change many attitudes. The women of the regiment became known as 'Stalin's Falcons', featuring in an exhibition on Soviet women in the war in 1944. These women flew 24,000 combat missions, and would win twenty-five Hero of the Soviet Union awards, the highest award the Soviet Union had for bravery—they also represented five-sixths of that same award given to women in the Red Air Force. Though their dangerous efforts, which caused significant casualties to the Night Witches themselves, were meant to be primarily psychological, the women caused very real damage—they dropped over 23,000 tons of bombs on the Germans.

One Po-2 navigator, Galina Dokutovich, summarised the Night Witches:

> In the beginning we fought for the right to be an independent military unit. Then we won the right to fight. They watched us with envy. But we achieved the right to be equal in battle. And when we achieved this, we showed that we could be in the front ranks of warriors.

Cardona and Marcwick, p. 84

The Germans came to have a nickname for the Po-2. So annoying were the night-time raids, and so regular, that the German enlisted men came to call it the 'duty sergeant'. The Duty Sergeant would do sterling wartime duty to harass and undermine the enemy's psychology, in addition to the very real damage that the bombing efforts would do.

The Polikarpov Po-2 served as a strong mount for the brave night bomber crews, women and men both. In the process it also created a legend for women's service in the Second World War. The Po-2 would continue in manufacture well after the war, serving as a crop duster and taking on a new role as a firefighter. This slow, antiquated biplane ended up carrying out nearly every necessary job, including night-time combat operations against the Germans—quite the achievement for an airplane that first flew in the 1920s, the oldest in this work by far.

The full story of the Night Witches has been documented extensively elsewhere, though as yet there is a regrettable lack of knowledge about their role and exploits in the general public consciousness. While there have been documentaries and dramatizations both within Russia and without, the story of these remarkable women (or indeed that of the 800,000 women who served in the Soviet armed forces in what Russia still terms the Great Patriotic War) is still one that many reading this entry will be hearing either for the first time or with only passing knowledge of it. Recent books on the subject are doing much to correct this, and the Night Witches recently had a graphic novel made about them by Dynamite Comics.

As for surviving Po-2s, it is remarkable, or perhaps not, given the Po-2's legend, that so many are still in flying condition. There are eight flying Po-2s at:

Fantasy of Flight, Florida, USA
Federation of Amateur Aviators, Tushino Airfield, Moscow
Flying Heritage Collection, Washington State, USA
Koroski Aeroklub, Slovenj Gradec, Slovenia
Metoděj Vlach foundation collection, Mladá Boleslav, Czech Republic
Military Aviation Museum, Virginia, USA
Museum of Transportation, Budaörsairfield, Hungary
Shuttleworth Collection, Bedfordshire, England

35

PZL P-11c

Poland's war history carries with it many unique, and indeed tragic, stories. Too often, the Polish contribution to the Allied war effort is remembered as their quick defeat on their native soil in 1939. Many authors have painted a picture of an obsolete force using obsolete tactics, easily defeated by the advanced German blitzkrieg. This view is both simplistic and extensively incorrect. In the larger sense, the fall of Poland was merely the beginning of Poland's war. Poles bravely fought on, and did so nearly everywhere. The highest scoring squadron of the Battle of Britain would be a Polish one:—the 303rd 'Kosciuszko' Squadron. It would be Poles that fought their way up Monte Cassino to finally dislodge German defenders in the most famed battle of the Italian Front. Parts of the Polish navy fought on from British ports, defending their allies and hunting their enemies. In Poland itself, there would be numerous uprisings, both by Jews fighting to survive the depravity and hatred of the Nazis and by the Polish Home Army.

In the midst of this, the contribution of the Polish air force could easily be overlooked, but it shouldn't be. In 1939, despite possessing mainly obsolete technology compared to the invading Luftwaffe, the Polish air force would strike back against the German invader until overwhelmed by attrition and the overrunning of Polish territory. Central to this effort was the gull-winged PZL P.11c, making up the majority of Poland's fighter strength. Valiantly employed, the outdated P.11c would nevertheless give solid account of itself, creating an enduring image of Polish bravery in the air.

Specifications

First Flight: 1931
Powerplant: Bristol Mercury V.S2 9-cylinder air-cooled radial-piston engine (560 hp), or a Polish Skoda Works Bristol Mercury VI.S2
Armament: Two KW Wz 33 or KM Wz 37 0.312-inch (7.92-mm) machine guns, optionally an extra two KW Wz 33 machine guns.
Top Speed: 242 mph (390 kph)
Range/Service Ceiling: 431 miles (700 km), 26,247 feet (8,000 metres)
Dimensions: Length 24 feet 9 inches (7.55 metres), height 9 feet 4 inches (2.85 metres), wingspan 35 feet 2 inches (10.719 metres)
Number Built: 325

Lost in the narrative of obsolescence and doom is the fact that, for a while, Poland had possessed the most advanced fighter force in the world. Poland was, in the 1920s and early 1930s, in something akin to luck because they possessed the designer Zygmunt Puławski. Puławski's distinctive gull-wings, mounted high and giving a pilot superb vision, were revolutionary for their time and became so associated with him that they were either called the 'Puławski wing' or even just the 'Polish wing'.

Puławski turned to building fighters and the result was first the PZL P.7, and then later the P.11. Poland would, in equipping such fighters, be at least briefly ahead of the rest of the world. PZL would build 150 P.7s for the Polish air force, and when the P.11 was brought into service, this would mean that Poland possessed the world's first all-metal fighter force. The tragedy of this would be that it was so rapidly outpaced by changes in design and, at this point, Puławski was unavailable to Poland—the genius designer had been killed in a plane crash in 1931.

The P.11 was Puławski's last fighter, and it began life as part of a series of development schemes for the P.7 to equip it with newer and better engines. Both the P.7 and P.11 were major leaps forward for Poland as they introduced Polish-designed monoplanes to replace aircraft such as the SPAD S.61 (a biplane with a reputation as a pilot-killer). The P.7 and P.11 shared the same essential design. Both were all-metal, high wing monoplanes, their wings of the standard Puławski type. They had progressively larger engines turning a two-bladed propeller, open cockpits, and fixed landing gear. The first P.11 flew in August 1931, a mere month after Puławski's death. It proved more than suitable, and a series of thirty were ordered as the P.11a; this was equipped with a Bristol Mercury IV S2 radial engine, which the Poles were building under license. This was considered an interim measure, until the main production version arrived, which was the P.11c.

The P.11c featured an improved fuselage, with the engine height lowered to further improve already superb pilot vision. Engines would change yet again, with the first fifty aircraft off the line equipped with Mercury V S2 engines (600 hp), and thereafter with the Mercury VI S2 (630 hp), and 175 aircraft were ordered for production, which began in 1934. Some P.11cs also featured provisions for a radio and a second pair of machine guns, though this was not usually fitted. The landing gear was designed in a scissor-type, with a damper built into the fuselage. One interesting feature the P.11 had was the ability to jettison the internal fuel tank in the fuselage, in case of an emergency. The P.11's high, gull wings were made of light and corrugated aluminium sheets, which kept the overall weight down.

Such a low level of production may seem to be strange, given the presence of the vast air fleets of the Soviet Union on the one hand—whom Poland had been at war with less than a decade before—and the resurgence of Nazi Germany on the other. In truth, there was confusion in the Polish command structure as to what the strategy would be regarding bombers and fighters, with much debate over which types would be used or ordered from abroad.

The PZL P.11 was officially debuted at the Paris Aviation Fair in December 1934, and it caused a sensation. Romania immediately purchased a license to make seventy of their own aircraft, which would be exported to Romania as the P.11f. Other interested parties were Greece, Portugal, Republican Spain, Turkey, and Yugoslavia, though they ultimately placed no orders. Bulgaria, Greece, and Turkey would all eventually buy PZLs, but they would purchase the new P.24, a further (and, as events would have it, final) version of the PZL line of gull-winged fighters.

When the P.11c began to enter service late 1934 to early 1935, it was superior to the best fighters then in service, such as the Gloster Gauntlet in Great Britain, or the Heinkel He 51 in Germany. It would, however, prove to be rapidly outpaced by the revolutionary second generation of monoplane fighters, especially the Bf 109 that would soon be coming for the P.11c rather directly. In the interim, however, the P.11c proved a very popular aircraft.

As war clouds began to gather, it became rapidly apparent that the P.11c was inadequate in terms of both design and most especially in numbers. Polish hopes were pinned on new designs and also foreign-ordered machines, but the former was clearly not going to arrive in time, and the latter had not arrived by the time war came. The decision was made to produce a last version of the P.11, with a Mercury VIII engine and an enclosed cockpit. The resultant version, known as Kobuz, only managed to fly in prototype form by the time the Germans invaded.

As a result of some poor command-level decisions regarding aircraft development, Poland was left with only a tiny force of PZL P.7 and P.11c fighters to meet the sledgehammer of the Luftwaffe. Here, however, the little P.11c was to demonstrate that, obsolete or not, it could still carry a powerful sting. Given the tiny number on hand, it was easy to underestimate the fighter, but the mistake was in misjudging the men flying her.

Poland had, at the time, one of the best trained cadres of pilots in the world. This was coupled to a certain knowledge at higher levels of the impending attack, and as a result the force of P.11c fighters was spread out to subsidiary airfields and airstrips. The rugged design could easily operate from these fields, which meant that the first German blows fell on mostly abandoned air bases. In addition, the badly outnumbered Poles quickly adapted their tactics to suit their very slow fighter.

There were 185 P.11 fighters on hand when the Germans struck, despite the pre-war Polish plan to concentrate on bombers as a key focus of their air strategy. Pilots knew that they could never match the speed of their opponents, with even German bombers being faster than their P.11cs. The fighter was already nimble, and its loaded weight of a mere 3,968 lb (1,799 kg) meant it could spring some nasty surprises on the Germans.

First, in attacking German bombers, the Poles would lance into bomber formations from head on, since they could not keep pace with the Germans otherwise. They also learned that by gaining altitude, they could dive down onto the German bombers, matching their speed. Within two days, the Poles had downed twenty-one enemy aircraft. These tactics would help them take their toll of Germany's best bombers. In terms of defending against the Bf 109 and Bf 110 fighters, the Poles adapted quickly. The slow speed was, in fact, potentially an advantage since it gave the P.11c a better turning circle. The Poles would allow enemy fighters to close on them from behind, then turn sharply and quickly, so the Germans were forced to make their broader turns to compensate. The P.11c, bravely piloted, could turn in a tight enough circle to come up behind the enemy and fire a burst or two before the enemy Messerschmitts managed to complete a turn.

At the start of the war, some of the P.11s were deployed as patrol aircraft along the border with the USSR, a role the PZL was unsuited for as it only had a patrol duration of forty-five minutes to an hour. Famed pilot Janusz Żurakowski took to tinkering with the design to improve this, adjusting fuel mixtures and settings. He also fell in love with the plane's agility, and it was known as 'Bee' amongst the pilots of his unit for its nimbleness. When war came, however, Żurakowski and the pilots of the Pursuit Brigade were more than ready around Warsaw.

The Germans immediately launched what they termed Der Spaziergang über Warsaw (Stroll over Warsaw), the P.11s of the brigade intercepted and shot down six Heinkel He 111 bombers, and one Sub-Lieutenant Borowski of 113 Eskadra brought down a Bf 109. The cost to the Poles was a single P.11. The Poles would lose a total of three more P.11s later that afternoon in a second attack, where the escorting fighters were able to intercept them before they hit the bombers, but they took two more 109s with them. Overall, in the first six days of the war, the Fighter Brigade shot down forty-seven planes, but had to be withdrawn from around the capital by attrition.

For an obsolete little fighter, overwhelmed by enemy numbers, the result should have been a clear-cut victory for German aerial arms. It was absolutely not so. The P.11c would shoot down 124 aircraft, while losing a 114 of its numbers to all causes. The lack of replacements meant, however, that the effort could not be sustained; two weeks into the German invasion, the P.11 was offering only light resistance. Ultimately, there were simply too few fighters to adequately defend Poland as needed, and the scattering of units that had preserved the plane also meant slow and difficult command and control.

Nevertheless, the P.11c and its brave pilots fought as long as they could, many flying their aircraft into neighbouring, neutral countries. The planes were interned, but the pilots would make their way to France and England where they would cost the Luftwaffe dearly. The summation of the PZL P.11c's story, then, is of yet another aircraft that bravely fought on despite its obsolescence. It is a story of bravery against impossible conditions, and a story well worth remembering.

A solitary PZL P.11c survives today, and is housed at the Polish Aviation Museum in Krakow. There is a fascinating story as to how this PZL came to be in the museum's possession. A damaged P.11c, which had been forced down, formerly belonging to the 121st Squadron, was shipped to Berlin, full of damage to the wings and engine. This war trophy was taken by Hermann Goering and placed in the German Air Museum, surviving the bombing of that museum by the British in 1943. The P.11c was loaded onto a train, managing to remain intact, and shipped back into Poland, where it was later found by the Soviets. It finally made it to the Krakow museum in 1963, and for twenty-five years remained in a decayed state, until PZL undertook a full restoration in the 1980s. It was an interesting process, and the odds against the P.11 surviving were long. Yet it still remains and can be viewed by the public as a testament and memorial to Polish bravery in the air.

36

PZL.37 Łoś

PZL did not produce just fighters. While it was designing and producing nimble fighters that would fight against all odds and despite their own obsolescence, they were also creating new and advanced designs. It was, in short, also producing bombers, and the mainstay of the Polish bomber fleet would be the PZL.37 Łoś ('Moose'). The Moose would also serve in minor part as part of the Romanian air force, but it will be best remembered for its brief service against the Germans in 1939. Forced into unplanned roles, the bombers would suffer heavy losses as they threw themselves, unescorted, against the oncoming German onslaught. If anything is worthy of remembrance, such bravery in the face of all odds most certainly is.

Specifications

First Flight: 1936
Powerplant: Two Bristol Pegasus XX radial engines, 970 hp each.
Armament: Three WZ 37 0.312-inch (7.92-mm) observer's machine guns, up to 5,690 lb (2,580 kg) of bombs.
Top Speed: 277 mph (445 kph)
Range/Service Ceiling: 1,615 miles (2,600 km), 23,000 feet (7,000 metres)
Dimensions: Length 42 feet 5 inches (12.92 metres), height 16 feet 9 inches (5.1 metres), wingspan 58 feet 10 inches (17.93 metres)
Number Built: 120+

The PZL.37 Łoś would prove to be the most modern design with which Poland went to war. It was designed in the mid-1930s by Jerzy Dąbrowski, and would go through two prototypes, though both would have substantial features in common. The aircraft was unusually compact and also very streamlined. The first prototype featured a single-fin tail design, which was replaced in the second prototype by the twin rudders that would be featured in all the production examples. The first prototype would fly in June 1936, and the aircraft that went into production surely ranked as one of the best medium bombers in the world.

While the wings were advanced enough to be considered precursors to the laminar flow wings that would follow, the similarities were largely the result of good fortune. However, there was another major benefit; the resulting aircraft profile had less drag than anticipated, and the 'A' versions had 10 per cent more speed than had been planned on. For its small size the design could also carry an unusually high payload at a decent range. The bombload was, in fact, nearly half of the aircraft's unloaded weight. The design also handled well in the air, with no problems being reported in its overall performance. Perhaps the type's only vice was an insufficient defensive armament of a mere three machine guns.

An order was placed for 180 production model by the Polish government. The first wave of these would be the PZL.37A, a total of ten aircraft that were built with the single tail surface. The next wave was designated the PZL.37A bis, with the twin tail. This batch would contain nineteen aircraft, and every aircraft came with a pair of Bristol Pegasus XII B radial engines, which were Polish-built under license. The main production variant, however, would be the PZL.37B, with the twin tails and the Pegasus XX engines. Production for the Polish Air Force began in 1937, and from the beginning PZL sought to gain foreign orders for this excellent bomber.

The bomber proved to be something of a sensation in the eyes of the world. When it went on display in 1938, it generated immediate interest and sales, in part owing to the fact that it won a prize at the 1938 Paris Air Show. Bulgaria purchased twelve aircraft as well as a production license, Romania purchased ten, and Yugoslavia purchased twenty. These were a purchase of the PZL.37C and 'D' aircraft, which were export models built with Gnome-Rhône 14N-0/1 and 14N-20/21 engines. Other countries such as Denmark, Estonia, Finland, and Iran also were interested, though in the case of the latter nations, the Poles ultimately declined owing to what was termed a lack of production abilities, as war was by then looming large. As such, Poland had to concentrate its limited production for domestic use.

The first of the bombers meant for Poland began to arrive in 1938. With production somewhat slowed by foreign orders, only ninety of this excellent bomber had been delivered to the Polish forces by September 1939, and a mere thirty-six of these were operational. While the operational aircraft were dispersed when war came, the aircraft that were yet to arrive from training were not so lucky. The training unit aircraft, and those at Małaszewicze air base in eastern Poland were meant to form a second operational bomber unit, but these aircraft were caught on the ground by the Luftwaffe and destroyed. This is where the legend of the Polish air force being destroyed on the ground may have had its genesis.

The thirty-six bombers in operation could not count on replacement and replenishment either. A total of perhaps ten were delivered to counter attrition, not enough to keep pace with losses, ultimately. And thirty-six bombers were entirely too few aircraft to stem the massive German tide that overwhelmed Poland in that dark September of 1939. It certainly did not help that the crews had not had the time to properly train in the use of the aircraft, nor was an advanced bomber likely to do well from the primitive fields that it would occupy.

One source, in summarising the problems the PZL.37 faced on the eve of war, stated:

> The training of the crews was uneven. The crews of the Łoś bomber were just equipping with the new plane and some 'bugs' had yet to be corrected. In particular, there was

trouble with the retractable landing gear. The maintenance crews were also still getting acquainted with a plane that was more modern and more advanced, and, therefore, more complicated than those to which they were accustomed.

Peszke, p. 84

The bombers were organised into the Bomber Brigade as part of the Lotnictwo Dyspozycyne (strategic aviation force). A total of four squadrons were equipped with the bomber—211, 212, 216, and 217. Initial strategy had been composed with a view towards strategic objectives being attacked within Germany, but in the event this was not carried out and the bombers were used exclusively to try to stem the tide with more tactical bombing within Poland itself. These bombers were destined to fly without any backup. The Poles had been scheduled to receive Fairey Battle light bombers from Britain to augment the PZL.37s, but these had not arrived before war was declared nor were they delivered afterwards. Also undelivered were the foreign fighter planes that the Poles had requested to escort the bombers, which were supposed to be Hawker Hurricanes from Britain and Morane-Saulnier M.S. 406 fighters from France. With the PZL fighters scattered to avoid the attentions of the Luftwaffe, the Łoś would be flying on its own.

This situation should have been one that resulted in nothing but tragedy, but if the Germans expected an easy time of it from these outnumbered bombers, they were in for a surprise. The Poles operated their bombers fearlessly in the event, making their bombing runs against advancing German columns. These attacks had an effect far out of proportion to what might be expected for their numbers. Several German columns were held up for a number of days, but given the pitifully small amount of bombers could not slow the German offensive. Their greatest achievement, however, is worth mentioning. On 4 September, they sprung upon the 3rd and 4th Panzer Divisions. The Polish attacks threw the panzers into confusion, and ended up costing the divisions 28 per cent of their strength.

Despite its light armament, the Łoś also proved capable of defending itself, with its gunners claiming two Bf 109E fighters. Unfortunately, twelve of these excellent medium bombers were shot down by the enemy, and one was tragically shot down by a Polish anti-aircraft battery. As the Germans advanced deep into Poland, this attrition, damage, and the overrunning of air fields ensured that the Łoś had little more role to play in the course of the campaign.

Despite their brave efforts, many factors ultimately brought the Bomber Brigade low. By the 7th, communication was becoming difficult, with frequent breaks between Polish units and their command structure. At the same time, upkeep became a critical problem, since the heavy duty maintenance companies needed for the aircraft had not been mobilised in time to get them into position before combat started and restricted their movements. Between the 10th and 17th, the unit essentially fell to pieces as the retreat meant that its units, including the PZL.37 squadrons, were moved to landing strips further to the south-east, where the obtaining of supplies and spare parts became nearly impossible.

The PZL.37, in addition to the older, lighter Karaś bombers, had still achieved a substantial result—the Bomber Brigade had dropped a total of 378,000 lb (171,458 kg) of ordnance on the Germans, and this despite the fact that the Łoś never carried its full bombload. A bomber that could drop a stunning tonnage of bombs given its weight was prevented in doing so by supply difficulties and the rapid advance of the campaign. The PZL.37s flew 100 bombing missions before two invasions made its work impossible, with the other aircraft carrying out another 130, but, owing to the terrible conditions and the fact that the bombers flew unescorted, the Bomber Brigade suffered a loss of 81 per cent of its operational strength in a campaign that, for them, lasted seventeen days.

Thirty-nine Łoś bombers would ultimately either escape to, or wind up in, Romania after the Soviet Union invaded Poland from the east, where the arriving aircraft were impounded by order of the Romanian government. These aircraft would be incorporated in to the Romanian air force and would go on to see combat in the Soviet Union. These aircraft may have been reinforced from aircraft the Germans captured at the PZL factory airfield. Ultimately, what few PZL.37 bombers survived after long service were destroyed in an air raid in September 1944. The Hungarian Air Force ambushed them on the ground at Câmpia Turzii airfield and destroyed all but two of them. These last two were used as target tugs by the Romanian air force until the early 1950s.

Even more than the PZL P.11c, the story of the Łoś bomber was one of being overwhelmed by the enemy. Although too few to alter the outcome of the battle, they carried on, launching daring raids on the enemy ground forces. It was also, when it took to the skies, one of the most advanced medium bombers in the world. With an excellent design, and brave pilots, the PZL.37 Łoś still did remarkable service for Poland in the worst of circumstances. Ultimately, it was an advanced aircraft that came too late to achieve the result it might have. Nevertheless, the type was employed with bravery, achieving success against terrible odds.

The PZL.37 is often written as PZL P.37, which is technically inaccurate, as the 'P' was kept for Zygmunt Puławski fighter designs.

There are no original PZL.37s that survive, but two replicas do exist. One is on display at the PZL factory at Mielec, while the other replicates a downed bomber and is located in the forest at Dłutówek, on the spot marking the crash site of a wartime PZL.37 bomber.

37

Savoia-Marchetti SM.79

The Italian Sparviero ('Sparrowhawk') is perhaps one of the biggest surprises of the war. The wood and metal design would serve everywhere the Regia Aeronautica fought, starting in Spain, and would remain in Italian service until 1952. While her hump would earn her the nickname 'Gobbo Maledetto', or 'damned hunchback', the Sparviero would prove to be an outstanding Italian design of the war, and was Italy's most-produced bomber. It would be perhaps Italy's most-famed contribution to the air war. The SM.79 would see service as a transport, a bomber, and most successfully as a torpedo bomber. Like Victor Hugo's more-famed French hunchback, the Sparviero would create an enduring legacy.

Specifications

(Note: Data is for the SM.79-I)

First Flight: 1934
Powerplant: Three Alfa-Romeo 128-RC18 radial engines, 860 hp each.
Armament: Two Breda-SAFAT 0.5-inch (12.7-mm) machine guns, two optional 0.303-inch (7.7-mm) lateral machine guns, one MG 151 20-mm forward-firing cannon, 2,645 lb (1,200 kg) of bombs, or two 17.72-inch (450-mm) torpedoes.
Top Speed: 286 mph (460 kph)
Range/Service Ceiling: 1,615 miles (2,600 km), 24,600 feet (7,500 metres)
Dimensions: Length 53 feet 2 inches (16.2 metres), height 13 feet 6 inches (16.2 metres), wingspan 66 feet 3 inches (20.2 metres)
Number Built: 1,240

Savoia-Marchetti had an interesting history of producing capable and sometimes unusual trimotor designs for Italy. The original purpose that the aircraft was designed for was as a transport and air racer, originally conceived of by the Italian government as something to establish national pride. Fascism, either in its Italian or German forms, placed a huge value on propaganda related to technology, and aviation was a critical part of this. Every feat performed by fascist arms was something that could be trumpeted to increase popularity domestically, and to attempt to intimidate foreign rivals.

An early Savoia-Marchetti SM.79. (*Courtesy of the Ron Dupas Collection, 1000aircraftphotos.com*)

In the case of the Savoia-Marchetti trimotor, however, Italy certainly got what it paid for. The aircraft that would become the SM.79 was meant to redeem Italian pride after Italian floatplanes were not ready for the final Schneider Cup race, which Mussolini had badly wanted to win. The trimotor would end up doing far more than that, but the design itself that resulted from this mix of practicality and pride was a curious combination of old and new.

It was a low-wing monoplane design, with retractable landing gear, which was a modern feature, even if the tail wheel did not retract. The fuselage had a steel, tubular skeleton covered in the forward section by duraluminium. In the upper fuselage section, construction was of mixed duraluminium and plywood, and all other fuselages were fabric covered—a throwback to older times. The wings were all wood, and relatively small in total size, which was compensated with leading-edge slats and trailing edge flaps. Internally, they were made of three plywood or spruce spars, linked by plywood ribs and then further covered in a plywood skin.

The first aircraft flew in 1934, officially given a civilian designation of SM.79P. It was an eight-seat passenger aircraft. This interesting combination of design elements certainly satisfied the need for glory: it would set twenty-six speed and distance records before Italy's war began in 1940. The first of these records was set on 2 August 1935 when the prototype flew from Rome to Italian Eritrea in twelve hours, with a brief Cairo stop-over. The SM.79P competed in the 1937 Istres–Damascus–Paris race, a long run from France to Syria and then back again. Six of the entrants would be SM.79Ps. Given the type's already demonstrated capabilities, the only real competition for the Savoia-Marchetti design would be a de Havilland Comet and a Caudron C.641. The result, however, more than justified the trimotor—the first three places were swept by the SM.79P. As an aside, the Comet would eventually be developed into the almost all-wood Mosquito of legendary fame.

The type had always been planned with an eye towards it becoming a bomber, and the second prototype was built as such, flying in 1935. It proved satisfactory and was slated for production as the SM.79-I. The main changes to create the bomber version were the replacement of the prototype's engines with Alfa Romeo 126 radial engines, and a large ventral gondola for the bombardier. The type also had a machine gun mounted in the fairing above the cockpit, forward firing, as well as a second firing backwards from the dorsal bump that would give the aircraft its famed nickname. Full-scale production began in October 1936, and by the time it ceased in June 1943, over 1,217 of this remarkable trimotor would be built, making it easily one of Italy's most important wartime aircraft.

These aircraft would receive their baptism of fire in the Spanish Civil War, despite the conclusion of many that the trimotor was already an obsolete concept. Here, these aircraft would help to set a dark precedent for what was to come. They were sometimes used to bomb cities, killing something on the order of 2,700 civilians—it was a small foretaste of what the Second World War would have in store. The first interception of the type came in October 1937, when three Sparviero were attacked by Polikarpov I-16 fighters. Despite bullets striking the fuel tanks, all three made it back to base, and subsequent attacks failed to down other Sparviero, and few were known to be lost in the conflict overall. Overall, it came to be known as an exceptional aircraft, which was fast, rugged, and particularly manoeuvrable for a bomber of its size. Naturally enough, as a result of all of these factors, the SM.79's performance as a bomber over Spain generated a good deal of foreign interest in the design. Yugoslavia purchased forty-five of them, and Brazil and Iraq also made purchases. These latter two sales, however, were of a twin-engined version, dubbed the SM.79B. Romania would also purchase this latter version.

In-flight Savoia-Marchetti SM.79. (*Courtesy of the Ron Dupas Collection, 1000aircraftphotos.com*)

They would also take the SM.79JR, a version that came with a pair of Junkers Jumo 211Da engines. These would come to serve on the Eastern Front.

The Regia Aeronautica, however, stuck to the trimotor design. This is not to say that they did not improve it, however. The engines were upgraded through progressive models, ultimately coming to mount the Piaggio P.XI RC40 engines, which generated 1,000 hp each. These aircraft were destined to become the workhorse of the Italian fleet, serving in every Italian theatre of war. The aircraft was known to be easily maintained, and its high manoeuvrability made it a favourite with pilots and crews. The wood and fabric construction, however, would mean the type was always vulnerable to fire, which would be a drawback. While Spanish combat had not revealed this flaw, the heavier weaponry of the aircraft it would face after 1940 would.

By 1939, the type was also available as a torpedo bomber, the SM.79-II. This role had sprung out of trials begun in 1937 at Gorizia, with the aircraft redesigned to launch a single 450-mm (17.7-inch) torpedo from an offset rack underneath the fuselage. On occasion, the type also carried a second torpedo, which was quite the potential punch against ships for a single aircraft. Even the Luftwaffe, normally dismissive of Italian aviation, recognised the Sparviero's abilities and studied closely from their Axis partner in the art of torpedo bombing.

When war came, the Sparviero was Italy's mainstay, ready to operate in the close-support, medium bomber, torpedo bomber, and transport roles. They had been built in heavy numbers for Italian industry, and equipped a total of fourteen Stormos when Italy went to war in 1940. The anti-shipping role took early precedence, with aircraft of the 9th and 46th Stormos attacking French shipping in the Riviera from 13 June onwards.

A small number of Sparviero served in Ethiopia, trying to stem the tide of the British advance there. There, in combat against older Gloster Gladiators, the type proved that, so long as it did not catch on fire, it could be relatively difficult to defeat, often surviving fighter assaults and returning to base damaged but intact. There were never enough of the aircraft, that far from the heart of the Italian empire, to stem the tide.

Over Malta, however, the aura that the Sparviero had would begin to lose its lustre against the redoubtable Gloster Gladiators and Hawker Hurricanes. The British craft employed superior tactics that negated Italian numerical superiority, and they started to take their toll of the SM.79. The Sparviero also operated in Libya, though in relatively limited numbers and with correspondingly slight success. It would also fight in Greece and over Crete, though the Royal Air Force would constantly dog its steps.

These were all, however, instances of the Sparviero serving as a conventional medium bomber. In the role of torpedo bomber, it would be significantly more successful and play merry hob with Allied shipping. It proved to be very capable of striking Allied warships from destroyers all the way up to battleships and aircraft carriers, many of these strikes requiring at best lengthy dockyard stays to repair the damage—though quite a few Italian strikes on British warships happened during the convoy delivery to Malta known as Operation Pedestal in 1942. As 1941 progressed, however, their use against merchant shipping became successful as well, hitting and sinking merchant ships while losing relatively few of their own aircraft. The total score for 1941 told a fairly good story for the Italians. Sparviero sank nine ships and damaged several others, losing a total of fourteen torpedo bombers. This was a fairly economical loss to the damage caused and was the best year for Italian torpedo bombing.

The greatest flaw in the employment of the Sparviero was that it was highly unusual for even half the aircraft to be available for flight at any given time. Italian support and maintenance was highly inadequate to the aircraft's needs, which meant that only relatively small numbers were used in any single operation in any single place. As time progressed, perhaps predictably, the effectiveness of the Sparviero decreased. This had much to do with weight of numbers, but also with the fact that anti-aircraft defences for aircraft kept increasing, and the Sparviero had no radar, meaning that even night attacks the Sparviero had to find and hit ships visually, and was opposed by ships with radar and increasingly powerful fighter cover.

With poor service and combat damage, the number of aircraft available dwindled. Despite its long production run and generally limited combat loss, only thirty-six operational Sparviero were on hand when Italy surrendered in July 1943. Following the Armistice, the Sparviero continued to serve with Italian forces on either side of the divide, both with the Co-Belligerent forces supporting the Allies, and with Mussolini's rump state.

Those fighting for Mussolini included the new production SM.79-III, a slight improvement over its fellows. These first saw action in opposing the landings at Anzio, though during the campaign losses began to escalate appallingly. Through attrition, the numbers of Sparviero bombers declined rapidly, with the last victory of the type being recorded in December 1944 when the last two flying Sparviero sank a 5,000-ton ship in the Adriatic.

In the post-war world, the Sparviero continued to serve, mainly because the aircraft in service as transports, trainers, and drone-control aircraft survived the war. They lingered in Italian service until 1952. Indeed, the Sparviero even managed one last foreign order. The Lebanese Air Force bought three aircraft, which soldiered on until at least 1959, a remarkable longevity for a trimotor aircraft.

The SM.79 Sparviero was an aircraft that seemed to surpass the limitations of its design as well as the time in which it was built. It was a world-beater when it was designed, but like so many Italian designs it was beginning to face obsolescence in the face by the time war was declared. Nevertheless, it performed magnificently despite numerous limitations on its effectiveness, not the least of which was inefficient and limited ground support. It is difficult to picture any aircraft succeeding under the conditions faced by the Sparviero, and the fact that it remained in service after the war testifies to the fact that it was a design that remained useful, despite age and obsolescence and the world passing the trimotor by.

There are two intact Sparviero aircraft. The first can be found at the Gianni Caproni Museum, located at Trento in Northern Italy. The second is to be found in the Italian Air Force Museum in Vigna di Valle, Rome. There is a third, however. A crashed SM.79 is preserved as if it were still in its crash site, and this can be found at the Volandia Park and Museum in Somma Lombardo, also in Northern Italy.

38

Vought OS2U Kingfisher

The role of the seaplane in the Second World War is all too often forgotten. There are, after all, so many stories to tell that such planes get pushed to the periphery. Yet the seaplanes and flying boats played a critical role during the war as transports, bombers, and reconnaissance aircraft. Some, like the PBY Catalina, would achieve enduring fame and be instantly recognisable to aviation enthusiasts. Others, like the Martin Mars, continue to serve to this day as firefighters. Still others would help Japan secure its vast island empire, providing air support to locations far too small or too remote for the construction of airfields. Amongst all these, the Vought Kingfisher needs to take its rightful place in our historical memory. It outlived its first successor, and was only supplanted in 1944, by which time it had done its duty as the US Navy's main shipboard observation aircraft, and further creating a legacy as a rescue craft, sometimes under unique and daring circumstances.

Specifications

First Flight: 1938
Powerplant: Pratt & Whitney R-985-AN-2 radial engine, 450 hp
Armament: To M1919 Browning 0.3-inch (7.62-mm) machine guns, up to 650 lb (295 kg) of bombs.
Top Speed: 164 mph (264 kph)
Range/Service Ceiling: 805 miles (1,296 km), 13,000 feet (3,950 metres)
Dimensions: Length 33 feet 10 inches (10.31 metres), height 15 feet 1.5 inches (4.61 metres), wingspan 35 feet 11 inches (10.95 metres)
Number Built: 1,519

The United States Navy had been relatively late to the concept of ship-borne aircraft. When the American 6th Battle Squadron arrived to reinforce the British Grand Fleet at Scapa Flow in 1917, they were quite surprised to find that every major British warship down to the size of cruisers came equipped with at least one aircraft for scouting—a concept the Americans had not adopted. They did not long remain behind, however.

In 1919, the US Navy began to carry out tests with aircraft as part of the arsenal of their capital warships, establishing that aircraft spotting increased the accuracy of battleship fire beyond 10 miles by a staggering 200 per cent. By 1925, the Navy had enshrined the concept of aerial gun spotting. It became a core part of how the fleet would operate, and, by the 1930s, the United States had equipped many of its ships with biplane scout aircraft. This number included equipping every single one of the fleet's battleships with catapult-mounted aircraft, though the cruiser-carried aircraft were focused on long-range scouting, given the differences in the roles of the ships. The arrival of monoplane fighters offered new opportunities both in terms of aircraft capability, as well as opportunities to sell designs to the Navy.

In 1937, the US Navy Bureau of Aeronautics issued a requirement to manufacturers to present them with designs for a new scout aircraft to equip the battleships and cruisers of the fleet. Three designs were ultimately submitted. The Naval Aircraft Factory produced the XOSN-1 biplane of mixed fabric and metal construction. Stearman also produced a biplane, of a similar construction. Their design, the XOSS-1, had the unique feature of being able to fit both floats and conventional landing gear.

Both aircraft were functional, but conventional, and the Bureau was dissatisfied with this. They turned their attention to the third design, submitted by Vought-Sikorsky. The design was labelled the XOS2U-1, with an internal designation of Model VS310, and had been supervised by Vought engineer Rex B. Beisel, who would later become the company's general manager. Beisel's design was a two-seat monoplane that was mostly metal, though it featured the fairly standard 1930s design feature of fabric-covered control surfaces. The design also featured a radial engine, a spacious cockpit, and a large 'glasshouse' over the rear of the fuselage and over the main float, making for excellent visibility. The design had some advantages that were not at first apparent. The design used spot welding, which meant that production would be significantly quicker, and the design would be easier to repair once in service. Additionally, the resulting airframe was very durable, able to withstand the stresses of many catapult launches—an operation involving quite a bit of force—and also could survive landings in even rough weather conditions.

The wing was perhaps the most remarkable feature of the aircraft, giving the Kingfisher a very unique ability. The wings were constructed with a broad-chord wing design. This came with large trailing edge flaps that spanned the entire length of the wing, which ensured that the Kingfisher would have a superb ability to get airborne at low speeds. There were also spoilers on the upper wing to help provide control for rolling. The overall result of all of this was an aircraft that could become airborne at a mere 55.6 mph (89.47 kph).

The Bureau was impressed, and issued a contract on 19 March 1937. This contract called for a single prototype to be built, which took to the air with wheels in March 1938, and the float version flew on 19 May. It was delivered in August for navy testing, after which it was handed over to the USS *West Virginia* for catapult trials. It successfully completed both of the trial sessions, and Vought was awarded a contract for fifty-four aircraft in late May 1939. The first production machines had been assigned to their duty stations by the end of 1940, with the first ship-based aircraft going aboard the USS *Colorado*.

The majority of this first batch of aircraft, designated OS2U-1, were distributed mainly between the Alameda NAS Battle Force, the Pensacola Naval Air Station, and most notably to the Pearl Harbor Battle Force. The OS2U-1 had a slightly newer engine, and some other minor changes to the shape of the aircraft, including a new float and the mount of a direction finding loop. The next development would be the OS2U-2, which became available before the OS2U-1 had even completed delivery. There would be 158 of this version, and this version concentrated on the more outwardly invisible changes. First and foremost was the addition of self-sealing fuel tanks, armour plating around vulnerable areas, and additional fuel tanks.

Most of these aircraft would be allocated to any number of US inshore patrol squadrons that would be produced, with the US Navy ultimately creating thirty total squadrons featuring the Kingfisher. These initially carried out what were termed 'neutrality patrols' before the United States entered the war. The last version of the aircraft to see service during the war would be the OS2U-3, which was in every way the best model. This craft was authorised as part of the Two-Ocean Naval Expansion Act, part of a major expansion plan for the US Navy. A thousand Kingfishers were authorised, and over 970 of them were manufactured, with deliveries starting in late May 1941. This aircraft was meant to service in both Army and Navy service, which meant that it came with numerous interchangeable

A Vought OS2U on the launching ramp of a US warship. (*Courtesy of the National Naval Air Museum*)

components to simplify the supply of parts to both services. The only other real change was the addition of more armour to the design, which brought down the maximum speed a little bit, but besides that had little impact on performance. It also came with increased fuel capacity and a switch to either the normal AN-2 or and AN-8 engine, depending on which batch it was. The last Kingfisher had been produced by September 1942.

Thanks to Lend-Lease, the Kingfisher would also be supplied to the British as well as the Royal Australian Air Force. These started to be shipped out in May 1942, employed in various duties and services—reconnaissance, scouting for the fleet, gunnery spotting, anti-submarine patrolling, ship-to-shore communications, and rescue of downed airmen. There was a total of 100 Kingfishers chosen for this duty.

An early use in combat was during Operation Torch, with the OS2U scouting for the American fleet in case of combat with French forces. When the OS2U arrived, it became clear that the Vichy Forces defending North Africa were very ready to fight, and the OS2U called in gunnery from the USS *Massachusetts* upon the French battleship *Jean Bart*. This singular Kingfisher, with Thomas Dougherty at the controls and Robert Etheridge manning the radio, was forced down by a French fighter, with both men taken captive.

It also proved an excellent anti-submarine patrol aircraft. They were slow, true, but they could carry a good amount of bombs and be up for a long time and the non-carrier operations of the Naval Aviation command were perennially short of aircraft. The Kingfishers that were part of the Inshore Patrol Squadrons flew many sorties up to 350 miles (563 km) from the coast. On 15 July 1942, with gunfire support from the USS *Unicoi*, a pair of Kingfishers dropped depth charges on the German submarine U-576 and sank her. They would continue to serve in this bombing role from Alaska all the way to the US Virgin Islands. The Kingfisher even took on shore installations in the Aleutian Islands. Perhaps most surprisingly of all, a Kingfisher even scored an aerial kill, downing a Mitsubishi Zero in February 1945 just off Iwo Jima. The greatest irony about the Kingfisher's service is that it never served in one of the ways in which it was originally conceived—the only time that battleships faced battleships at sea, in the Surigao Strait in late 1944, radar-controlled gunnery did the work of the Kingfisher, already replacing it in its designed role at this early stage.

Kingfishers also, perhaps unexpectedly, equipped American carriers as well. Seaplane carriers of the *Barnegat*-class carried them, but so did fleet carriers, namely *Hornet*, *Saratoga*, and *Wasp*, which used them as scout and utility aircraft. The Kingfisher also excelled as a trainer. Its handling was found to be so gentle and easy that, in its use as an intermediate trainer, the usual arrangement of installing dual controls was not followed. It was unnecessary, given that the Kingfisher was just that forgiving of pilot mistakes.

One pilot recalled the Kingfisher:

It was a very stable craft. Very slow, but very stable. They said you could loop it, but with those big floats, I wasn't going to push it. The Kingfisher was a good airplane for its purpose because you could see everything that was going on.

Noles, p. 69

The Kingfisher could stay airborne for nine hours, with a radius of 400 miles (643 km), and, given the Kingfisher's wide dispersal, it became the eyes of the Navy before radar replaced spotter aircraft in that role. It was well-liked by the ground troops and it helped to spot Japanese positions throughout the Pacific.

In the role of search and rescue, however, the Kingfisher did still more excellent service. It was well-noted for its abilities as a rescue craft. In November 1942, one Kingfisher even picked up Eddie Rickenbacker, the American First World War fighter ace who had been adrift at sea for twenty-four days. In another remarkable incident, in April 1944, a Kingfisher landed in Truk lagoon and picked up nine downed aviators, with each man holding onto the wings. Then the aircraft taxied out of the lagoon to the submarine USS *Tang*. Though the Japanese forces at Truk had been massively damaged, the island would remain in Japanese hands until the surrender in August 1945, so the Kingfisher's errand of mercy was quite the brave one.

The Kingfisher survived one successor, the Curtiss SOC Seagull, before it started to be replaced in the late days of the war by the Curtiss SC Seahawk. Ultimately, however, it was the advent of radar and the helicopter that spelt the end not just for the Kingfisher, but catapult aircraft in general. The end of the war wasn't the end of the Kingfisher, however. It continued to serve under other flags for several years thereafter, as the Kingfisher had also been exported to Australia, Chile, Cuba, the Dominican Republic, Mexico, and Uruguay.

The Vought OS2U Kingfisher, known as 'old, slow and ugly', did a great deal, in spite the slow speed of the aircraft. It was an example of what was, ultimately, a dying breed—a type of aircraft that was slowly being supplanted by events. In the meantime, however, the Kingfisher would carry on until the end of the war, carrying out rescues and reconnaissance missions of superb value to the fleet.

There is a grand total of eight Kingfishers that survive today. One example is awaiting restoration at Whale World in Albany, Australia. Another is located at the *Museo Nacional Aeronáutico y del Espacio de Chile*, at Santiago. A version with fixed landing gear is in Cuba, at the *Museo de la Revolución* in Havana. Five more are located in the United States. One is with the USS *Alabama* in Mobile, Alabama. A second is at the Smithsonian Air and Space Museum, while a third is at the National Naval Air Museum in Florida. A fourth is still mounted on a battleship, the USS *North Carolina*, in North Carolina, and the last is in storage at the Yanks Air Museum in California.

39

Westland Lysander

Perhaps one of the more recognisable inclusions in this book, the Westland Lysander fulfilled interesting roles during the war. Designed as an army co-operation and liaison aircraft, the Lysander would find itself involved (with great success) in a role that had all the hallmarks of British derring-do and cloak and dagger mystique. The Lysander's stunning short-field capabilities would make it the workhorse of clandestine operations, carving out a legend that would make the Lysander's story one of the more remarkable ones of the Second World War.

Specifications

First Flight: 1936
Powerplant: Bristol Mercury XX radial engine, 870 hp.
Armament: Two Browning 0.303-inch (7.7-mm) machine guns in wheel fairings, another Lewis 0.303-inch gun for the observer, plus potentially four 20-lb (9-kg) bombs under the rear fuselage, and optionally 227 lb (500 kg) of bombs on the stub-wings occasionally fitted.
Top Speed: 212 mph (341 kph)
Range/Service Ceiling: 600 miles (966 km), 21,500 feet (6,550 metres)
Dimensions: Length 30 feet 6 inches (9.29 metres), height 14 feet 6 inches (4.42 metres), wingspan 50 feet (15.24 metres)
Number Built: 1,786

The aircraft that would come to be beloved as the 'Lizzie' started as a new specification, A.39/34, which called for a new army co-operation aircraft to replace the aging Hawker Hector biplane. Little did Westland know that it was producing a design that would, perhaps more than any other, define the company's historical image and public memory. The specification wanted a new aircraft for army co-operation that had good STOL (short take-off and landing) capabilities, to give it maximum versatility in the field. The response from the chief designer, W. E. W. Petter, was in essence to 'keep it simple', an approach that would work spectacularly.

The design that Westland created to fulfil the requirement was unique, to say the least, and may be one of the most distinctive aircraft of the Second World War. The aircraft that would become the Lysander was a monoplane, but with the wing high and braced. The wheels were spatted and also very large, and the fuselage was strangely rotund with an emphasis placed on visibility. The structure of the aircraft was made up of a steel tubing skeleton, braced with wooden formers, the entire thing swathed in fabric. The uniquely shaped wing was something of a hybrid, a mixture of metal and fabric—the metal covering from the leading edge to the main spar, with fabric covering the rest. The leading edge also had slotted flaps, which gave the Lysander the unique and impressive ability to land or take-off at a mere 65 mph (104 kph). The gunner/observer's seat was designed to swing around as needed, and the gunner could double as a bombardier as there was a bomb sight facing downwards through the fuselage. The Lysander was also designed to both take and give punches, coming with self-sealing fuel tanks as well as two fixed forward-facing machine guns, which were mounted in the large wheel spats. The observer had access to another machine gun.

Work proceeded very rapidly, and the prototype was taken up for the first time by pilot Harald Penrose on 15 June 1936. The various marks that the aircraft went through would mainly be slight improvements with larger engines, reaching to the Mk IIIA, which came with a Mercury XXX engine and a pair of Browning machine guns in the rear cockpit for the gunner/observer.

The design was rapidly selected as the fulfilment of the specification, with the aircraft being ordered in late January 1937, and production beginning the next year. There were seven squadrons of Lysanders active with the Royal Air Force by the time it went to war in 1939. These would travel to France along with the British Expeditionary Force, experiencing what many have term the 'Phoney War', before the German invasion of France and the Low Countries. In this time the Lysander even managed to down a Heinkel 111, which had strayed into BEF airspace, in addition to normal duties.

When the onslaught came, however, the Lysanders would be badly mauled. The problem was, in the main, that the aircraft was designed to operate single and unescorted. This was all well and good, as the Lysander could perform superbly as an artillery spotter and reconnaissance aircraft—so long as the RAF ruled the skies. Unfortunately, when the Luftwaffe was swarming the skies in an attempt to establish supremacy, the Lysanders that were encountered were very vulnerable. The Lysander gunners ensured the enemy did not have it all their own way, accounting for six enemy aircraft, but the toll would be heavy indeed. As the campaign progressed and the British retreated towards Dunkirk, Lysanders were pressed into service dropping supplies and attacking German forward positions. Out of 174 Lysanders that arrived in France, eighty-eight were shot down with another thirty destroyed on the ground.

This prompted the Lysander's withdrawal from frontline operations, with aircraft being pushed into training and glider-towing duties. Elsewhere, it was used for air-sea rescue and the aircraft would see service in the Mediterranean and Middle East, sometimes as a light bomber. In Europe, however, the relegation was total. There it might have stayed, too, if it were not for the Lysander's absolutely superb STOL capabilities. The British would find another use for the Lysander, that of a clandestine operations aircraft.

In August 1941, training commenced in night-landings, with a view towards carrying out missions in Occupied France. The Lysander was thus reborn into a second life as one of the best clandestine aircraft ever constructed, dropping supplies to resistance cells in German-occupied Europe as well as both dropping off and extracting agents. By the time France had been liberated, Lysanders had delivered 293 agents to French soil, while bringing out more than 500—and in all that time they lost a mere three aircraft.

The first mission involved delivering an agent and extracting another from central France. The mission nearly came to naught when the returning agent was delayed by local police, but he made it to the landing area and the agents were exchanged, with the Lysander on the ground for a total of only four minutes. The take-off was destined to be rougher, however. The pilot aimed for a break in the trees that lined the field, which turned out to have telephone wires. The Lysander passed through without damage, but it returned to England trailing some of those wires.

One of the rare losses was when a Lysander was forced down by storm icing and ran into a ditch. The people involved made it back to England through other surreptitious means, but the Germans were alerted to the operations of the Westland aircraft in their territory. Yet they seemed unable to do much to stop the flights, with the only other losses being two sadly fatal crashes in England. In the main, these duties were carried out by No. 161 squadron, all through late 1941 until the Liberation of France. It was an astonishing effort, and the Lysander continued to operate in the covert role in the Mediterranean right up until the end of the war in Europe; it carried out sorties into Greece, Italy, as well as Yugoslavia, and in the same role those black-painted Lysanders even infiltrated behind Japanese lines until Japan's surrender. The aircraft was retired very shortly thereafter, in 1946, though it would continue for a short time longer in foreign hands.

The Westland Lysander is indeed the most famous of Westland's many aircraft, with the possible exception of some of the company's later helicopters. However, in terms of the Second World War, the Lysander stands apart. It was conceived for one role, although in the event it was found to be exceedingly vulnerable in that role, and in the process was given another role for which it proved to be nearly invulnerable. It was, and is, a curious set of circumstances, but the Lysander can call upon a brave and ultimately successful service history. From valiant, but doomed service in France, to spectacularly successful clandestine operations, the Westland Lysander wrote a proud page into the history books of aviation.

Of all the aircraft in this book, the Lysander has survived in the highest total numbers. Three Lysanders can be found in her native England, with one held at the RAF Duxford museum, another at Hendon, and a third—in flying conditions and beautiful night-time colours—is held by the Shuttleworth Collection. Westland itself was known to have a Lysander, but the author has been unable to trace it as of the time of writing. Another four Lysanders are to be found in the author's native Canada, one of which he had the pleasure to see in person at the Canadian Aviation and Space Museum in Ottawa. Another is held, in flying condition, at the Canadian Warplane Heritage Museum in Hamilton, and the third is at the Canadian Museum of Flight in Langley. The fourth is the most recently restored, held by Vintage Wings of Canada in Gatineau.

Two more Lysanders are to be found in the United States. One, naturally enough, is held by the Smithsonian in Washington, with another owned by the Fantasy of Flight Museum in Florida. Further afield, the Indian Air Force Museum in New Delhi has a Lysander, though it has been painted in fanciful colours. A last pair of Lysanders, one apparently still under restoration, are held by the Sabena Old Timers association in Zaventem.

40

Westland Welkin

The Westland Welkin is a superb example of a well-constructed technological solution to a problem that never, in point of fact, materialised. The project that resulted was a technological marvel, a leap forward in aircraft design that would be of crucial importance to aircraft that came thereafter, but is today mostly forgotten. Yet, by the time the Welkin first soared to amazing heights, it was faced by an utter lack of opposition in the skies over England. The result was an aircraft without a role, and as a result the Welkin never entered widespread service. Yet the aircraft remains an important example of a little-known area of Second World War aviation—the high-altitude war.

Specifications

First Flight: 1942
Powerplant: Two Rolls-Royce Merlin 76/77 liquid-cooled piston engine, 1,233 hp each.
Armament: Four Hispano 20-mm cannon
Top Speed: 385 mph (625 kph)
Range/Service Ceiling: 1,480 miles (2,380 km), 44,000 feet (13,420 metres)
Dimensions: Length 41 feet 6 inches (12.67 metres), height 15 feet 9 inches (4.8 metres), wingspan 70 feet (21.3 metres)
Number Built: 77 complete aircraft, 26 airframes without engines

Perhaps unusually, the Westland Welkin came into existence in response to the existence of another specific aircraft. The Junkers Ju 86 had first flown in 1934, constructed as a competitor to the Heinkel 111. In both testing and combat, the standard Ju 86 proved inferior to the He 111 and saw only limited production. However, in 1940 the Luftwaffe tested a new prototype, designation Ju 86P. The Ju 86P had longer wings, a pressurised cabin, and turbocharged Junkers Jumo engines. It was rated as having a service ceiling of 39,000 feet (12,000 metres), and could go even higher than that. By comparison, a Spitfire Mk V could ascend as high as 36,500 feet (11,125 metres). Thus the Germans considered the Ju 86P to be immune to fighter interception, and could carry out high-altitude bombing or photoreconnaissance with impunity. It was the existence of such a craft that prompted the development of the Westland Welkin.

The British Air Ministry issued a specification in 1940 for a high-altitude fighter to be a counter-aircraft, and Westland responded with designs for what was initially designated

The Westland Welkin in flight. (*Courtesy of the Jacques Trempe Collection, 1000aircraftphotos.com*)

the P.14. Designed by W. E. W. Petter, the aircraft would require an enormous new wing—the production models would speed aloft with a wingspan of 70 feet (21 metres). A major improvement over Westland's previous twin-engined design, the Whirlwind, was made by replacing the troublesome Peregrine engines with two Merlin engines, the superb engine synonymous both with high-performance and the Royal Air Force.

The vast majority of effort, however, would go into designing a pressurised cockpit, and this ultimately delayed matters. The Royal Air Force authorised two prototypes of the P.14 in 1941, but the first Welkin did not fly until late 1942. For its day, the Welkin was astonishingly advanced. Its electrical system alone was highly complex, taking an experienced electrician who knew the plane well over four hours to perform all the requisite pre-flight checks.

Despite this complexity, the Welkin was more than ready to fulfil its role—a role that had, by that time, already disappeared. In 1942, specially modified Spitfire Mk Vs had begun to intercept the high-flying Ju 86, which was subsequently withdrawn. Thus the Westland's reason for being had ceased to exist by the time it reached active service. The Welkin had been ordered into production 1943 after tests against a modified de Havilland Mosquito and another Welkin at up to 40,000 feet (12,190 metres), and in the end the RAF ordered 100 Welkin Mk Is, eighty of which were delivered by the time the contract was cancelled. None of them were issued to combat squadrons, instead a very small number were devoted to high-altitude research. The Welkin also proved to be not as manoeuvrable against other fighters as had been hoped for, as the Welkin ran into problems faced by all subsonic, high-altitude designs. While not perfect by any means, the Welkin provided invaluable knowledge and technical experience that would serve the British well, and the Welkin remained a secret project until the end of the war, though it was retired by the end of 1944.

A single Welkin was redesigned as a two-seater night fighter, complete with radar. This was designated the Welkin NF Mk II and was never ordered into production. There would be some use for Westland out of the experience, even if the aircraft did not reach the potential they might have wished. The experience with creating pressurised cockpits resulted in a contract to modify cockpits of around thirty Gloster Meteors for high-altitude work. A small consolation, perhaps, but at least the Welkin's work was not wasted.

People at the time understood this too. The magazine *Nature*, writing in July 1945 when the secret project became known to the public, noted the Welkin's importance and the apt fact that it was a Westland design:

> It is appropriate that this, the first stratosphere fighter to be adopted by the R.A.F. as a standard type, should have been designed and produced by the Westland Aircraft Co., which has specialised in the problem of high flying and was responsible, in pre-war years, for the equipment of the Mount Everest flying expedition. Many problems upon the design of pressure cabins have been solved in the experimental work on the 'Welkin'

A Westland Welkin Mk II, side view. Note the additional nose extension for radar. (*Courtesy of the Nico Braas Collection, 1000aircraftphotos.com*)

that will be equally important to civil aviation…. The temperature control has been found to be such that no special clothing was needed even at an outside temperature of -78°F.

Nature, July 1945

While it may seem like an out-of-place failure for the RAF, it is critical to note that this was at the time a developing area of warfare, as much theoretical as it was practical. As aircraft continued to gain higher and higher altitudes, the complexity of the aerial battlefield increased. The Welkin, though never entering service and never proving an unmitigated success, nevertheless was a step in the advancement of aviation knowledge, one mirrored by research and development amongst the other powers.

The British were not the only ones to develop a countermeasure aircraft to the Ju 86; the Soviet Union also deployed a modified Yakovlev fighter, designated Yak-9PD to counter the threat that, owing to events over England, never truly developed. It is believed that a handful of Yak-9PDs were developed, seeing limited service against high-altitude German aircraft.

Furthermore, the Germans developed their own high-altitude fighter as a counter aircraft. Work began in 1942 to prepare for the eventual attack of B-29 Superfortress bombers. The Blohm und Voss Bv155 would have had an incredible maximum altitude of 56,102 feet (16,950 metres). In this case, however, it was not the withdrawal of the craft's reason for existence that halted work. Only three were ever built as prototypes, with the end of the war halting already protracted design work. The second prototype, V2, is currently in storage at the Smithsonian's Gerber facility.

In addition, it is worth mentioning that the Westland Welkin was, in itself, the next step from another Westland design worthy of mention: the Westland Whirlwind. Conceived as a twin-engined heavy fighter, the Whirlwind was plagued by development problems with its Rolls-Royce Peregrine engines, and ultimately only saw limited service. Aside from a high approach and landing speed, it was praised by its pilots and gave good account of itself. Interestingly, it took part in the combat involved with the 'Channel Dash' of the German heavy cruisers *Gneisenau* and *Scharnhorst* in 1942.

Epilogue

What has been written here is but a partial story. Each of these aircraft, and indeed many, many others, have far more tales to tell. This book was a partial telling, but one that will hopefully spark interest in finding more, and with a bit of luck telling a few stories that you, the reader, have yet to hear.

The war saw many aircraft rise and fall, and they often would clash in titanic numbers in ways that, a few scant years before, nobody had even predicted could exist. The pace of change is utterly remarkable—a point that writing this book has reinforced for me personally. The transitional speed from biplanes to monoplanes to superior monoplanes to jet aircraft happened in an incredibly short span of time, vast technological change that was accelerated beyond all measure by the greatest conflict in human history.

We must never forget the very human cost, either. The people who flew and maintained these aircraft, the people who built them—all of these contributions were and are more important than any technical history could ever be. These were aircraft that were shaped by human hands, designed to be the best that technology and the minds of humankind could create. They represent a strange combination of dream and necessity, of national needs and the brilliance of human engineering. There is a terrible irony to the fact that the best and most creative minds tried to create aircraft that could rise higher and go faster than ever before, and then used them to destroy each other and human beings on the ground, in great number. The numbers of casualties were truly catastrophic. One estimate of the aircraft losses on the Eastern Front alone speak to 70,000 Soviet aircraft destroyed and 77,000 Axis aircraft. This says nothing about the casualties these aircraft caused, but this is merely one front—an example of the sheer slaughter of the skies.

It is difficult to reconcile these two things in the human mind. War is, in every way, the failure of humanity, a hell made manifest by our failings and historical mistakes. In some cases, it becomes necessary, or events have gained too much momentum to make the result be otherwise. On the other hand, creation can be our highest and greatest trait. That we can make something new, or refine something, that changes the course of events. This, in the end, is the general conclusion that one can reach regarding the air war—it unleashed terrible tragedy, tested the mettle of human beings, but also advanced human understanding of flight and airborne technology beyond any measure that anybody could have imagined before. It accelerated an already breakneck pace of development, even when the lessons it created were more cautionary tales.

Of the aircraft contained in these pages, however, we can come to certain conclusions. On the Axis side, most of these aircraft arrived far too late, or in too small of numbers, to make any meaningful impact on the course of the conflict. Even if they had, it is extremely doubtful that the historical outcome would have been any different, though people will always be fascinated by 'what ifs?'. This should not take away from the technical achievement of such aircraft, and some of the examples go a long way to countering stereotypical beliefs about the aerial prowess and technical innovation of nations such as Italy or Japan. In history, the simplistic view is almost always wrong, and there are almost always exceptions to the rule.

On the Allied side, the story is frequently that of utilising older, outdated designs until newer ones could be tested and brought into service, with varying degrees of success. Each nation had differing construction priorities and strategies, and this is reflected in its aircraft.

Lastly, I tried to be inclusive in my selections, to demonstrate that the frequently forgotten nations who participated in the war had vibrant and innovative aircraft industries of their own. My own journey into the field of lesser-known aircraft began this way, when I first discovered stories about the PZL P.11c, many years ago.

This work has been a long time in coming, and it has been a labour of love, as indeed this field tends to be for those who participate in it. In conclusion, then, I would like to thank you for your interest, your time, and most of all to say thank you to those of you reading this who participate in aviation. The restorers, mechanics, pilots, engineers, volunteers, museum staff, writers, artists, and enthusiasts who ensure that these stories are not forgotten. You not only keep these airplanes flying, you keep their stories alive. History is very definitely a story, a tale of people and events and developments that should be told with enthusiasm and thoroughly enjoyed.

The stories of these aircraft, of the people who flew and maintained them—and keep them so today—are all fascinating, and each is worthy of telling. It has been an honour to play a very small part in this particular story.

Bibliography

Books

Aldrich, R., *Witness to War: Diaries of the Second World War in Europe and the Middle East*, (London: Corgi Books, 2013)

Angelucci, E., and Matricardi, P., *World Aircraft: World War II, Volume I (Sampson Low Guides)*, (Maidenhead: Sampson Low, 1978)

Arena, N., Borgiotti, A., and Gori, C., *Savoia Marchetti SM 79 Sparviero*, (Modena: Mucchi editore, 1994)

Armitage, M., *The Royal Air Force: An Illustrated History*, (London: Brockhampton Press, 1998)

Axelrod, A., and Kingston, J., *Encyclopedia of World War II, Volume 1*, (New York: Infobase Publishing, 2007)

Barker, R., *The Epic of Flight: The RAF at War*, (Alexandria: Time-Life, Books, 1981)

Belcarz, B., *GC 1/145 in France 1940*, (Sandomierz, Poland/Redbourn, UK: Mushroom Model Publications, 2002)

Bergerud, E., *Fire in the Sky: The Air War in the South Pacific*, (Colorado: Perseus Books Group, 2000)

Berliner, D., *History's Most Important Racing Aircraft*, (South Yorkshire: Pen & Sword Aviation, 2013)

Bernád, D., *Rumanian Aces of World War 2 (Aircraft of the Aces 54)*, (Botley: Osprey Publishing, 2003)

Bishop, C., *The Encyclopedia of Weapons of World War II*, (New York: Friedman/Fairfax Publishers, 2002)

Boer, P. C., *The Loss of Java*, (Singapore: NUS Press, 2011)

Bourne, M., *The Second World War in the Air: The Story of Air Combat in Every Theatre of World War Two*, (Leicestershire: Matador, 2013)

Boyne, W. J., *Beyond the Wild Blue: A History of the United States Air Force, 1947-2007*, (New York: Macmillan Publishers, 2007)

Boyne, W., *Clash of Wings: World War II in the Air*, (New York: Touchstone, 1994); (ed.), *Air Warfare: An International Encyclopedia*, (California, ABC-CLIO Ltd, 2002)

Brew, A., *The Turret Fighters: Defiant and Roc*, (Wiltshire, UK: Crowood Press, 2002)

Brindley, J. F., *Caproni Reggiane Re 2001 Falco II, Re 2002 Ariete & Re 2005 Sagittario: Aircraft in Profile Vol. 13*, (Berkshire: Profile Publications, 1973)

Brotzu, E., Cosolo, G., and Garello, G., *Aerei Italiani nella 2° Guerra Mondiale: Caccia Assalto 3*, (Rome: Edizioni Bizzarri, 1972)

Canwell, D., and Sutherland, J., *Vichy Air Force at War: The French Air Force that Fought the Allies in World War II*, (South Yorkshire: Pen & Sword Aviation, 2011)

Cardona, E., and Markwick, R., *Soviet Women on the Frontline in the Second World War*, (New York: Palgrave Macmillan: 2012)

Carruthers, B., *Poland 1939: The Blitzkrieg Unleashed*, (Warwickshire: Coda Books Ltd, 2011)

Caygill, P., *Flying to the Limit: Testing World War II Single-Engine Fighter Aircraft*, (South Yorkshire: Pen & Sword Aviation, 2005)

Chant, C., *A Century of Triumph: The History of Aviation*, (New York: The Free Press, 2002)

Cull, B., and Shores, C., *Air War for Yugoslavia, Greece and Crete*, (London: Grub Street, 1987)

Cynk, J. B., *Polish Aircraft 1893-1939*, (London: Putnam & Company Ltd, 1971); *P.Z.L. P.37 Łoś (Aircraft in Profile number 258)*, (Windsor: Profile Publications Ltd, 1973)

Dahl, R., *The Wonderful Story of Henry Sugar and Six More*, (New York: Penguin Books Limited, 2011)

Dancey, P., *Boeing: Plane-Makers of Distinction*, (Lulu.com, 2013)

Danel, R., and Cuny, J., *Docavia n°4: le Dewoitine D.520*, (Paris: Editions Larivière, 1966)

Darling, K., *Vought Sikorsky OS2U Kingfisher*, (Vale of Glamorgan: Big Bird Aviation, 2009)

Davies, G., *From Lysander to Lightning: Teddy Petter, Aircraft Designer*, (South Carolina: The History Press, 2014)

Donald, D., (ed.), *Bombers of World War II*, (London: Brown Books, 1998)

Dressel, J., Griehl, M., and Menke, J., (ed.), Force, Dr E., (transl.), *Heinkel He 280*, (West Chester: Schiffer Military History, 1991)

Dunning, C., *Solo coraggio! La storia completa della Regia Aeronautica dal 1940 al 1943*, (Parma: Delta Editrice, 2000)

Evanier, M., *Blackhawk, Part 2*, (San Diego: Comic-Con International, 2000)

Fitzsimmons, B., (ed.), *The Illustrated Encyclopedia of 20th Century Weapons and Warfare*, (New York: Columbia House, 1967)

Fredriksen, J., *International Warbirds: An Illustrated Guide to World Military Aircraft, 1914-2000*, (California: ABC-CLIO Ltd, 2001)

Garello, G., *Il Piaggio P.108*, (Rome: Edizioni Bizzarri, 1973)

Garzke, W. H., and Dulin, R. O., *Battleships: Axis and Neutral Battleships in World War II*, (Annapolis: Naval Institute Press, 1985)

Gerrard, H., and Zaloga, S., *Poland 1939: The Birth of Blitzkrieg*, (Oxford: Osprey Publishing, 2002)

Gibbings, D., *A Quiet Country Town: A Celebration of 100 Years of Westland at Yeovil*, (South Carolina: The History Press, 2015)

Glass, A., *Polskie Konstrukcje Lotnicze Vol. 3*, (Sandomierz: Wydawnictwo Stratus, 2008)

Goñi, U., *The Real Odessa: Smuggling the Nazis to Perón's Argentina*, (London: Granta Books, 2002)

Gordon, Y., and Rigamant, V., *OKB Tupolev: A History of the Design Bureau and its Aircraft*, (Hinckley: Midland Publishing, 2005)

Gordon, Y., *Soviet Airpower in World War 2*, (Hinckley, England: Midland Publishing, 2008)

Graff, C., *Flying Warbirds: An Illustrated Profile of the Flying Heritage Collection's Rare WWII Aircraft*, (Minneapolis: Zenith Press, 2014); *Images of Aviation: Boeing Field*, (Charleston: Arcadia Publishing, 2008)

Gray, P. L., *No. 025—The Fokker D-VII—Profile Number 25*, (Leatherhead, England: Profile Publications, 1965)

Green, W., and Swanborough, G., *The Great Book of Fighters*, (St. Paul, Minnesota: MBI Publishing, 2001)

Green, W., *Warplanes of the Third Reich*, (North Hollywood: Galahad Publishing, 1990)

Griehl, M., and Dressel, J., *Heinkel He 177—277—274*, (Shrewsbury: Airlife Publishing 1998)

Griehl, M., *German Bombers over England, 1940-44*, (Barnsley: Frontline Books, 1999)

Grujic, Z., *Airforce of Serbia and Yugoslavia 1901-1994*, (Belgrade: Military book, 1997)

Gunston, B., *The Illustrated Directory of Fighting Aircraft of World War II*, (London: Salamander Books, 1988); *The Osprey Encyclopedia of Russian Aircraft 1875–1995*, (London: Osprey Publishing, 1995); *Tupolev Aircraft since 1922*, (Annapolis: Naval Institute Press, 1995)

Gustavsson, H., and Slongo, L., *Gloster Gladiator vs CR.42 Falco*, (Botley: Osprey Publishing, 2002)

Hata, I., Izawa, Y., and Shores, C., *Japanese Army Fighter Aces, 1931-45*, (Pennsylvania: Stackpole Books, 2012)

Herwig, D., and Rode, H., *Luftwaffe Secret Projects: Strategic Bombers 1935-1945*, (Leicester: Midland Publishing: 2000)

Higham, R., *Unflinching Zeal: The Air Battles over France and Britain, May-October 1940*, (Annapolis: Naval Institute Press, 2012); (ed.), *Why Air Forces Fail: The Anatomy of Defeat*, (Kentucky: University Press of Kentucky, 2006)

Hooftman, H., *Fokker G-1, Tweede druk (Nederlandse Vliegtuig Encyclopedie, deel 12)*, (Bennekom: Cockpit-Uitgeverij, 1981)

Jablonski, E., *The Epic of Flight: America in the Air War*, (Alexandria: Time-Life Books, 1982)

Jackson, R., *101 Great Bombers*, (New York: The Rosen Publishing Group, 2010); *Messerschmitt Me 109 A-D Series*, (Oxford: Osprey Publishing, 2015)

Jacobs, P., *Aces of the Luftwaffe: The Jagdflieger in the Second World War*, (Yorkshire: Frontline Books, 2014)

James, D. N., *Gloster Aircraft since 1917*, (London: Putnam & Company Limited, 1971); *Westland Aircraft since 1915*, (London: Putnam & Company Limited, 1991)

Janić, Č., and Petrović, O., *Short History of Aviation in Serbia*, (Beograd: Aerokomunikacije, 2011)

Johnson, E. R., *American Flying Boats and Amphibious Aircraft: An Illustrated History*, (North Carolina: McFarland & Company Inc., 2009)

Johnson, E. R., and Jones, L., *American Military Transport Aircraft since 1925*, (North Carolina: McFarland & Company, Inc., 2013)

Joseph, F., *The Axis Air Forces: Flying in Support of the German Luftwaffe*, (California: ABC-CLIO, LLC, 2012)

Kaplan, P., *Big Wings: The Largest Aeroplanes Ever Built*, (South Yorkshire: Pen and Sword Aviation, 2005)

Koehler, H. D., *Ernst Heinkel: Pionier der Schnellflugzeuge*, (Bonn: Bernard & Graefe, 1999)

Koskodan, K., *No Greater Ally: The Untold Story of Poland's Forces in WWII*, (Oxford: Osprey Publishing, 2009)

Lake, J., *The Great Book of Bombers: The World's Most Important Bombers from World War II*, (St Paul: MBI Publishing Company, 2002)

Lewis, P., *The British Bomber since 1914*, (London: Putnam & Company Limited, 1980)

Lucabaugh, D., and Martin, B., *Grumman XF5F-1 & XP-50 Skyrocket, Naval Fighters Number Thirty-one*, (California: Ginter Books, 1995)

Lyman, R., *Iraq 1941: The Battles for Basra, Habbniya, Fallujah and Baghdad*, (Oxford: Osprey Publishing, 2006)

Manchester, W., *The Arms of Krupp*, (Boston: Little Brown and Company, 1968)

Maslov, M. A., *Polikarpov I-15, I-16 and I-153 Aces*, (Oxford: Osprey Publishing, 2010)

Matricardi, P., *Aerei Militari: Bombardieri e Transporti*, (Milan: Mondadori Electa Editori, 2006); *Aerei Mililtari: Bombardieri e da Trasporto 2*, (Milano: Electa Mondadori, 2006); *Aerei Militari: Caccia e Ricognitori*; (Milan: Mondadori Electa, 2006)

McNiece, M., and Murphy, J., *Military Aircraft, 1919-1945: An Illustrated History of Their Impact*, (California: ABC-CLIO, 2008)

Mičev, S., (ed.), *Slovak National Uprising 1944*, (Múzeum SNP, Banská Bystrica, 2009)

Miller, R., Time-Life Editors, *The Epic of Flight: The Soviet Air Force at War*, (Alexandria: Time-Life Books, 1985)

Mohan, P. V. S. J., *Westland Lysander in Indian Air Force Service*, (Hyderabad: Warbirds India, 2010)

Molesworth, C., *57th Fighter Group: 'First in the Blue'*, (Oxford: Osprey Publishing Limited, 2011)

Mondey, D., *The Concise Guide to Axis Aircraft of World War II*, (New York: Bounty Books, 1996); *The Hamlyn Concise Guide to Axis Aircraft of World War II*, (London: Bounty Books, 2006)

Motum, J., *The Putnam Aeronautical Review, Volume 2*, (London: Conway Maritime Press Limited, 1990)

Murray, W., *An Interview with Chuck 'Blackhawk' Cuidera*, Comic Book Marketplace No. 68 (Timonium: Gemstone Publishing, 1999)

Neulen, H., *In The Skies of Europe: Air Forces Allied to the Luftwaffe 1939-1945*, (Ramsbury, (Marlborough, UK: The Crowood Press, 2000)

Nevin, D., *The Epic of Flight: Architects of Air Power*, (Alexandria: Time-Life Books, 1981)

Nijboer, D., *Gunner: An Illustrated History of World War II Aircraft Turrets and Gun Positions*, (Shrewsbury: Airlife Publishing Company Limited, 2001)

Oštrić, Š. I., and Janić, Č. J., *Ik Fighters (Yugoslavia: 1930-40s): Aircraft in Profile, Volume 13 (nos. 241-246)*, (Windsor: Profile Publications Ltd, 1973)

Penland, D., and Van der Linden, F. R., *The Nation's Hangar: Aircraft Treasures of the Smithsonian*, (Washington: Smithsonian Books, 2011)

Pigott, P., *Taming the Skies: A Celebration of Canadian Flight*, (Toronto: Dundurn Press, 2003)

Rickenbacker, E. V., *Rickenbacker: An Autobiography*, (Englewood Cliffs: Prentice-Hall, Inc., 1967)

Ross, A. T., *Armed and Ready: The Industrial Development and Defence of Australia 1900–1945*, (Wahroonga: Turton & Armstrong, 1995)

Savic, D., and Ciglic, B., *Croatian Aces of World War II (Osprey Aircraft of the Aces-49)*, (London: Oxford University Press, 2002)

Sgarlato, N., *Great Planes Monographes N.27—P.108, la Fortezza della Regia*, (Parma: West-ward edizioni, 2007); *Sparviero (The Great Historical Planes series) N.2*, (Parma: West-ward editzioni, 2002)

Skaida, H., *Heroines of the Soviet Union 1941-45*, (Oxford: Osprey Publishing, 2003)

Smith, J. R., and Kay, A. L., *German Aircraft of the Second World War*, (London: Putnam & Company Limited, 1972); *German Aircraft of the Second World War: Including Helicopters and Missiles*, (Annapolis: Naval Institute Press, 2002)

Stenman, K., and Keskinen, K., *Finnish Aces of World War 2*, (Oxford: Osprey Publishing, 1998)

Stenman, K., and Thomas, A., *Aircraft of the Aces: Brewster F2A Buffalo Aces of World War 2*, (Oxford, UK: Osprey Publishing, 2010)

Stoff, J., *Picture History of World War II American Aircraft Production*, (New York: Dover Publications, 1993)

Sutherland, J., and Canwell, D., *Air War East Africa 1940-41: The RAF Versus the Italian Air Force*, (Barnsley: Pen and Sword Aviation, 2009)

Taylor, J. W. R., *Combat Aircraft of the World from 1909 to the Present*, (New York: G.P. Putnam's Sons, 1969)

Thetford, O., *Aircraft of the Royal Air Force 1918-57*, (London: Putnam & Company Limited, 1957)

Thomas, A., *Gloster Gladiator Aces*, (Botley: Osprey Publishing, 2002)

Thompson, J. W., *Italian Civil and Military Aircraft 1930-1945*, (New York: Aero Publishers Inc., 1963)

Time-Life Books, (eds), *The Epic of Flight: The Luftwaffe*, (Chicago: Time-Life Books, 1983)

Van der Klaauw, B., *The Fokker G-1 (Aircraft in Profile, Volume 6, number 134)*, (Windsor, Profile Publications Ltd, 1966)

Wagner, R., and Nowarra, H. J., *German Combat Planes: A Comprehensive Survey and History of the Development of German Military Aircraft from 1914 to 1945*, (New York: Doubleday & Company, 1971)

Walker, B., *The Epic of Flight: Fighting Jets*, (Chicago: Time-Life Books, 1983)

Wheeler, K., *Bombers over Japan*, (New York: Time Life Books, 1982)

Widner, R., *Searching for Lost Warbirds in Florida, Volume 1*, (Lulu.com, 2012)

Yenne, B., *The World's Worst Aircraft*, (Maryland: World Publication Group, 2001)

Yronwode, C., *Who's Who: An Interview with Will Eisner—Blackhawk No. 260*, (New York: DC Comics, 1983)

Zabecki, D., (ed.), *World War II in Europe: An Encyclopedia*, (New York: Routledge, 2015)

Zuk, B., *Janusz Zurakowski: Legend in the Skies*, (St Catharines: Vanwell Publishing Limited, 2004)

Magazines and Articles

'British Fighter Plane Has Turrets That Fire Broadside', *The Science News-Letter*, 1940, 37(24), p. 373-374

'Hans von Ohain', *The Times*, 6 April 1998

'In Science Fields', *The Science News-Letter*, 1940, 37(25), p. 390

'New Stratospheric Aircraft', *Nature*, 1945, 156 (3950), 44

'Technology and Legitimacy: Soviet Aviation and Stalinism in the 1930s', *Technology and Culture*, 1976, 17(1), pp. 55-81

'The Elegant Elk... Poland's Unfortunate Bomber', *Air International*, 1988, 35(4), pp. 193-198, 216-218

'The Last Swallow of Summer... The Extraordinary Story of the Ki-100', *Air International*, 11 (4), 1976, pp. 185-191

'Twenty-One Gun Warplane Pours Fire in All Directions.' *Popular Mechanics*, September 1940: 391

'Wedell Sets Speed Mark at Air Races', *St. Joseph Gazette*, 5 September 1933: 1. Print

'What Army and Navy Planes Are Being Furnished Allies', *The Science News-Letter*, 1940, 37(25), p. 390

Bignozzi, G., 'The Italian "Fortress" (part 1).' *Air International*, 31(6), 1986, pp. 398-305; 'The Italian "Fortress" (part 2).' *Air International*, 32(1), 1986, pp. 23-31, 47-49

Caruana, R., *Allez le Gosse: The Dewoitine D.520*, (Scale Aviation Modeller International, 1998), 4(11), pp. 28-730

Cattaneo, G., 'Macchis across the Med: Macchi C.202/205s in Egyptian Service', *Air Enthusiast*, 1996, 57, pp. 75-77

Fischer, C. M., 'Flying the Airacomet', *Flying Magazine*, (1944)

Gigli-Cervi, A., *D.520, la tecnica*, Aerei nella Storia, 2015, 99, pp. 26-33

Green, W., (ed.) 'Le Faucheur... Fokker's Formidable G.1', *Flying Review International*, 1967, 22(8)

Gueli, M., 'Spitfire con Coccarde Italiane.' *Storia Militare Magazine*, 62, p.4-10

Guttman, J., 'Based on a Racing Plane, Caudron's Promising Lightweight Interceptor had a Short, Disappointing Combat Career', *Aviation History*, 1999, 10(3), pp. 16-21; 'Last of the Buffalos', *Aviation History*, 2009, 19(1), p. 10; 'Scaling New Heights: Conceived to Combat Germany's High-Altitude Bombers, the Westland Welkin Arrived on the Scene too Late to Fulfil its Mission', *Aviation History*, 2012, 23(1), pp. 14-16

Harvey, A. D., 'The French Armee de l'Air in May–June 1940: A Failure of Conception', *Journal of Contemporary History*, 1990, 25(4), pp. 447-465

Hervieux, P., 'Le Operazioni Degli Aereosiluranti Italiani e Tedeschi Nel Mediterraneo', *Storia Militare*, 1997, 42

Johnson, E. R., 'Workhorse of the Fleet', *Aviation History*, 2011, 22(2), pp. 44-50

Lembo, D., 'Luigi Gorrini', *Ali Tricolori*, 2002, 23

Michalek, P., 'Polish Fighter's Odyssey', *Aviation History*, 2008, 18(6), pp. 18-20

Noles Jr, J., 'Old, slow and ugly', *Air and Space,* 2005, February-March, p. 66

O'Leary, M., (ed.). 'XP-75: Spare Parts Fighter', *America's Forgotten Wings*, 1994, Volume 1, 85

Pedriali, F., 'Le Fortezze Volanti Italiane', *RID Magazine*, 1991, pp. 60-66

Perry, J. K. J., 'Powerless and Frustrated: Britain's Relationship with China during the Opening Years of the Second Sino-Japanese War, 1937-1939', *Diplomacy and Statecraft*, 2011, 22(3), pp. 408-430

Peszke, A., 'The Bomber Brigade of the Polish Air Force in September, 1939', *The Polish Review*, 1968, 13(4), pp. 80-100

Peszke, M. A., 'The Polish Armed Forces in Exile: Part 2 July 1941-May 1945', 1987, 32(1), pp. 33-69

Petrone, K., 'Soviet Women's Voices in the Stalin Era', *Journal of Women's History*, 2004, 16(2), pp. 197-208

Picarella, G., 'Database: Kawasaki Ki-100. Article, scale drawings and cutaway', *Aeroplane Magazine*, 2995, 33(11), 391

Post, C. A., 'Forward Air Control: A Royal Australian Air Force Innovation', Air Power History, 2000, 14(5), pp. 68-77

Sankowski, W., 'Intrygujące Spady', *Lotnictwo z Szachownicą*, 2001, 6

Saxon, T., 'Kehl: The German use of Guided Weapons against Naval Targets 1943-44', *Defence Studies*, 2003, 3(1), pp. 1-16

Sgarlato, N., 'La Produzione Aereonautica Italiana 1943-45', *Aerei Nella Storia*, 1998, 28; 'Macchi Folgore', *Aerei Nella Storia*, 1998, 8, pp. 8-20

Swanborough, G., 'S.79 the Hunchbacked Sparrow', *Air International*, 1984, 21(1), p. 27

Temple, T., 'Red Mule', *Aviation History*, 2008, 18(6) pp. 56-60

Thomas, A., 'Oriental Gladiators: The Combat Debut for the Gloster Biplane', *Air Enthusiast*, 1996, 121, pp. 73-75

Trumbull, R., 'The 'Graveyard' Lure of Truk Lagoon', *New York Times*, 30 April 1972,
Vasicek, R., 'Czech Ace Vaclav Cukr, Who Flew Fighters for France in 1940, Kept a Diary
  Describing...', *World War II*, 2000, 14(5), pp. 68-71
XX10. Print

Websites

Bell XP-59A Airacomet, (Smithsonian National Air and Space Museum, 2015) [viewed 27 June 2015]
  Available from: airandspace.si.edu/collections/artifact.cfm?object=nasm_A19450016000
Boeing P-26 Peashooter, The Aviation Internet Group, 2014, [viewed 29 June 2015]. Available from:
  www.aviation-history.com/boeing/p26.html
Danish Military Aviation in Relation to the Second World War, (Rathbone Museum, 2011) [viewed 2
  July 2015]. Available from: www.rathbonemuseum.com/DENMARK/DKPhotos/DKPhotos.html
Future's uncertain for Martin Mars waterbombers, (Alberni Valley Times, 2013), [viewed 11 July 2015].
  Available from: www.albernivalleynews.com/news/216126261.html
IAR 80: Romania's Indigenous Fighter Plane, (HistoryNet, 2006), [viewed 18 July 2015]. Available
  from: www.historynet.com/iar-80-romanias-indigenous-fighter-plane.htm
Ilmari Juutilainen, (Century of Flight, 2007), [viewed 20 June 2015]. Available from: www.century-
  of-flight.net/Aviation history/WW2/aces/Ilmari Juutilainen.htm
Magnificent Men who Built a Vital Flying Machine, (The Weekend Australian, 2010), [viewed 2 July
  2015]. Available from: www.theaustralian.com.au/news/inquirer/magnificent-men-who-built-a-
  vital-flying-machine/story-e6frg6z6-1225857293144
Martin Mars Coming Back, BC News, 2015, [viewed 11 July 2015]. Available from: www.castanet.net/
  news/BC/143564/Martin-Mars-coming-back
Quest for Performance: The Evolution of Modern Aircraft, NASA History Office, 1985, 2004, [viewed 1
  July 2015]. Available from: www.hq.nasa.gov/pao/History/SP-468/cover.htm
The Gloster Gladiator in the Norwegian Army Air Service (Hærens Flygevåpen), (Håkans Aviation
  Page, 2004), [viewed 2 July 2015]. Available from: surfcity.kund.dalnet.se/gladiator_norway.htm
*The Qualitative Composition of Combat Aircraft Long-range Aviation in the Most Important Dates
  of the Great Patriotic War of 1941-1945*, Ilpilot, upload date unknown, [viewed 20 July 2015].
  Available from: ilpilot.narod.ru/vvs_tsifra/gl_3/3.118.html
The Real Genocide in Yugoslavia: Independent Croatia of 1941 Revisited, R. Archibald Weiss Institute
  for Serbian Studies, 2014, [viewed 22 July 2015]. Available from: www.reiss-institute.org/
  truehistory/the-real-genocide/
Vought OS2U-3 Kingfisher, Museo Aeronautico, 2015, [viewed 1 July 2015]. Available from: www.
  museoaeronautico.cl/espanol/pop-ficha.php?id=29
Zukowsky, J., 'Kurt Tank', *Encyclopædia Britannica*, (2015), retrieved from www.britannica.com/
  biography/Kurt-Tank